M000223468

DIVIDED LOYALTIES

DIVIDED LOYALTIES

Young Somali Americans and the Lure of Extremism

Joseph Weber

MICHIGAN STATE UNIVERSITY PRESS | *East Lansing*

Copyright © 2020 by Joseph Weber

⊛ The paper used in this publication meets the minimum requirements
of ANSI/NISO Z39.48-1992 (R 1997) (Permanence of Paper).

Michigan State University Press
East Lansing, Michigan 48823-5245

LIBRARY OF CONGRESS CATALOGING-IN-PUBLICATION DATA
Names: Weber, Joseph (Professor of journalism) author.
Title: Divided loyalties : young Somali Americans and the lure of extremism / Joseph Weber.
Description: East Lansing, Michigan : Michigan State University Press, 2020.
| Includes bibliographical references and index.
Identifiers: LCCN 2019048854 | ISBN 978-1-61186-372-7 (paperback) | ISBN 978-1-60917-646-4
| ISBN 978-1-62895-407-4 | ISBN 978-1-62896-408-0
Subjects: LCSH: Trials (Terrorism)—Minnesota—Minneapolis.
| Somali Americans—Minnesota—Social conditions.
Classification: LCC KF221.P6 W43 2020 | DDC 345.73/02317—dc23
LC record available at https://lccn.loc.gov/2019048854

Book design and typesetting by Charlie Sharp, Sharp Designs, East Lansing, Michigan
Cover design by David Drummond, Salamander Design, www.salamanderhill.com.

Michigan State University Press is a member of the Green Press Initiative and is committed to developing
and encouraging ecologically responsible publishing practices. For more information about the Green
Press Initiative and the use of recycled paper in book publishing, please visit www.greenpressinitiative.org.

Visit Michigan State University Press at *www.msupress.org*

■

For Donna and our children,
all of whom battle for justice and peace

■

Yusuf Jama
Hamsa Kariye—"Farmer"
Hersi Kariye—"Abu Zabayr"
Douglas McAuthur McCain—"Tooth"
Hanad Mohallim
Mohamud Mohamed Mohamud
Abdi Mohamud Nur
Mohamed Amiin Ali Roble—"Rose"

Would-Be ISIS Members

Zacharia Yusuf Abdurahman
Hamza Naj Ahmed
Abdirahman Abdirashid Bashir—"Cali"
Abdirahman (*or* Abdurahman) Yasin Daud
Adnan Abdihamid Farah
Mohamed Abdihamid Farah
Hanad Mustafe (*or* Mustofe) Musse
Guled Ali Omar
Abdullahi Yusuf—"Bones"
Abdirizak Mohamed Warsame—"Zak" *or* "A-Zak"

Prosecutors

Julie E. Allyn
John F. Docherty
Charles J. Kovats Jr.
Andrew M. Luger (*former US attorney*)
William M. Narus
Andrew R. Winter

FBI Agents

Carson P. Green
Daniel P. Higgins

Defense Attorneys

Manny Atwal
Bruce D. Nestor

Glenn P. Bruder
Marnie Fearon
Jon M. Hopeman
Murad H. Mohammad
Kenneth Ubong Udoibok

Former Chief US Probation and Pretrial Services Officer, US District Court of Minnesota

Kevin D. Lowry

Senior Judge

Michael J. Davis

INTRODUCTION

Flanked by a pair of FBI agents as he strode through the overhead skyway system in Minneapolis, twenty-year-old Abdirahman Abdirashid Bashir could easily have been mistaken for a Hollywood celebrity.[1] Other young Somali American men, spying him from the street below, dogged the slender, well-dressed Bashir. Like hungry fans desperate to pursue the latest megastar, they tracked him, following along and pointing at him as he walked from the federal courthouse in Minneapolis to his hotel.

But this was no lovefest over the latest young phenom. Earlier, Bashir had fallen under the often-hostile glare of a spillover crowd of Somali Americans, who packed two courtrooms as three of Bashir's friends stood trial for attempting to join the Islamic State of Iraq and Syria (ISIS).[2] The crowd included women dressed head-to-toe in colorful, tent-like "jilbab" dresses, their heads modestly covered by scarves. They were among parents and other relatives of the accused, as well as Bashir's family, who jammed the seats, each group coldly eyeing the other. Marshals stood by to make sure the groups stayed civil. The young men pointing at Bashir on his walk were taunting him, not greeting him.

For five days in May 2016, Bashir took center stage as he was questioned, prodded, and challenged on the stand in a drama that riveted many in Minneapolis. Just a little over a year before, in April 2015, he and two friends had driven halfway across the country, leaving Minneapolis for what his friends thought was a way station to ISIS, a short stopover in San Diego. There, they expected to collect passports that would help them travel first into Mexico and then on to Syria, where they would join other friends who had taken up arms to defend and expand the so-called Islamic State. The trio was among thirteen young men who plotted between 2013 and 2015 to make their way to Syria, a place they had idealized as an Islamic Utopia. They were part of an extraordinary phenomenon in the core of the American heartland in which at least fifty-four people—mostly young men—joined, tried to join, or supported the terrorist groups al-Shabab in Somalia, ISIS in Syria, and al-Qaida, as far back as 2007. Some died on battlefields or in attacks on innocents, and some are serving prison terms.[3]

The fact that the distant countries were killing fields on which some Minneapolis men were slaughtered only added to the allure in their young minds. With the naivete of adolescence and the suicidal fervor of Islamist fanatics—hyped up by seductive videos from ISIS propagandists—some of the men craved martyrdom. Like others among the former Minnesotans before them, they would become "shahids," heroically sacrificing their lives for Islam and, in the process, attaining Paradise for themselves and their families. Indeed, three of the thirteen in Bashir's group snuck into Syria and died there, much to the envy of some of those left behind in Minneapolis.[4]

But, now that nine of the remaining plotters in Bashir's circle had been stymied and were in the hands of federal jailers, what would happen to them? Where did their loyalties lie? Where did they lie for Bashir, the gangly five-foot, ten-inch Californian who loved basketball and played it as he and his friends plotted on courts across Minneapolis? And how had these young Somali Americans—who dressed, talked, learned, and played so much like other Americans, particularly African Americans—become so entranced with a group that Westerners and others across the globe reviled as murderous, as an incarnation of modern evil that had unnerved the world? Despite abundant media coverage of ISIS atrocities—indeed because of the cruel beheadings, burnings, and shootings the group celebrated in its internet propaganda videos—the Minnesota men had been infatuated with the AK-47-toting terrorists. How could their allegiances be so twisted? How could they be so seduced?

The questions loomed over the stories of all the Minnesotans who had over a dozen years disregarded American authorities, and authorities the world over, to support Islamist terrorism in al-Shabab, ISIS, and al-Qaida. Almost all were Somali or Somali American. They were immigrants or the children of immigrants who had fled the horrors of the never-ending warfare and chaos of Somalia for the haven of the United States. Most had lived their formative and teen years in America, in places such as San Diego and Minneapolis, where they moved through US school systems and entered college. They seemed well on their way to attaining the American dream of professional and personal success.

So, how could they turn their backs on that? Why would they be willing to take up arms against fellow Americans in remote, unfamiliar lands, especially in the shadow of the three thousand American deaths on September 11, 2001, in the World Trade Center attacks staged by other radical Islamists, as well as the scores of terrorist attacks worldwide since? Why would so many be willing—indeed, eager—to give up their lives, especially after their parents had so desperately struggled to give them good and safe ones?

Divided loyalties coursed through the thirteenth-floor federal courtroom where Bashir took the stand in May 2016. Would Bashir, born in San Diego to a couple who had fled Somalia for the safety and opportunities America promised, prove loyal to his friends or his country? To protect his friends, he had lied to grand juries before, so would he do so in open court? And what of the crowd that packed the hard benches in the courtroom? Did the loyalties among the Somali Americans in the room lie with the young men whom US authorities had caught red-handed in their plotting and had arrested after a sting operation that seemed straight out of the movies? Or did they have faith in the system they had fled into? Many seemed as mistrustful of the FBI and the US government as they understandably had been of the brutal and bloody government they had left in Somalia a couple decades before.

Abdirahman Abdirashid Bashir's story and the stories of his friends—and of the twoscore others from Minnesota who involved themselves in various ways with terrorism—are at base tales of divided and strained loyalties. Warfare, Islamic devotion, anti-Islamic hatred, racism, troubled economic conditions, and confused and blended senses of identity all figured into the stories. All those elements played a role in the drama that unfolded in the courthouse and outside. All those factors, too, have scarred in various ways the 46,000 or so Somali Americans of Minnesota, the overwhelming majority of whom want nothing more than to make their way up the American economic and social ladder—carving out a place in American society even as they struggle to preserve the legacy and culture of their forbears.

Follow along as we trace the origins, development, and—for some—the resolution of the fractured loyalties that marked the tales of a surprising number of Somalis in the core of the American heartland. Along the way, we'll depart from the narrative at times to explore the genesis of the chaos in Somalia, the development of the Somali American community and its integration into American society, the perverse appeal of terrorism for some alienated young people, the seductive nature of ISIS recruitment techniques, the group's peculiar treatment of women, and the strengths and weaknesses of the court and rehabilitation systems in handling terrorism-related matters. Bashir's story, in which his five days on the witness stand played an important but small part, offers a unique window onto the perverse appeal of groups likely to long trouble the world, despite recent successes by the West in battling the so-called Islamic State.

While ISIS has been subdued, it hasn't been destroyed. Much as when one strikes a ball of mercury with a hammer and it breaks into tiny bits and scatters, the group has largely dispersed. The hammer that forces of the West and their allies brought down on ISIS in Syria has driven its thousands of fighters far and wide, some to find homes in other like-minded groups across Africa and elsewhere. Radicalization in the West remains a thorny problem, especially in European prisons, and fears about homegrown terrorist attacks remain high even as officials fret that directed attacks could resume in time. As a United Nations report in July 2019 warned, terrorists will continue to pose a threat across much of the world.[5] Experts writing for the Institute for the Study of War similarly have cautioned that ISIS is far from defeated.[6] The lessons of Minnesota will be relevant for years to come.

CHAPTER ONE

The Seeds of Jihad

To understand Bashir's complex story, let's look back to his time in San Diego. Even before high school, he told me, he began wrestling with the idea of jihad, the Islamic concept of struggle that includes the obligation to defend Muslims against invaders and oppressors.[1] As early as age fourteen, he was puzzling over whether groups such as the Taliban in Afghanistan were fulfilling the obligation of jihad. It was also around then, meanwhile, that a fervor for helping Somalis in the homeland was taking root among other young men in Minneapolis.

Bashir, who was just a few years younger than the Minneapolis men, like them was asking tough questions. Were American military personnel in Afghanistan foreign oppressors, as Russian troops had once been? Was Osama bin Laden a hero or villain? Was al-Qaida a liberating force defending Islam against an oppressive West? During his 2009–10 school year in high school, Bashir was learning the ways of traditional Sunni Islam—and, particularly, the radical Islamist variety of it—from beloved cousins, one just a few years older than he. They took the view that groups derided in the West as terrorists were actually following the religion's dictates. Such groups, they said, were recasting for a modern time the defenses that companions of Prophet Muhammad mounted when they were persecuted in Mecca in the early seventh century and fled to another Arabian city, Medina.

Abdirahman Abdirashid Bashir at first wanted to join ISIS, following relatives and friends who did so. After several of them died in Syria, he spurned the effort and wore a wire for the FBI. He is shown here in the fall of 2017, eighteen months after three of his friends stood trial on terrorism-related charges.

The Prophet's history, Bashir said, seemed "encouraging . . . inspirational." Relying on his cousins and the videos he saw online, he drew connections between the defensive battles the Prophet and his companions fought and modern events. "When we're young, we think, 'wow, I wish I was there, defending the oppressed ones, the weak ones.' Then you try to put it in this time. That's when it's really a big turn," he said. "There's a lot of radical clerics who are preaching."

As he imagined himself heroically defending Islam, he would watch videos made by one such cleric, New Mexico–born Anwar al-Awlaki, who argued in persuasive, American-inflected English that Muslims are obliged to throw non-Muslims out of their lands. For Bashir and his cousins, images of women and children being bombed fueled their anger at foreigners in Afghanistan and laid a foundation for looking on al-Qaida, al-Shabab, and, later, on ISIS, not as terrorist groups but as liberators and defenders of Muslims.

Bashir's cousins, in fact, were convinced that the correct path for Muslims was to drive out "kuffar"—non-Muslims, including American soldiers—from Afghanistan. But Bashir wasn't so sure. He went to his father, Abdirashid Bashir Hassan, who argued that the fight in Afghanistan was not jihad and that al-Qaida was anything but heroic.[2] He told Bashir that some Muslims, such as the Taliban, were in the wrong, and that it was they who triggered and perpetuated the war.

Before fleeing the civil war and famine in Somalia, Hassan had studied Islam for three years in Saudi Arabia. In San Diego, Bashir's father for a time had attended Masjid Ar-Ribat al-Islami, the mosque where al-Awlaki served as imam for four years until 2000, and he had seen al-Awlaki in action there. Hassan had told his son that al-Awlaki was constantly "head-butting" with respected scholars who would visit the mosque. "The guy was crazy," Hassan said of the al-Qaida propagandist. "He misinterprets Quran, hadith [reports of the Prophet]. He has an ideology that's wrong." Two of the perpetrators of the September 11, 2001, attacks that leveled the World Trade Center towers in the United States also attended the mosque and were close to al-Awlaki.[3]

For Bashir, the split in views between his father and his cousins was troubling, and the torment played into his adolescent desire to take his own path. As a young teen and the oldest boy in his family, Bashir looked up to one cousin, Hersi "Abu Zabayr" Kariye, then in his mid-twenties, as an older brother. For their part, Hersi and Hersi's brother, Hamsa "Farmer" Kariye, kept trying to make Bashir and a younger brother, also called Hamsa, more observant.[4] The older cousins bought Bashir and his brother koofiyad head coverings and ankle-length traditional Somali robes known as khameez when Bashir was in ninth grade.

Those efforts put them at odds with Bashir's father, Hassan. Hassan, a tall thin man who favors dark business suits, had yearned to attend an American university in San Diego as a high school student in Somalia in the 1980s. It was by happenstance that he was able to bring his family to San Diego in 1992. Hassan was infuriated when the cousins once showed up and started praying on Bashir's front lawn, prompting his family's San Diego neighbors to call the police.

But others Bashir knew in San Diego would, in time, reinforce the young teen's radical views. Among them was another cousin, Hanad Mohallim—a boy of about the same age as Bashir. Mohallim was "like my brother," Bashir would testify in court in his May 2016 appearance. "We would go everywhere together, do activities, play basketball, grew up in the same city."[5] Bashir and Mohallim would get together and watch videos such as "Fighting for Jannah (Paradise)" together. That video told of how two friends competed with one another to be more virtuous, outdoing one another in praying and fasting. The pair went out to fight to defend Muslims and one was captured and tortured, but he only laughed at his tormentors, explaining that he was glad to die a martyr, beating his friend—his brother, as he called him—to Paradise. Later, the video said, the pair met in Paradise.[6]

In San Diego, the young Bashir also spent a lot of time with an older family friend from Minnesota, a non-Somali man named Douglas McAuthur "Tooth" McCain. Back when Bashir was in middle school, he also briefly met another older non-Somali man, Troy M. Kastigar, a close friend of McCain's. The three—Mohallim, McCain, and Kastigar—over the following few years would prove crucial in helping shape Bashir's political views.

But, back in 2009, Bashir's father saw danger mainly in the approaches by the Kariye brothers. He told them to stay away from his sons. Later, Hamsa Kariye traveled to Africa to join al-Shabab, Bashir said. He returned to the West only after his mother, sister, and brother traveled there and persuaded him to come back, forcing the family to move to Canada to avoid prosecution in the United States.

For a time, the move to Canada by the Kariye brothers seemed to solve the problem of Bashir's nascent radicalization. But it was to prove temporary.

CHAPTER TWO

A Land of Chaos

Before following Bashir's road into terrorism, let's understand the baggage that Somalis and first-generation Somali Americans carry as they look at groups such as al-Shabab and ISIS. Far more than their white American neighbors in such cities as Minneapolis, San Diego, Columbus (Ohio), Portland (Oregon), Portland (Maine), and other cities across the United States where tens of thousands of Somalis have settled, the immigrants of Bashir's parents' generation know what war, poverty, and life as a newcomer to a foreign land mean.

For their part, younger Somali Americans have seen the strained lives their parents lead, as those parents are tied to Somalia by language, culture, and, sometimes, financial obligations to relatives. Even as their elders negotiate the demands, opportunities, and challenges of American culture, many of the young people themselves lead double lives. They often seem as American as any native-born citizen outside the house but Somali through and through inside.

Their ancestral homeland, a sprawling, poor, and long-troubled country, forms the tip of the Horn of Africa. It fills a landmass that would equal most of the east coast of the United States, a band that would stretch south from the northern border of Massachusetts to the middle of Florida and westward from the coast as far as central Pennsylvania in the north and to the Alabama border in the south.

Jutting out into the Arabian Sea with the Gulf of Aden separating it from Yemen in the north, this sad, tormented stretch of a country was long dominated by foreign powers; its mix of nomadic and agrarian people arose from a blend of Africans and Arabs who traded in the area for millennia. Indeed, Somalis see themselves as different from Africans and speak of "going to Africa" when they visit other parts of the continent. They often even look different from many other Africans, and are sometimes notable for narrow chins more typical of their Arab forbears. They can be so distinctive, in fact, that refugee-camp screeners in the early 2000s applied physical tests to differentiate between Somalis and Somali Bantus, a subgroup from the Jubba Valley in southern Somalia.[1]

Unlike the Christians who predominate in neighboring Kenya and the mixed population of Ethiopia, Somalis almost exclusively adopted Islam. This crucial difference continues to separate them from many of their neighbors. Much to their detriment in forming a nation, they also clung to the Arab custom of valuing their clans—sprawling extended families—above nation or other forms of self-identification.

Somalia, like the rest of the Horn of Africa, tossed off its colonial rulers in 1960, at a time when many African nations were being born. Britain, which controlled northwest Somalia, and Italy, which reigned in the south and northeast, both then gave up their longstanding hold on the area (the French did so later, in 1977, yielding the area that became Djibouti).

But the effort to knit together disparate clans and forge a cohesive nation proved ill fated. Blame this in part on continuing meddling by outsiders, particularly the Soviet Union and the United States, as well as Kenya and Ethiopia, whose eastern regions Somali leaders coveted as historically Somali territory. Indeed, the Somali flag still sports a five-pointed star that refers to Greater Somalia, comprising the south, north, and northwest regions, as well as northeastern Kenya and the Ogaden region of Ethiopia.[2]

When the Western nations pulled out in the 1960s, the Soviet Union moved in to militarize Somalia in a bid to extend its influence in Africa. Somalia, for its part, supported a guerrilla movement in Ethiopia called the Western Somali Liberation Front (WSLF) and wound up, in 1964, under assault by Ethiopian bombing raids.[3] These raids triggered years of tit-for-tat actions between the neighboring countries.

In the late 1960s, a new Somali government tried to make peace with the Ethiopians. It wound up being criticized for abandoning the original Somali intentions of ruling over all traditional Somali land. After President Abdirashid Ali Sharmarke was assassinated in 1969, an expansion-minded military junta, led by Mohammed Siad Barre, took control, installing a blend of Marxism and Islam known as "scientific socialism" and further deepening the country's ties to the Soviet Union.[4]

Much of the anguish of current-day Somalia—and the tortured history so many Somalis brought with them to the United States—originated in the long-lived regime of Siad Barre, who held sway until 1991. His mixed legacy spawned the brutality and chaos that has dogged the country ever since and that has scarred many of those in the expanding Somali diaspora. On the one hand, he modernized much of Somalia, which was still largely composed of farmers and camel-herders. He introduced a written form of the Somali language, adopting Latin script,[5] and pushed for greater literacy by sending convoys of young, educated urbanites into the countryside to teach.[6]

On the other hand, he led the country into foolhardy military escapades, renewing support for the WSLF and backing other insurgent groups battling Ethiopia. Siad Barre pushed his military to invade Ethiopia in the Ogaden War in 1977, initially capturing land that was long inhabited by Somalis, only to be forced to retreat when the Soviet Union decided, in 1978, that it was better off backing the strategically important Ethiopians. The defeat triggered a major refugee crisis, as several hundred thousand Ethiopians with Somali clan ties fled into Somalia, and led to a military coup attempt that Siad Barre brutally crushed, in part by executing seventeen plotters publicly in April 1978.[7] This was the earliest of many refugee crises to beset Somalis, driving them far outside their homelands.

Conditions then just got worse for Siad Barre and Somalia. Furious at the Soviet turnabout, the dictator threw out Soviet advisers, and the United States leaped into the breach, pumping in huge amounts of foreign aid. But the support couldn't stabilize Somalia's feeble economy or quell rising resistance to Siad Barre's increasingly brutal approaches to governing. The dictator, like other tyrants in Africa and outside it, before and since, had his opponents jailed, tortured, raped, and murdered.

Soon, breakaway movements arose. One, based in Ethiopia and supported by Addis Ababa, led Siad Barre to punish clans in the central part of Somalia that he deemed hostile. Meanwhile, in the northwest—in the area once controlled by Britain—the Somali National Movement (SNM) stirred. The SNM became so troublesome to Siad Barre that, in 1988, he sent his military into cities such as Hargeisa and Burao, killing thousands and creating thousands more refugees.[8] As one witness told the Africa Watch Committee, a branch of Human Rights Watch, in 1989: "Who could believe that planes belonging to the Somali army would take off from Hargeisa airport to bomb Hargeisa itself and its population? From dawn to dusk, day in and day out, and intermittently during the night, there was shelling, bombing, people being slaughtered by soldiers in the streets, in their homes and in all the places they sought refuge."[9]

As his critics grew more desperate and bolder, Siad Barre responded with still more military raids, imprisonment, torture, and murder. He compiled what the United Nations Development Programme called "one of the worst human rights records in Africa."[10] The Somali military, Africa Watch reported, resembled "a foreign occupation force that recognizes no constraints on its power to kill, rape, or loot."[11]

Resistance mounted against Siad Barre, and, despite American backing, he was forced out of power in 1991 by a coalition of armed groups. This ushered in the current failed state, the rise of al-Shabab, as a Somali-focused, religiously based insurgency at first (though in time it adopted Islamist terrorism and a transnational focus), and the clan-dominated tumult that has reigned since. In 1993, two years after Siad Barre's fall, Americans learned how unpopular their involvement in Somalia was when President Bill Clinton sent attack helicopters into Mogadishu to capture military commanders working for Habr Gidr clan warlord Mohamed Farah Aided. Aided, who had played a key role in ousting Siad Barre, was then battling United Nations forces.

Two Black Hawk helicopters were shot down, prompting a rescue effort that took the lives of an estimated seven hundred Somalis and eighteen American soldiers whose bodies were dragged through the streets by enraged Somalis—much of that televised and later made infamous by the book *Black Hawk Down* and a movie of the same name.[12] Clinton pulled American forces out of Somalia, putting the brakes on US military involvement there until about 2001, when the United States began stepping up covert military and Central Intelligence Agency actions against American nemesis al-Qaida and, later, against al-Shabab, the Somali-based group.[13] Meanwhile, beginning in about 2000, Somali pirates began bedeviling fishing and cargo vessels in the Arabian Sea and Indian Ocean, later moving on to yachts; the pirates kidnapped crews, killing and torturing some, and they collected hefty ransoms. Multinational efforts, including the use of US Navy ships, were launched to squelch the armed seagoing thieves.

From 2017 on, American involvement in the country accelerated. That led to the death in May 2017 of a US Navy SEAL, the first American combat fatality there since the Black Hawk debacle.[14] This was followed, in June 2018, by the killing of an

American Green Beret in a mortar assault on an outpost in the country's Jubaland region.[15]

The United States military in November 2017 struck an al-Shabab camp by air, claiming to kill more than one hundred members of the group. That assault followed a truck bombing in mid-October in Mogadishu, apparently by the group, that the Associated Press reported killed 512 people, wounded another 312, and left sixty-two other people missing; it was called Somalia's 9/11.[16] That attack was followed two weeks later by a suicide bombing at a hotel in the city that killed at least twenty-three people and in which al-Shabab claimed responsibility.[17] Even as President Trump in December 2018 ordered a withdrawal from Syria (though he later delayed full withdrawal) and a sharp drawdown in Afghanistan, he declared parts of Somalia "areas of active hostility" and authorized an escalation of military action. The *Wall Street Journal* reported that US airstrikes against al-Shabab positions and fighters had tripled since 2016, to forty-seven in 2018, according to US Africa Command. The US military said it killed 338 of the group's fighters in 2018, and it reported it had conducted five airstrikes and killed twenty-six militants in the first eight days of 2019.[18]

As of the fall of 2019, the United States had more than five hundred military personnel in the country, led by a one-star general, US Army Brigadier General Miguel A. Castellanos. As deputy commanding general for the Combined Joint Task Force–Horn of Africa and Mogadishu Coordination Cell director, Castellanos served as the senior US military liaison to the government of Somalia, the Somali National Security Forces, and to international partners.[19] On the diplomatic front, the United States reestablished what the US Department of State called "a permanent diplomatic presence" in Mogadishu in December 2018, a month after Ambassador Donald Y. Yamamoto presented his credentials to the Somali president, Mohamed Farmaajo.[20] Shortly before meeting with Farmaajo in Mogadishu, Yamamoto nodded to the importance of Minnesota's Somali community by visiting Minneapolis.[21]

Involvement in Somalia by the United States has waxed and waned over the years. At times, American military actions enraged Somalis who intentionally or unintentionally were targeted. Still, for many Somalis, the United States throughout has remained a magnet, a locus of order and opportunity in a chaotic world. Regardless of Washington's pro–Siad Barre policies and its military actions, ordinary Somalis have long seen America as a safe haven and a place of freedom and opportunity, a shining city on a hill where they yearned to live.[22] Journalist Andrew Harding told of how Mohamud "Tarzan" Nur, Mogadishu's mayor from 2010 to 2014, grew up in a Mogadishu orphanage dreaming of going to the United States. He even kept a map of America taped to the underside of a dormitory bunk above him.[23] Indeed, the future mayor was thrilled in 1972 when Milwaukee Bucks stars Oscar Robertson and Kareem Abdul-Jabbar visited, and Abdul-Jabbar played on Nur's orphanage team in a basketball match.[24]

Later, in the 1990s, as their country collapsed, rising numbers of Somalis fled, and many made their way to the United States, with an estimated 89,000 Somali immigrants living in the country as of 2015, according to the Migration Policy Institute.[25] Citing United Nations' estimates, the Pew Research Center pegged the current number of Somalis in the United States somewhat higher, at between 140,000 and 150,000, or about 7 percent of the Somali diaspora. Immigrants from the war-ravaged country still were pressing to get into the United States as of 2015 when nearly nine thousand sought refuge in America.[26]

Those figures dwindled in the wake of moves by the administration of President Trump to ban admissions to the United States of people from a half dozen Muslim-majority countries, including Somalia. The US Department of State's Refugee Processing Center put the number of Somalis arriving in the United States at 2,770 in calendar year 2017, just 139 in calendar 2018, and 272 in 2019. By contrast, 10,786 Somalis made their way into the United States in 2016, according to the processing center. After much legal wrangling over details in initial proposed restrictions, the White House in September 2017 imposed a permanent ban on eight countries, including Somalia, suspending immigration from it and subjecting visitors from Somalia to tougher screening.[27] That measure came under legal assault later in the fall of 2017, but the Supreme Court in June 2018 upheld the White House's final approach in *Trump v. Hawaii,* calling it "squarely within the scope of Presidential authority."[28]

Trump capped the overall number of refugees welcome in the United States at 45,000 for the fiscal year that began in September 2017, the lowest figure in decades and a cut from 84,995 accepted by President Barack Obama in 2016 (and from the 110,000 Obama aimed for in 2017).[29] He also indefinitely suspended the "follow-to-join" program (labeling it "chain migration"), in which spouses and children were rejoined with migrant family members. The restrictions would choke off immigration from Somalia, which the *Star Tribune* reported accounted for 45 percent of immigrants to Minnesota in 2016.[30] Later, in 2019, Trump capped the overall number of refugees welcome from Africa at 11,000. Nonetheless, Somalis are in the United States to stay and births in the community, of course, will inexorably drive up the population of Somali Americans in Minnesota and elsewhere in the country each year.

For complicated reasons, the Minneapolis–St. Paul area became home to the largest concentration of Somalis and Somali Americans in the United States, though estimates of the population in the state vary widely. The total has been estimated as low as 33,000 and as high as more than double that.[31] Minnesota Compass, a nonprofit that keeps track of immigrant data, put the total number of Somalis and Somali Americans statewide in Minnesota in 2016 at 46,622, plus or minus 6,165. This included about 21,000 Somali Americans, seventeen or under, who were born in the United States.[32] The Minnesota State Demographic Center, in a January 2016 report titled "The Economic Status of Minnesotans," similarly estimated the Somali population in the state at about 46,300, plus or minus 6,100. The population included some 14,600 or so ethnic Somalis born in Minnesota, plus another 2,800 or so born elsewhere in the United States.[33] Minnesota state demographer Susan Brower said most of the Somalis and Somali Americans live in the seven-county region that includes the Twin Cities of Minneapolis and St. Paul.[34]

It was in this tumultuous and troubling world that Bashir and his friends came of age. They were part of a community that fled violence but, as we shall also see, continues to struggle with it in different forms. And it was against this backdrop that they became entangled in the world of online radicalism and distant terrorists who had the power to reach deep into the American heartland.

CHAPTER THREE

The First Wave

E ven before Bashir and his cousins in San Diego mused about martyrdom and heroism, young men from Minneapolis were making their way to battlefields in Africa where they thought they would find both. Bashir's radical cousins, it turned out, were not alone in their views.

Toward the end of the first decade in the 2000s, Somali Americans from Minnesota were leaving to become foreign fighters. It was not ISIS that enthralled these young men, but al-Shabab, the homegrown Somali group that American authorities—with good reason—labeled a terrorist organization.

For some young Somalis and Somali Americans in the years following the attacks of September 11, 2001, al-Shabab was far from such a terrorist organization, however. Rather, they saw it as a noble Islamic guerrilla force that was the last and best hope to rid their homeland of corrupt secular rulers and warring clan leaders, some of whom had supported an infuriating invasion by neighboring Ethiopia. To them, al-Shabab was an archetypal heroic band of brothers—an image its propaganda videos reinforced—and some Somalis in Minnesota eagerly signed on to join them.

Much like the Taliban of Afghanistan, al-Shabab sought to set up a government based on Sharia, Islamic law. Supporters hoped that by hewing to the principles

The Abubakar as-Saddique Islamic Center was a meeting place for some of the men who made their way to Somalia to join al-Shabab. While a janitor at the mosque was convicted of terrorism-related charges, leaders were not implicated.

of strict Islam, al-Shabab would bring the peace and stability to Somalia that had eluded the country from the time that these young Somalis and their parents fled. Some warmed to the idea of returning to a land where they would live in accord with the strict Salafist doctrines that hailed from Saudi Arabia (a contrast, oddly enough, with the more relaxed Sufi-influenced form of Islam long common among Somalis).[1] Indeed, some saw the group's Utopian vision for Somalia and beyond as a way to free themselves of lives in the United States that were marred by sin, poverty, and confusion and, in some cases, by drug use and gang violence. Perhaps rebellion against the less savory elements of American culture drove them to warm to the most oppositional form of Islam they could find, the Islam of the resistance fighter.

Al-Shabab, Arabic for "the youth," sprang from a group of clerics and Islamic judges known as the Islamic Courts Union (ICU). The ICU evolved out of the chaos in and around Mogadishu in the 1990s to run local courts, police services, education, and healthcare. By 1999, it had gained enough power to take control of the central commercial area in Mogadishu, the Bakara Market. Then, by 2004, it had grown strong enough to formally organize itself as an alternative to Western-backed leaders who, in 2000, formed the short-lived Transitional National Government (TNG) and, later, in 2004, its successor, the Transitional Federal Government (TFG).[2] Also in 2004, the ICU elected a former schoolteacher widely seen as moderate, Sheikh Sharif Sheikh Ahmed, as chairman.

To the warlords who dominated Somalia, though, the ICU was a threat. They organized themselves into the Alliance for Restoration of Peace and Counter-Terrorism, apparently trying to tie themselves—at least rhetorically—into the West's war on terrorism. But the ICU's militia routed the warlords in Mogadishu. Then, as Cedric Barnes of London's School of Oriental and African Studies and Harun Hassan of London's Somali Media Centre argued in a 2007 article in the *Journal of Eastern African Studies:* "The Courts achieved the unthinkable, uniting Mogadishu for the first time in 16 years, and re-establishing peace and security." Rubbish was cleared, the main Mogadishu airport and seaport were reopened, squatters were driven from government buildings, and property rights were dealt with.[3]

But, for all that seeming progress and the presence of moderate leaders, the ICU was too big of a tent for the West, especially the United States. Its broad umbrella covered radicals who were believed to give refuge to al-Qaida operatives in Mogadishu, and it welcomed such leaders as Aden Hashi Ayro, a longtime militant who came to lead the ICU's militia as it evolved into al-Shabab. Under Ayro, al-Shabab's brutal attacks drew condemnation from much of the ICU's leadership and from outside the country, according to the Mapping Militant Organizations project at Stanford University.

Al-Shabab's early activities allegedly included multiple killings of international workers between 2003 and 2005 in Somaliland, the northwestern region formerly occupied by the British that, in 1991, seceded from Somalia. Reflecting its loathing of the West and the area's former colonial masters, the group in 2005 disinterred an entire Italian cemetery. The same year, it also supported violent retaliation against members of Somalia's Transitional Federal Government after ICU members were assassinated, allegedly by that transitional government.

As the ICU arose, al-Shabab members were sheltering al-Qaida members, and in 2008, al-Shabab formally aligned itself with al-Qaida. While some ICU leaders tried to keep their focus on Somalia, Ayro pushed the group to link Somalia's battles to a global jihadist agenda.[4] After Ayro was killed in a May 2008 US missile attack, his successor, Ahmed Abdi Godane—also called Mukhtar Abu Zubeyr—published a statement praising al-Qaida and declaring affiliation with global jihad. The group then stepped up suicide attacks and welcomed al-Qaida members into its leadership.[5]

Together, the ICU and al-Shabab threatened neighboring Ethiopia as well. The government in Addis Ababa backed the Somali Transitional Federal Government (TFG), which sought to rule from the city of Baidoa, some 140 miles to the northwest of Mogadishu. Ethiopia, with its history of battling Somalia and its own problems with a restive Somali ethnic population, steadily built up its forces on Somali soil.

Ethiopia enlisted the United States and together they persuaded the United Nations to authorize troops from the African Union to enter the country as a peacekeeping force. The United States backed Ethiopia's invasion and opposed the ICU in the main because of al-Qaida's influence in the ICU. After the ICU leaders demanded that the outside forces leave, Ethiopian and TFG troops overran Mogadishu, shutting down the ICU's brief reign at the end of December 2006, a move that left al-Shabab to regroup and grow into the deadlier freestanding Islamist force that allied itself with al-Qaida.[6]

By refusing to deal early on with the ICU in ways that could have encouraged its moderate elements, the United States may have missed a chance to foster stability in Somalia and to isolate the Islamists in the group's midst. But American authorities, making policy while the wounds of 9/11 were still raw and as American soldiers were battling Islamists in Afghanistan and Iraq, may have seen no palatable alternative.

Tragically, however, this played into the hands of supporters of al-Shabab and their beliefs in global jihad, along with resistance to anything but the most Islamist-oriented approach to Somalia. The group then became a magnet for naive young Somalis in the United States, who struggled with undifferentiating hostility to Islam from many of the Americans around them.

Indeed, for the Somalis of Minneapolis and elsewhere, news of the Ethiopian invasion of 2006 landed like a bombshell. Many young Somalis who had fled the country little more than a decade before had been raised expecting that their exile in the West was a temporary thing, according to Jaylani Hussein, a Somali American who served as executive director of the Minnesota chapter of the Council on American-Islamic Relations (CAIR-MN). [7] They saw the invasion as a betrayal, he said, and, taking heart from the anti-Ethiopian sentiment of others across the Somali community, felt it was their nationalistic duty to defend the homeland. For some, that meant supporting al-Shabab even after the United States declared it a foreign terrorist organization in March 2008, making it a crime to support the group with money or to join it, conspire to join it, or attempt to join it.[8]

The reaction in the Somali diaspora, in turn, triggered efforts by federal authorities in Minneapolis to prevent Somalis from backing al-Shabab, including prosecuting those who made moves to join or financially support it. FBI surveillance and a string of prosecutions—conducted under the moniker of "Operation Rhino," apparently referring to the Horn of Africa—bred mistrust and suspicion among Somalis that lingers today. Even though only a fraction of the Somali and Somali American population in Minnesota actively supported al-Shabab, it also led to rising friction between the newcomers and some other Minnesotans.

In the first wave of Minnesotans to support terrorism—the al-Shabab wave—at least twenty-four men traveled to Somalia from Minnesota to join the group between 2007 and 2012, according to court records. As of early 2020, ten of the men were dead, while five had returned to face prosecution and imprisonment. At least eight others were believed to be alive and were wanted by US authorities—although military actions against al-Shabab made their status uncertain.[9] At least eight other people from Minnesota supported efforts by people to join al-Shabab, including three women who donated to the organization or raised funds for it, in part through an internet chat room that reached Somali communities outside the state.[10]

Most of the travelers left the Minneapolis area between the fall of 2007 and late 2009 to train and fight in Somalia with the terrorist group. Many of them ultimately fought with the group against Ethiopian forces, African Union troops, and the Transitional Federal Government (TFG). Before leaving, in December 2007, some of the travelers raised money in Minnesota for their trips, either tapping into the anti-Ethiopian sentiments of their fellow Somalis or misleading them by suggesting the young men would use the money to go to Saudi Arabia to study the Quran.[11]

Some of the travelers saw the move overseas as a way to align themselves with a global jihadist movement, one that gave them a sense of belonging and an identity that apparently eluded them in their adopted country. Once in Somalia, the men attended an al-Shabab training camp with dozens of other Somalis from across Africa and the United States. Somali, Arab, and Western instructors schooled them there in the use of small arms, machine guns, rocket-propelled grenades, and military-style tactics, according to court records. The trainees also were indoctrinated with anti-Ethiopian, anti-American, anti-Israeli and anti-Western beliefs, according to indictments brought against several of the men.

For all the sense of solidarity the move generated for some of the men, for others the journey just proved to be tragic. In fact, it was something they wanted to turn their backs on. According to court documents, on October 29, 2008, Shirwa Mohamud "Timaweyne" Ahmed, an early traveler from Minnesota, blew himself up in one of five simultaneous suicide attacks on targets in northern Somalia. Ahmed's role was to drive an explosive-laden Toyota truck into an office of the Puntland Intelligence Service in Bossasso, Puntland, an area in the northeast of Somalia that declared itself an autonomous part of the country in 1998. Other targets in the coordinated group of attacks included a second Puntland Intelligence Service Office in Bossasso, the Presidential Palace, the United Nations Development Program office, and the Ethiopian Trade Mission in Hargeisa, the capital city of Somaliland.[12] Ahmed was believed to be the first American suicide bomber in Somalia, part of an effort that killed more than twenty people.

Ahmed, who was twenty-six at the time of his death, didn't want that gory distinction, according to one of his fellow travelers. He had tried to quit al-Shabab, according to testimony in a 2012 court case against another man accused of aiding efforts by the Minnesotans to join the group. Islamic scholars whom Ahmed met in Saudi Arabia had urged him to stay away from al-Shabab, but the woman who ran one of the group's safe houses refused to give him back his passport, and he was then persuaded by others to stick with the group, according to his friend.

"He wanted to come back to the United States, but they wouldn't let him. He was trapped," his friend Salah Osman Ahmed testified before a federal jury, according to an account of the court action in the *Pioneer Press*. "That is the last person I ever thought about doing that," he said of his comrade's suicide bombing. "He didn't want to stay with al-Shabab."[13]

Like Shirwa Ahmed, Salah Osman Ahmed and another 2007 fellow traveler to Somalia, Abdifatah Yusuf Isse, wanted out of al-Shabab after spending only a short time with the group. Before they became disillusioned, the three were among a group of young men who complained about the Ethiopian invasion of their homeland in gatherings at Abubakar as-Saddique, a large Somali mosque in a rundown corner of Minneapolis. After raising money from Somalis in Minnesota to finance their travels, the trio of travelers made their way to Somalia and found themselves in early 2008 clearing land to build the al-Shabab training camp and getting military training.

They soon regretted their decision, however, and Salah Osman Ahmed and Abdifatah Yusuf Isse fled the camp after Ahmed developed a skin rash and an al-Shabab leader let them leave for medical treatment, as reported by Laura Yuen of Minnesota Public Radio News.[14] The pair made their way back to the United States, were arrested, and pleaded guilty to providing material support—themselves—for terrorism. US law allows for sentences of up to twenty years for such offenses. The men, who cooperated with authorities, were both sentenced in 2013 to three years in prison, far less time than they could have gotten.[15]

The men proved to be unsettling examples of recruitment and disillusionment. Isse, for instance, was born in Somalia and fled the dysfunctional country with his family when he was eight years old. His family made its way to Seattle, Washington, where he graduated from a public high school and, for four years, studied economics at Eastern Washington University near Spokane, leaving in 2007 without earning his degree. One teacher there, quoted by reporters for the *Seattle Times,* described Isse as a nice young man interested in graduate school and aspiring to work for the United Nations or the World Bank. He had lofty ambitions, despite some challenges he had with upper-level economics classes.

But Isse had met a young woman from Minnesota, moved there, and was out of work and living with the girlfriend in the Minneapolis suburb of Robbinsdale when he fell in with a crowd that attended the Minneapolis mosque. He was never especially religious, his mother—described as a devout Muslim herself—told the paper's reporters. Still, he proved to be easy prey for recruiters who also visited the mosque, according to Omar Jamal, director of the Somali Justice Advocacy Center in Minneapolis. "These people came here and took these boys right under the noses of the FBI," Jamal said at the time.[16]

Recruiters played a substantial role in Minneapolis, especially in the cases of people attracted to al-Shabab. For those drawn to ISIS a decade later, online recruitment through videos generated by al-Awlaki and by ISIS figured heavily, together with "self-recruitment" through peer-pressure, according to authorities. Several men in Minnesota, and later in Somalia and Syria, were key in the recruitments, but the young men, furious at the news and videos they saw and heard about Somalia or Syria, also seemed to talk themselves into signing up. Others—including some young women—were enticed by at least one woman who recruited online.

For their part, leaders at Abubakar as-Saddique staunchly denied that the mosque was a hotbed of radicalism or that anyone there preached violence.[17] Federal prosecutors in Minneapolis, furthermore, found no evidence that the leaders of the mosque were involved in recruiting efforts that secretly took place there.

But federal authorities and some Somalis in Minnesota singled out the guiding roles that others, especially older men, played in the decisions that men in their twenties or younger made to try to take up arms with al-Shabab in Somalia. The US

Attorney's Office in October 2012 won a conviction on terrorism-support charges of a then forty-six-year-old Minneapolis man, Mahamud Said Omar, who worked as a janitor at the Abubakar as-Saddique mosque. With wiretaps, testimony from four others who had pleaded guilty in related cases, and other evidence, the government showed how Omar conspired with others to raise money for the al-Shabab recruits to travel, and that he visited a Somali safe house the group ran to turn over hundreds of dollars to buy AK-47 assault weapons for the men.[18] He was sentenced to twenty years in federal prison.

The prosecution maintained that Omar, also known as Sharif Omar, was integral to the conspiracy—though he may have been more of a facilitator than a mentor. At his sentencing hearing, he addressed the judge in what one journalist called a "rambling screed" that at times was incoherent.[19] His lawyers painted him as mentally impaired.

Nonetheless, Omar was competent enough to help an initial group that left Minneapolis in late 2007 and then, in the fall of 2008, to help another half dozen men—some as young as seventeen—to take the trip. As Assistant US Attorney John F. Docherty noted in an interview with me, Omar proved capable of helping the men get money and tickets to travel and carefully tracked them as they traveled by phoning them during airport layovers. He maintained contacts with al-Shabab members and was trusted enough by the group be allowed into its safe houses.[20] After helping the second group travel from Minnesota that fall, Omar left the United States for Saudi Arabia and, in time, unsuccessfully sought asylum in the Netherlands before being extradited to Minnesota.

Yet another man from Minnesota who wielded heavy influence on the younger recruits, according to authorities, was Omer Abdi Mohamed, nicknamed "Brother Omer" or "Galeyr." A few years older than most of the others, he was described by witnesses in court papers as charismatic and knowledgeable about Islam. Mohamed shared al-Awlaki's videos with the men and often took the lead in meetings, arguing that the men had a religious duty to fight for al-Shabab. He also helped the men get their plane tickets. He called one key secret meeting at Minneapolis's now-defunct Ainu Shams restaurant in which the potential recruits spoke by cell phone to an al-Shabab facilitator in Somalia, according to court papers in the case against him. Mohamed also provided strategic advice, telling would-be terrorists, for instance, that they should not travel in groups of four or more in order to avoid drawing notice.

Before he headed out to his death in his 2008 suicide bombing, Shirwa Ahmed phoned his sister from Somalia to say goodbye. He also called Mohamed. Three years later, in 2011, Mohamed pleaded guilty to federal charges of conspiring to provide material support to a conspiracy to murder, kidnap, and maim abroad.[21] But, as the *Star Tribune* reported, he was out on bond soon after and volunteering or working at an Islamic school, or "dugsi," the Essential Learning Institute of Minnesota (ELMI), where more than one thousand students attended culture and language classes after school and on weekends. There, he reportedly told a parent about an exorcism ritual in which a troubled student was held down while verses of the Quran were recited over her to purge her of a "jinn," or evil spirit.

Aside from his religious efforts, Mohamed was involved in more sinister things that touched the school: two of the al-Shabab recruits—Mohamed Guled Osman, then nineteen, and Omar Ali "Khalif" Farah, then twenty—had attended ELMI before leaving for Somalia in July 2012. After learning of Mohamed's activities at the school in October 2012, Judge Michael J. Davis revoked his bond and ordered him jailed, saying that his trial had exposed "the web that has been weaved in dealing with the secret indoctrination" of al-Shabab recruits.[22] In 2013, Davis sentenced Mohamed to twelve years in prison, plus twenty years of supervised release, during which authorities would monitor him.[23] Prosecutor Charles J. Kovats Jr. called Mohamed "the most culpable" al-Shabab defendant the US Attorney's Office in Minnesota had prosecuted as of the end of 2017.[24]

Wooing young men into supporting terror—persuading them it was justifiable, even heroic—took a certain sinister skill. Framed in the right way, terrible violence, even against innocents, could be made to seem righteous—which may have been the radical Islamists' most noxious talent.

Still another Minnesota man implicated as a recruiter, Cabdullaahi Ahmed Faarax, appeared to dazzle his younger listeners with tales of how he had been injured while fighting on one trip to Somalia. He met with potential recruits in the fall of 2007, when he was about thirty years old, in a Minneapolis mosque and at a private home, according to a criminal complaint brought against him, in absentia, by the US attorney in Minnesota. Faarax, known as "Smiley," in one meeting told the younger men that he had "experienced true brotherhood while fighting in Somalia and that travel for jihad was the best thing that they could do," according to an October 2009 affidavit in the case by FBI Special Agent Michael N. Cannizzaro Jr.

Faarax's pitch seemed ideally suited to the idealistic, angry, and easily swayed young men. He claimed to be involved in guerrilla fighting on the Somalia-Kenya border, where he suffered a leg injury. Citing cooperating witnesses, Cannizzaro said Faarax told his young listeners that traveling to their homeland would be "fun," and that "they would get to shoot guns in Somalia." After his time in combat, Faarax traveled to Kenya and married two women in Nairobi before returning temporarily to the United States.[25] Later, in the fall of 2009, Faarax made his way to Mexico, crossing the border below San Diego, from which he could return to Somalia. His activities earned him a spot on the FBI's "Most Wanted" list.[26]

Faarax's story took a mysterious turn in the fall of 2013 when family members in Minnesota told a reporter for *Time* that he might have been involved in the savage attacks that killed sixty-seven shoppers at Nairobi's Westgate Mall in September 2013. The family members said they would be relieved if Faarax were one of the al-Shabab attackers who were killed because "then he can kill no more, taint our names no more."[27] Such was the split that al-Shabab and, later, ISIS caused in families. While some relatives acquiesced to or even supported their sons' efforts to ally themselves with terrorists, others were appalled and embarrassed, and struggled to understand their children's actions.

Federal authorities dismissed as baseless, however, the reports that Faarax was among the attackers at the Nairobi mall. In the absence of confirmation of his death, Faarax remained on the FBI's "Most Wanted" list as of early 2020 for providing material support—himself—to al-Shabab.

The recruits were aided by Somalis in Minnesota who raised the money they needed for travel and weapons. One who was prosecuted by federal authorities and pleaded guilty, Ahmed Hussein Mahamud, worked with co-conspirators between 2008 and 2011 to raise $1,500 in four fundraising events in Minneapolis and Eden Prairie, Minnesota, according to court papers. He wired money to one of the Minnesotans who joined al-Shabab, Abdikadir Ali Abdi, so he could buy a gun. The men involved in the scheme met, among other places, at the Abubakar as-Saddique mosque.

The evidence against Mahamud included a recorded phone conversation with an unidentified friend in which Mahamud said: "You must take them all non-Muslims as your enemies. You must take all non-Muslims as your enemies." Mahamud, who flipped and testified for the government in the trial of mosque janitor Mahamud Said Omar, pleaded guilty to conspiring to provide material support to a foreign terrorist organization. Because of his cooperation, Judge Davis sentenced him to a comparatively light three years in prison and twenty years of supervised release.

As some Somalis in Minnesota struggled to fathom the motivations of the recruits, they focused on coaxing by older men and, beyond that, the early religious training that some recruits got. Osman Ahmed, a Minnesota political activist who became a staffer for former US Senator Al Franken, served in March 2009 as a spokesman for the families of some Somalis whose sons had joined al-Shabab. He provided a statement to the US Senate Committee on Homeland Security and Governmental Affairs, which conducted hearings on the recruitments, and was unsparing of those he blamed for skewing the minds of the young men and enticing them to become terrorists.[28]

Ahmed's nephew, Burhan Ibrahim Hassan, known as "Little Bashir," was one such recruit. Hassan had not shown up for classes one day in early November 2008 at Roosevelt High School in Minneapolis, where he was a seventeen-year-old senior. His absence triggered a frantic search by his relatives. "We roamed around the metropolitan area and even beyond, nationwide," Ahmed wrote in his statement to the Senate committee. "We went to [Abubakar as-Saddique] mosque and Dawa Mosque, called our building security, called Hennepin County Medical Center, hospital emergencies, and the airport. After that, his mother looked into his room and found that his travel luggage was missing, his clothes were not there and his passport was missing. We immediately notified respective law enforcement agencies. We immediately contacted the local police office MPD and the FBI office in Minneapolis, MN. We have been up on our heels since we have realized that our children were mentally and physically kidnapped on November 4, 2008, on Election Day!!"

Ahmed spoke on behalf of the families of five teens he said "were sent" to Somalia, sharing their ages at the time of their departure. Along with his nephew, he listed Mohamoud Ali Hassan (eighteen, studying engineering at the University of Minnesota), Abdisalan Hussein Ali (nineteen, studying health at the University of Minnesota), Jamal Aweys Sheik Bana (nineteen, studying engineering at Minneapolis Community and Technical College [MCTC] and at Normandale Community College in Minnesota), as well as Mustafa Ali Salat (eighteen, a student at Harding High School in St. Paul).

"These Somali American kids were not troubled kids or [in] gangs. They were the hope of the Somali American community. They were the doctors, lawyers, engineers, scientists and leaders of the future of our strong and prosperous nation," Ahmed told the Senate committee. "For instance, Burhan Hassan was a brilliant student with straight As and on top of his class. He was taking college course[s], i.e., Calculus, Advanced Chemistry etc., as he was about to graduate from high school. These classes were sponsored by the University of Minnesota. He was an ambitious kid with the hope to go to Harvard University to study medicine or law and become a medical doctor or a lawyer."

Conventional wisdom holds that those most likely to be drawn to terrorism hail from the lowest socioeconomic and educational strata. As ill-schooled and isolated loners, it has been said, they turn to violence to vent their anger, reflecting their alienation from society. But much of the academic literature offers a more nuanced portrayal of recruits to radical groups: they often come from modest, though not destitute, backgrounds, and tend to be bright and sophisticated enough to be politically aware, as reflected by their academic achievements in college or, as in the cases of some of the Minnesotans, at least in high school.

With some exceptions, they tend not be involved in gangs, even when they come from lower middle-class or poor families and sometimes have relatives who are involved in gangs. Often, they are idealists, young people with options and few obligations and who thus are free to ally themselves with groups that promise to change conditions that trouble them, such as anti-Muslim sentiments or the perceived victimization of Muslims. As Alexander Lee, a political scientist at the University of Rochester, explained in his 2011 article, "Who Becomes a Terrorist?," recruits to such groups tend to be "lower-status individuals from the educated and politicized section of the population." Further, he reported: "Terrorists, like members of other political groups, are drawn not from a random sample of the population but, rather, from those who have acquired information about the political process, are connected to politicized social networks, and are able to devote time and energy to political involvement."[29]

The young Somali Americans Ahmed referred to had all left Somalia as infants. His nephew was just eight months old when his family made its way to a refugee camp in Kenya, and he was under four when they brought him to the United States in 1996. The boys' knowledge of Somalia was based on what they heard from their parents and teachers, particularly those at the Abubakar as-Saddique mosque, Ahmed said. Burhan Hassan studied Islam there, as did the other boys, and, beginning in 1998, at a predecessor mosque in an area of Minneapolis known as "Little Mogadishu"—the Cedar-Riverside area that is home to thousands of Somalis.

"He attended its youth group. These kids have no perception of Somalia except the one that was formed in their mind by their teachers at the Abubakar Center," Ahmed said. "We believe that these children did not travel to Somalia by themselves. There must be others who made them understand that going to Somalia and participating [in] the fighting is the right thing to do. To address the issue from a factual perspective, it is the dream of every Somali parent to have their children go to the mosque but none of them expected to have their children's mind programmed in a manner that is in line with the extremist's ideologies."

Importantly, however, prosecutors did not tie the recruitments to imams or other mosque leaders. They determined that the recruiters appeared to have simply used rooms in the mosques and deliberately concealed their activities from the leaders, who were unaware of them.

Secrecy was paramount to the recruiters. The departures of the recruits, for instance, stunned and confounded their families, Ahmed said. "No one can imagine the destruction this issue has caused for these mothers and grandmothers. They are going through the worst time in their lives," he told the senators. "Imagine, how these parents feel when their children are returned back to the country were they originally fled from the chaos, genocide, gang rape and lawlessness."

All the young men Ahmed spoke of, except for Mustafa Ali Salat, are dead or believed dead, according to prosecutor Kovats, who monitored the Somali travelers' cases for years. The exact circumstances of their deaths are not altogether clear, although photos on the internet and a video celebrating the "martyrdom" of one of the five—along with two other dead Minnesotans—offered disturbing evidence to their grieving and befuddled families.

Family members of one traveler, Jamal Aweys Sheikh Bana, learned of his death in July 2009, when they checked the internet. There, they saw photos of the young man with a bullet wound in his head and his body being carried on a stretcher in Mogadishu. Sheikh Bana was described as someone with "movie-star looks" and, as a promising engineering student and the eldest of seven children in his family, someone the immigrant family pinned its hopes on.[30] Over three years later, in October 2012, Abayte Ahmed, Sheikh Bana's mother, had to look at the photo again as she testified in court at the trial of one of the men later convicted of aiding Sheikh Bana and others in getting to Somalia, Mahamud Said Omar, the mosque janitor. She, like other parents of the travelers, had alerted police when her son went missing back in 2008. She didn't learn of Sheikh Bana's departure for Somalia until he got there and called to tell her he was in Somalia before hanging up, moving fast for fear the call could be traced.[31]

Another recruit, Mohamoud Ali Hassan, epitomized the shifting nature of youthful idealism, the potent influence of peers, and the insidious influence of recruiters. While in his first year as an engineering student at the University of Minnesota in May 2007, Hassan posted a thoughtful essay on Facebook defending the Ethiopian invasion of Somalia, saying the country's forces moved in at the request of the Transitional Federal Government, which he called "the sole legitimate authority of the country." Friends said Hassan, who posted his essay under the name of Bashir Maxamed Caydid, was related to the president of the Somali government at the time. Hitting a patriotic note, he wrote: "Our nation first needs to be freed from the forces of darkness," and he argued that the ICU and its allies were embarked on an unjust cause "no matter how much religious/nationalist rhetoric you use to portray otherwise." He told the ICU and al-Shabab: "Therefore, I would advise you to stop sending young Somali boys on suicide missions against well armed and well trained troops."[32]

But Hassan's convictions soon changed, shifting along with a personal religious transformation, as his friends told *New York Times* reporter Andrea Elliott. In the fall of 2007, she reported, Hassan began downloading sermons onto his iPod and soon was attending the Abubakar mosque. Reports of rapes in Somalia troubled him, and he started learning more about the rebels in the country. When a friend from the mosque left for Somalia, he wanted to join him. Then, in May 2008, he was infuriated by the United States air strike that killed al-Shabab leader Aden Hashi Ayro and at least ten civilians. "How dare they?" Hassan demanded one afternoon at the university student center, the newspaper reported. "Who is the terrorist?"[33]

Hassan readily found jihadist videos from cleric Anwar al-Awlaki and others, as well as chat rooms, Elliott reported. By November 2008, he quit school and left Minnesota for Somalia. There, propagandists for al-Shabab told his story in a 2013 al-Shabab recruitment video, "The Path to Paradise: From the Twin Cities to the Land of the Two Migrations." The reason for his change of heart: a narrator on the video claimed that "the enchanting siren of jihad reached him."

Hassan, addressing the camera, urged would-be recruits to "support jihad in any way you can." Suggesting that joining the cause would be personally fulfilling, he said: "You are the one in need, you are the one in need, we are all in need of Allah." While it's not clear, in fact, who or what changed Hassan, he was reported to be deeply troubled by the shooting death in Minneapolis of an uncle he was close to.

The video claimed Hassan was killed in battle in Mogadishu in 2009, fulfilling his "dream" of becoming a martyr, or "shahid." The video showcased images of his body and that of Troy M. Kastigar, another Minnesotan who had converted to Islam and traveled to Somalia, only to die apparently at Hassan's side. Kastigar was the same man Bashir, then a middle-schooler, had briefly met in San Diego. Over those images, a rapper on the slickly produced video intoned: "your West is a test and so's your family. This world is an illusion, don't be deceived, call on Allah and never retreat. . . . Islam is our faith, jihad is our peak, the best of our end to be a shahid."[34]

All the deaths were crushing to the families and friends of those seduced into the "shahid" mythology, of course. Perhaps one of the most unsettling of the fatalities, though, was that of Osman Ahmed's nephew, Burhan Ibrahim Hassan. Hassan, who hadn't even finished high school when he left for Somalia in November 2008, had no interest in Somali politics or clan issues, according to his uncle. Instead, his main interest was doing well in school—until, by Ahmed's account, he fell into the angry group that met at the Minneapolis mosque.[35] Family members said Hassan had been ill in Somalia and wanted to quit the group but was shot by al-Shabab members in June 2009 as he was trying to leave.[36]

Like so many others—and like the plotters in Bashir's circle later on—the young Hassan had been played by the gunmen whose self-created heroic images belied their vicious intents.

CHAPTER FOUR

Blind Devotion

Nationalism, a naive appetite for adventure, and/or religious fervor seemed to draw the Minnesotans who left for Somalia between 2007 and 2009. Their motives echoed those of earlier generations of immigrants to America and their descendants who felt called to liberate their homelands or to fight oppression with force. Irish Americans supported the anti-British Irish Republican Army, for instance. Young American Jews backed such groups as the anti-British Irgun in Israel. And American leftists took up arms in the Spanish Civil War or, earlier, in the Russian Revolution.

The Somali travelers appeared to respond to strong sentiments among many Somalis in Minnesota that the Ethiopians, most of whom were Christians, were invaders. They saw al-Shabab as a liberating force, irrespective of the American stance against the group and of the group's anti–United States position. Some, however, did see the group as a vehicle that could help them attain martyrdom and the Paradise they thought it promised, a message the propagandists repeatedly drove home.

To CAIR's Jaylani Hussein, the men's story was tragic. He argued, in an interview with me, that many Somalis saw the Islamic Courts Union, the group from which al-Shabab emerged, as a moderate force. Hussein contended that the ICU had sought to negotiate with the displaced Somali government in Baidoa to join forces to run the country. But the United States, he maintained, couldn't brook the ICU because Americans, at the time, were in "full 9/11 special-war-on-terror mindset."[1] For the Somali Americans in Minneapolis drawn to the fight in their homeland, that stance put them on the wrong side of the battle line.

Whatever their motivations for joining al-Shabab, though, the recruits from Minnesota could not long harbor illusions about its brutal methods and intentions. One has only to hear the stories of the group's victims to understand that. For instance, Yusuf Hassan Abdi, a member of Kenya's parliament from Nairobi who won reelection for a third time in August 2017, learned firsthand how ugly the outfit's violence can be. His story and his insights into the nature of terrorist recruitment are worth pondering.

The bloody attack came five years earlier, during Hassan's reelection campaign for a second term. On December 7, 2012, just moments after he spoke to more than two hundred people at a mosque in his district, someone detonated a bomb stuffed with ball bearings and nails near him. Eight people, including two children, were killed around him. He nearly lost both his legs and was saved only by being rushed to a hospital.

His attackers have never been positively identified, but security officials told Hassan they were believed to be members of al-Shabab, which repeatedly reached outside Somalia to attack targets in Kenya and elsewhere. Hassan told me he was targeted because he is a moderate Muslim—the first Muslim Somali to be elected from Nairobi, his hometown—and he advocates unity among various religious groups, especially with Christians who predominate in Kenya.

"My election had built a bridge," Hassan said, as we sat in a comfortable coffee shop at an affluent Nairobi shopping mall.[2] "I have been working to bring religious, social, and political harmony in the constituency. I am a regular visitor to Christian communities. I speak at churches, which has been condemned by some radicals. I don't think they want a bridge-builder, someone who breaks barriers. They want a divided society, a society divided on religious grounds."

As he underwent repeated surgeries over the years and avoided amputation of one of his legs by traveling to New York for specialized treatment, Hassan had much time to ponder the motivations of the people who likely attacked him. He represented the Kamukunji district of Nairobi, an area that is home to at least 290,000 people—including both Somalis and non-Somalis, and not including tens of thousands more temporary migrants—and is the sort of multicultural melting pot that groups such as al-Shabab abhor. The terrorist group, he said, wants to drive wedges between religious communities and particularly to provoke Christians into an apocalyptic holy war with followers of their brand of Islam.

Attacks such as the one he suffered are "a form of incitement," he said. The bombers target mainly churches and Christian organizations, but they pursue anyone who advocates peaceful coexistence. The attack outside Nairobi's Al Hidaya mosque that day was, to Hassan, a bloody statement against unity and part of an attempt by ill-schooled idealists to destroy the existing order in hopes of building some divinely ordained society out of the ashes of the current one. "Their objective is to destroy what is in existence, to destroy and to create chaos," he said. "Everything that exists now [to them] is dirty, so there [is] nothing they need to preserve. Everything must be destroyed and out of that chaos would emerge something new, something more likeable to their philosophy and their way of thinking."

Along with his message of coexistence, Hassan's background represents the sort of life that al-Shabab and similar groups cannot abide. Born in Nairobi in March 1958 to parents who were also native Kenyans of Somali descent (like many in northeastern Kenya), Hassan attended secondary school in the city and then headed to the West for higher education, earning degrees at the University of Middlesex in the United Kingdom and later at the Fletcher School at Tufts University in the United States.

Hassan worked in journalism, reporting, writing or announcing for the Kenya Broadcasting Corporation, the *Arab Times,* and for many years, the British Broadcasting Corporation, then the Voice of America. He cofounded and edited a monthly magazine, *Africa Events.* He also served as the director of the Namibian national radio and television network, shortly after the country attained independence in 1990. He later worked for the United Nations, representing its refugee commission in areas including Central Asia, East Timor, and Southern Africa. He served as a senior spokesman for the United Nations in Kabul and then as a senior adviser to the UN Secretary General in New York City before returning to Nairobi in 2006 to run IRIN, a UN news organization that focuses on humanitarian topics.

Hassan was politically active during much of his time in journalism. Early on, he served as an executive member of the Committee for the Release of Political Prisoners of Kenya (CRPPK), which he had cofounded. He chaired a group that in the late 1980s opposed the one-party government of longtime Kenyan president, Daniel arap Moi, exposing human rights abuses in the country. He kept his journalistic and political pursuits separate for much of his career by covering areas outside

Kenya, even as he followed events there closely. In 2007, he ventured into electoral politics in Nairobi, though seats in Parliament eluded him on his first attempts (the 2007 election in Kamukunji was cancelled by the electoral commission because of violence and widespread irregularities). He finally won office in 2011 and sought re-election in 2013, a race he won while recuperating in a South African hospital from the injuries he suffered in the late 2012 mosque bombing.

While Hassan advocated peace and coexistence, when we spoke he did not see a future for Somalia that included al-Shabab as a partner in the Somali government. "Their thinking is shockingly different to the organization of normal society in the world, regardless of religion and ideology," Hassan said. "They have never shown any interest whatsoever [in a negotiated resolution of grievances]. They have demonized and degraded and degenerated every other group, every other political organization."

The choice for Somalis and the rest of the world in dealing with al-Shabab was stark, as Hassan saw it. He said: "They either get defeated, and the reasonable elements among them can become part of a new dispensation, or they win and they impose on society their ways, their philosophy, their ideology, what they believe, which I don't understand. I don't think there's anything in-between."

He allowed for the possibility, however, that some al-Shabab recruits could be rehabilitated. Naive Westerners, for instance, who signed up for the group or its ideological kin, such as the Islamic State, should not be jailed, he said, so long as their hearts and minds can be won away. Such recruits are often damaged idealists, confused about the different cultures they live in, and seduced by dreams of glory and a perverse interpretation of religion.

They often hail from families that have been broken, sometimes as a result of experiences the recruits' parents endured in Somalia or in refugee camps, Hassan said. Often, there is no father who could anchor a rebellious teen's emotional and intellectual wanderings. The parents of the recruits often don't even speak the language of the countries they settled in, whether that be English, Dutch, or another language. "They don't understand the culture," Hassan said. "A little box in the house, the TV, gives them a picture of it."

But he saw how the recruits have grown up, in effect, as dual citizens outside and inside their homes in such cities as Minneapolis and San Diego. "The children are conflicted," he said. "From morning to afternoon and evening, they are in American society, American culture. By nightfall, they come back to this island, Somalia island, which is driven by the divisions and the problems which are affected daily by the social, political, and economic upheavals of Somalia."

As a result, the potential recruits often did poorly in school, felt alienated, and may have suffered from racial discrimination. "They don't have a place they can call home," Hassan said. "And it is very easy, when you have a demagogue who tells them, 'your parents are like this, your parents are poor, you are not accepted into this society, you are not doing very well because of your religion, because of your culture. And you can liberate your country, you can have your own country and culture back. That is the only way you are going to be liberated from the shackles, the problems you face.' The kids are manipulated. They are not aware of the atrocities, the violations and the falsehoods of these organizations until they go, until they see the reality."

Al-Shabab won over recruits with such pitches from about 2007 through at least 2012. After that, Somali youths—such as Bashir and his friends—and others were drawn more to Islamic State, a group that Hassan said potential recruits saw as "more glorious." Islamic State offered them the chance to rebuild the glory of Islam in one of its historic centers, Syria. Recruits saw themselves liberating Syrian Muslims from a tyrannical regime and restoring a long-lost and long-promised caliphate. They also fell for a retelling of recent events that framed Christian America as an invader in Muslim Iraq, another historic center of Islamic civilization when it was at its peak. Such a recasting of events, along with stories of oppression Palestinian Muslims feel in Israel and in the occupied territories, can prove irresistible for pliable minds.

"As a young person, the combination of these factors can lead you to want to go and help the underdog, the poor Muslims who have been trampled upon by dictators," Hassan said. The concrete examples, shared in videos online or perhaps by propagandists in mosques, can prove enticing, especially when paired with the dissatisfactions the recruits may feel because of their poor domestic conditions and perhaps the inability of their families to rescue other relatives from refugee camps in Kenya or elsewhere. Said Hassan: "If you are reading this in Minnesota or Columbus as a young Muslim, it doesn't require a lot of push to convince you."

The enticement, of course, proved fatal for many. The recruits often suffered early deaths "in a struggle they have very little understanding of and a cause that turns out be a false cause," Hassan said. Some were killed in internal feuds, others used as suicide bombers because leaders in al-Shabab and the Islamic State saw them as disposable. Some, disillusioned by their experiences, were killed trying to flee, while some who returned faced jail in the West or in parts of Africa.

CHAPTER FIVE

A Cautionary Tale

As he moved forward in high school in California in 2010, Bashir's interests in jihad waned. Politics and rigorous observance took a backseat, especially when his family moved to the Balboa area of San Diego and got involved in the large and moderate Abu Bakr Masjid mosque at the Islamic Center of San Diego.

Instead, Bashir turned his attention to familiar high school pursuits, including basketball and football, in the new neighborhood. Such ways of belonging gave him the sense of community he craved. He and his cousin, Hanad Mohallim, forgot about politics for a time. That held true for Bashir even after Mohallim in 2011 moved to Minnesota and an American drone killed their online video guru, al-Awlaki, that year in Yemen. The Kariye cousins, who had by then moved to Edmonton in Canada, rarely stayed in touch with Bashir at that time. (Because Bashir's mother had nine sisters, he had a lot of cousins, spread across San Diego, Minneapolis, and Edmonton.)

But soon, a big change in Bashir's life would upend his routine and drive him into a different circle of friends. It would plunge him, too, into a complex and larger Somali American community, one in which some immigrants found great

Several of the men who plotted to join ISIS attended Heritage Academy, a public school in Minneapolis that caters to Somalis. Critics say the school works against assimilation, while defenders say conservative Muslim parents prefer it to diverse public schools because it helps preserve Somali identities and they fear exposing their children to drugs and even to clothing they regard as improper.

success and others—the vast majority—struggled to find their way socially and economically.

Looking for a tighter-knit Somali community and better economic prospects, Bashir's father moved the family in 2012 to Minneapolis. There, Bashir joined Mohallim and another cousin, Abdihafid Maxamed. They all attended the Heritage Academy, a publicly funded school that catered exclusively to Somalis, where the incoming senior, Bashir, soon made friends as the "kid from California." By his own account, he was a popular figure, someone whom everyone wanted to know. Like many other young Somalis, Bashir acquired a nickname—"Cali," an homage to his San Diego roots. "Good high school year, nothing really happened," Bashir recalled to me, though he did meet a girl at the school whom he courted (and later, in March 2016, married).

To make up for a shortfall in his credits, Bashir also attended Minnesota Transition School after school and in the fall of 2012 switched to the school fulltime. He graduated high school the following June. He then took a summer job cleaning airplanes with Maxamed at Minneapolis International Airport, got a car, and made plans to attend Minneapolis Community and Technical College that fall to study pharmacy (though he would later switch his major to law enforcement). Like hundreds of other Somali young men—including a particular group of a dozen or so—he also played a lot of basketball. The city's recreation department and a mosque gym gave the men plenty of opportunity to play.

Despite those bland outward appearances, the summer of 2013 was when "everything changed," Bashir recalled. The shift started when Bashir and Mohallim made plans to visit their Kariye cousins in Canada. Bashir's father, still troubled by the Kariye men's efforts to radicalize Bashir in high school, forbade Bashir from going. This was part of two years of fevered arguments and stony silences between Bashir and his father, Hassan.

Abdirashid Bashir Hassan's life should have been a cautionary tale for his elder son. His experiences as a refugee had taught him as much about desperation and struggle, both in Africa and in the United States, as his studies of Islam in Saudi Arabia had taught him about religion. Hassan had fled the poverty and anarchy of Mogadishu when he was about twenty-three years old in 1991. After spending some time in Nairobi, he, his wife, and their young firstborn daughter made their way in 1992 to San Diego, home to a large number of Somali refugees, under the sponsorship of a sister-in-law.

The move to San Diego fulfilled a dream for Hassan because as a high school student, in 1984, he had wanted to go to college in the city. Despite his poor English skills at the time, he wrote San Diego State University to get information about applying. Later, as Mogadishu collapsed, college seemed like a distant fantasy. There were days when he didn't eat, and looting, killing and rape abounded as civil war ripped the country apart, Hassan recalled in an interview with me.[1] By contrast, San Diego offered law and order, peace, and the chance at financial success, and he leapt at the chance to move there. "I came to live in peace and prosperity," said Hassan, one of tens of thousands of Somalis who made their way to the United States and across the world in the early 1990s.

To be sure, life in America wasn't easy—as it continues to be challenging for many Somalis. Hassan drove a taxi (and in 2019 was driving a car for Lyft). He worked in a grocery store. He did whatever he could to feed a family that grew to include six children. Bashir, his third child and first son, came along in San Diego in 1995. At one point, Hassan pooled his efforts and money with friends and colleagues from across the Somali diaspora to build a business producing samosas, the deep-fried or baked pasta treats that Somalis and many in the Middle East, Africa, and Asia crave, especially for meals during festivals such as Ramadan. The business failed, however, costing Hassan longtime friendships and alienating some Somalis in Minnesota. Hassan's travels in connection with it, moreover, gave him an unpleasant personal taste of America's war on terrorism, a run-in with the Department of Homeland Security.

Hassan recalled his problem with the authorities with anger and sadness. He had flown in 2005 to Columbus, Ohio, another big resettlement area for Somalis, to raise funds for the samosa factory. As he headed to the plane to return to San Diego, he was detained at the airport. The authorities questioned him for eleven hours, he recalled, apparently because his name had shown up on a list of suspected terrorists. It turned out, he said, that the suspect had a name similar to his—something not surprising because many Somalis share similar names, especially "Hassan" and variations of "Abdirashid." Even though he was released, he couldn't fly and had to rent a car to drive several days home. He said he had to hire a lawyer to get the matter straightened out.

If the Homeland Security department's system had registered Hassan's full name—which includes the family names of ancestors going back for 13 generations—the problem might not have shown up for him. Names, it seems, are part of the cultural clash between Somalis and Americans. Typically, Somali children's names often begin with three parts: the first name is a chosen name; the second is the first name of the father; and the last name is the paternal grandfather's first name.[2] Hassan's son, Abdirahman Abdirashid Bashir, uses Bashir as his last name.

Cultural collisions, financial struggles, and educational challenges make life difficult for refugees in any new country, and the United States is no exception. The United States celebrates its capacity for giving opportunity to newcomers—and history shows how immigrants make their way up the social ladder, some quickly and others across generations—but the climb is often difficult and slippery. Certainly, this has been true for Somalis, most of whom are immigrants who have been in the United States for less than twenty-five years or are first-generation Americans who straddle both the Somali and American worlds.

Many Somalis are poor. Many left their country with little more than the clothes on their backs and skills ill-suited to the modern American economy. Many older

Somalis, for instance, were farmers or nomads with little education who made their way for years through refugee camps in Kenya or other places before finding passage to the United States. They and their children have a long way to go to feel financially comfortable in the country.

Perhaps because of their nomadic backgrounds or because they were forced, as refugees, to move often, Somalis have been quick to pick up and leave when opportunities arose around the United States. Minneapolis author and playwright Ahmed Ismail Yusuf, in *Somalis in Minnesota,* told of how small numbers of Somali refugees initially moved to San Diego in the early 1990s to join a handful of families from the Ogaden region of Ethiopia that had settled there. When they heard of meatpacking jobs at a poultry company in Marshall, Minnesota, a small city about three hours west of Minneapolis by car, they flocked there.[3] While the weather differed dramatically from what Somalis were accustomed to—the equator passes through the southern tip of Somalia—the economy did offer low-skilled jobs in meatpacking and other areas with which the immigrants could earn a living. Soon, Somalis found their way to Minneapolis, where social service agencies, such as Lutheran Immigrant and Refugee Services, Lutheran Social Services of Minnesota, Catholic Charities, and others, helped them settle, much as such groups had aided other immigrants, such as the Vietnamese and Hmong after the Vietnam War.

Even within Minnesota, Somalis have tended to be on the move. From 2010 to 2014 the Minnesota State Demographic Center surveyed state residents and found that some 24 percent of Somalis changed addresses every year. The center's January 2016 report, "The Economic Status of Minnesotans," suggested the moves may have reflected "financial and housing instability."[4]

Poverty remains a huge issue for the Somalis of Minnesota. Minnesota Compass estimated that some 49 percent of Somalis in the state live below the poverty line. This is the case even though some 62 percent of the adults in the group work, often getting by on menial jobs. With some 40 percent of the community lacking even high school degrees, it's little wonder that getting good jobs are difficult, especially for older Somalis. Some 27 percent speak little or no English.[5]

"The median Somali household income level is staggeringly low," reported Stefanie Chambers, an associate professor of political science at Trinity College in Hartford, Connecticut. The American Community Survey in 2010 pegged the median household income for Somalis at $11,414 in Minneapolis and $13,370 in St. Paul, as Chambers recounted in *Somalis in the Twin Cities and Columbus,* her comparative study of the American cities with the largest Somali communities. This compared to a median household income for whites of $54,339 in Minneapolis and $52,665 in St. Paul. It also fell short of the median income figures for non-Somali blacks of $21,478 in Minneapolis and $23,508 in St. Paul.

The figures for Somalis may understate the group's income level because of undercounting of the population and because they don't account for such informal businesses as day care and home health care, Chambers acknowledged. Still, she argued that poverty is endemic in the group. "Despite the possible problems with these numbers, the overwhelming poverty in the Somali community is both undeniable and staggering," Chambers wrote. "This level of household poverty adds to the forces already stacked against Somali economic incorporation and financial security."[6]

Somalis tend to work in home health care, the food industry, housekeeping, and security, as well as in their own businesses, including restaurants scattered around the city of Minneapolis. Several Somali shopping malls dot the Minneapolis area, where shoppers can buy traditional food, clothing, and fabrics, often from small shops run by women clad in traditional flowing robes known as "jilbab" as well as hijab headscarves. Indeed, the traditional clothing has been an obstacle to employment outside the Somali community, according to University of Minnesota sociologist Cawo M. Abdi. Women have been denied jobs by factory employers who cited safety concerns because of the long robes, with some noting that some women refused for religious reason to wear uniforms.[7]

The forces working against Somali economic gains are both external and internal. Somali families, for one thing, tend to be large—a half dozen children per family is not uncommon.[8] According to the 2016 report, "The Economic Status of Minnesotans," some 41 percent of Somali families in the state have four or more people living in each household.[9]

Single-parent households are also not uncommon, moreover, though reliable statistics are difficult to find. Large numbers of Somalis are on public assistance in Minnesota, but some measures of them—such as figures that suggest the "married but separated" population among beneficiaries has been as high as 32.3 percent—may be inflated, since the welfare system tends to favor single mothers. As some women feel forced to hide their husbands, the system tends to create tensions in families and between men and women, unsettling "Somali gender power dynamics" by minimizing the man's traditional breadwinning role, according to sociologist Abdi.[10] Statistics compiled by Minnesota state demographer Susan Brower suggest that the share of women with children at home without a spouse present could range as high as 48 percent, with a relatively large number reporting they were married but their spouse was absent.

No matter what the precise figures are, poverty and family dysfunction have brought crime, as has happened with native-born Americans and with other immigrant groups throughout American history. Somalis in the Twin Cities were appalled when federal authorities in 2010 brought sex-trafficking charges against twenty-nine people (later adding a thirtieth person)—most of whom were allegedly active in three related gangs, the Somali Outlaws, the Somali Mafia, and the Lady Outlaws. Prosecutors in the US Attorney's Office in Nashville, Tennessee, charged that the gangs took young Somali and other African women, some thirteen years old or younger, from Minneapolis to Nashville to engage in prostitution between 2000 and 2010.[11] But the government's case fell apart after a jury acquitted six of the men charged, and a federal judge later threw out the convictions of three others, ruling that prosecutors had not proved there was a single overarching conspiracy.[12]

Still, police in Minneapolis have kept tabs on gang activity among Somalis. In 2011, they reported that seven Somali gangs were active in Minneapolis, with about two hundred members in all. Some one hundred or more gang-related crimes were reported each year in the Cedar-Riverside area of the city between 2008 and 2010. "They were trying to find identity," Hassan Mohamud, the imam at Islamic Da'wah Center of St. Paul, told a reporter. "They do not belong to Somalis. They do not belong to Islam. They do not belong to America. So they found their own system. . . . They had good intention. At first, the good intention was to help and support each other and protect. But they eventually changed that support system to harm."[13]

For some Somali teens, one of the downsides of assimilation into American society has been falling prey to the seductions of gangs and crime. Many second-generation Somali Americans have emulated the styles of dress, mannerisms, and ways of speaking of African Americans—even though tensions have arisen between non-Somali black Americans and Somalis, particularly in some Minnesota high schools. A fraction of such Somali Americans have found their way into Somali American gangs. In some ways, this echoes the experience of many other ethnic groups in which poor young people, usually men, banded together in criminal enterprises, often as a defensive reaction to rival ethnic groups. Irish gangs such as the Dead Rabbits, Forty Thieves, and the Bowery Boys terrorized New York in the mid-nineteenth century, for instance. Some Jews in the same period organized themselves into such groups as the Eastman Gang as well.[14] Long after such gangs disappeared, the Italian outfit, La Cosa Nostra, continued to trouble law enforcement, enduring into the early 2000s at least.[15] Latin American gangs and nativist white American gangs remain a major problem for authorities,[16] as do African American gangs such as the Crips and the Bloods, which have moved beyond their 1960s and 1970s California roots into cities across the United States.[17]

For some Somalis, the growth of gangs has had a peculiar international effect. In the Eastleigh suburb of Nairobi, a largely Somali neighborhood, young toughs who moved back to Kenya after learning criminal ways in the United States now sometimes terrorize locals. Residents of the area refer to them as "Americans," according to Chinese University of Hong Kong anthropologist Gordon Mathews, who has done research in the Eastleigh community.[18]

CHAPTER SIX

Don't Let the Caravan Leave You

Bashir's cousin Hanad Mohallim had no father to rein him in. So, when the idea of visiting the Kariye cousins in Canada struck the boys in 2013, and Bashir's father forbade Bashir from going, no one stood in Mohallim's way. Mohallim spent the month-long Ramadan holiday with the Kariyes.

He returned to Minnesota in late August "changed," Bashir said. He told Bashir, for one thing, that it was improper for Bashir to have a girlfriend and that he needed to go to the mosque more often. Mohallim took to wearing traditional clothing, and as Bashir would testify in court, "he was more religious, more devoted to Islam."

Mohallim's newfound strictness would affect Bashir profoundly. While Bashir's flirtation with radicalism in San Diego was intellectual—a matter of watching videos online and debating ideas with relatives—in Minneapolis it would grow much more tangible. After all, Minneapolis had a history with radicalization of its young men.

Indeed, the history of recruitment to al-Shabab made Bashir's father wary of certain mosques in the city because they were known for their recruits and for FBI surveillance. When Bashir and another cousin Abdihafid Maxamed visited one mosque in Little Mogadishu one day soon after Bashir moved to Minneapolis, his dad told him about the al-Shabab links to Minnesota and told him to stay away—and Bashir complied. "I didn't know there [was] a radical problem in Minnesota," Bashir recalled. "In San Diego, this [was] just like, 'Oh, my cousins were just talking.'"

But the talk and debate would soon lead to action for Bashir. While he spent most of the fall of 2013 focusing on class work at Minneapolis Community and Technical College, which he had begun attending, Mohallim, then in his senior year in high school, was deepening his commitment to radical Islam. Every so often, Mohallim talked to Bashir about Syria and the fighting there, echoing themes he had heard from the Kariye brothers and another Canadian cousin Mahad Hirsi. In late November that year, Mohallim stunned Bashir when he told him that one of the Kariye brothers had made his way to Syria to join ISIS and the other was on his way with Mahad Hirsi.

Bashir had coaxed the admission out of Mohallim after Bashir had a short FaceTime chat with Hersi Kariye—the cousin whom Bashir regarded as an older brother—while Kariye was waiting for a flight at an airport with Mahad Hirsi. Chillingly, Hersi Kariye told Bashir then, "Yo man, I heard you got off the path. . . . Don't let the caravan leave you." Being left by the caravan—a phrase perfectly pitched to an adolescent's fear of abandonment by friends—was one Bashir said the radical Islamists used a lot.

All through that rainy, dreary late fall, Bashir and Mohallim spent hours combing Twitter for signs of their cousins. They came across one photo online of Hersi Kariye with his face obscured by a mask, sitting down with an AK-47 rifle next to him, holding up an index finger in a kind of Islamist salute. "We could see . . . his eyes and eyebrows," Bashir recalled. "He was wearing sweatpants, and we remembered those sweatpants he used to always wear and the mask . . . a turban [that] they wrapped around their faces. . . . Hanad told us that was the exact one we bought in Canada." That image made his cousin's move to Syria all too real. "That was when it really hit me. I was shocked. My stomach hurt. It looked scary, it looked scary where he was."

Soon, Bashir and Mohallim were watching propaganda videos from ISIS regularly, and the pair argued as Mohallim vowed to go to Syria. Still in their teens, they were touched by images of children dying and mothers crying, as the narrators pleaded for help, urging Muslims to come to the aid of endangered fellow Muslims.

Bashir resisted, but the emotional tug was powerful. "I had seen a verse in the Quran saying why wouldn't you defend those who are weak, the oppressed ones that call out to God, saying, 'help us, give us protectors,' and it hit me," Bashir recalled.

He went to his dad and asked about jihad in Syria. He told Bashir that the battle in Syria was among splintered Muslim groups and that it was a civil war. "He was like, 'civil war is never, ever, jihad. It's a bunch of Muslims fighting each other, killing each other over territory, and that is haram [forbidden], and it's a big sin in Islam to kill your brothers and sisters.'"

Uncertain about who was right, Bashir bounced such arguments off Mohallim. Citing other sections of the Quran, Bashir said children are obliged first to care for their parents. As the eldest boys in their families, Bashir argued, he and Mohallim had a special obligation and that was their jihad, their struggle. "We can't just go," Bashir told him, adding that the Kariye brothers had older brothers who could care for their parents.

But Mohallim insisted he would go, in early 2014, with an older friend the boys knew from San Diego—Douglas McAuthur McCain. McCain, known as "Tooth" because of a missing front tooth, was a Chicago-born African American who had converted to Islam, had attended high school in the Minneapolis area, lived in San Diego, and married a Somali woman. Mohallim also pressed Bashir's then sixteen-year-old brother Hamsa to join them. Mohallim's religious commitment deepened still further, and he tried to press radical Islam on casual friends from the nearby suburb of Burnsville, at times irritating the Bashir brothers and provoking fears that someone would tip the federal authorities to his intentions.

By March 2014, Mohallim had locked in his plans to join ISIS. He told Bashir he had bought his ticket for a flight that would ultimately lead him to Syria, even though he was anxious about it. Mohallim dismissed his personal doubts as nothing more than "the devil talking," and steeled himself by reflecting that their Canadian cousins had promised that once he got to ISIS territory there would be nothing but "peace and tranquility in your heart." They warned him that the devil—"Shaytan" in Islam—would come up with excuses for him not to join them, such as an eldest son's obligation to care for his mother. Months earlier, Mohallim had touched Bashir by arguing that the Canadian cousins were "like our brothers to us, and they went over there. If they're saying it's good, don't you trust them? That's our brothers, man. They wouldn't want us to waste our lives over there."

Bashir was still skeptical, but Mohallim persuaded Bashir and his brother to help him on his way from Minneapolis, on March 9, 2014, to Syria, by way of Turkey. Facing the departure of a fourth cousin intent on joining ISIS, Bashir's skepticism wavered. He told Mohallim that if he found that the ISIS fighters were involved in true jihad, he would join him there. "I trust you with my life," Bashir said. "If you go there and you see that it's real jihad, true jihad, over there, I'm going to come later on." Mohallim then gave him a password to a shared Yahoo email account that ISIS fighters used to avoid federal government eavesdroppers.

The time on the way to the Minneapolis airport was poignant for the young men, as Mohallim screwed up his courage by listening to audio versions of "Under the Shades of Swords" and "In the Hearts of Green Birds: The Martyrs of Bosnia," accounts of the Bosnian War of the early 1990s. Bashir had learned of the accounts from his Canadian cousins as a ninth-grader and was taken by the descriptions of Western young men who had sacrificed their lives defending Muslims. The accounts described miracles, telling of how the martyrs' bodies would glow.

For the Bashir brothers and Mohallim, the scheme to get to Syria was a clumsy bit of *Spy vs. Spy,* with a pathetic twist. Nervous about her son's interests in radical Islam and mindful of other young Minnesotans who had left the United States, Mohallim's mother kept his passport away from him. He persuaded her to give it to him by applying for jobs and claiming he needed the passport for identification. Wary of cameras at the airport, the men initially planned for Bashir to take Mohallim to a train stop at the Mall of America from which he could get to the airport. But, worried about the time, they wound up driving to the airport anyway. And the men cooked up an alibi in which Bashir would say he last saw Mohallim at a mosque where they prayed a morning prayer together.

As the Bashir brothers went home just afterward, Bashir fretted that his mother could sense that something was amiss. Though burning to share the news of Mohallim's departure, he stayed silent, even with a sister and another visiting cousin. And when Mohallim's mother, Bashir's aunt, called late that night, panicked about her missing son, Bashir crafted a lie about Mohallim hanging out with a fictional Ethiopian.

Mohallim had masked his departure with a text to his mother saying he was playing basketball at a YMCA, only leading her to chase after him there, to no avail. "She looked for him all night," Bashir said, checking in with all her son's friends. Aware that her son's politics were "getting radical," as Bashir put it, she could see that his passport and clothes were gone, and she feared the worst.

Bashir's family then grilled him in a family meeting, figuring that Mohallim had tried to make his way to ISIS. His sisters said they would review the videotapes from cameras in the mosque to see whomever Mohallim had been with. "My heart dropped," Bashir recalled. Meanwhile, Mohallim's mother reached out to the FBI, desperate to get her son back. Bashir's lies soon crumbled, as his mother pressed him for the truth. "I told her everything," he said. Mohallim's mother then traveled to Turkey, spending two months trying to get him back, again to no avail, as ISIS moved him deep into Syria.

CHAPTER SEVEN

Why ISIS?

When the first wave of Minnesota Somalis chose to affiliate with al-Shabab, the connection was obvious: the group was rooted in their homeland and seemed to promise stability there, however problematic, after years of chaos. But the shift to ISIS by Bashir, his dozen friends, his relatives in Canada, and others was perplexing.

The young Minnesotans in the second wave had no connection to Syria, which lay more than three thousand miles to the north of Somalia by land. Further, the Syrian civil war was largely a matter of Arabs fighting other Arabs, a battle that was at least one step removed from Somalis, despite their distant Arab ancestry. For Somali Americans such as Bashir, who had been born in the United States, or who had come as toddlers, the appeal of ISIS was even more difficult to understand because of the group's explicit anti-Americanism and the brutality that so publicly marked its actions, particularly its ghoulish beheadings of Westerners.

But it was the religious nature of the fight that tugged at the young Somalis and Somali Americans. To them, it seemed like a battle for the restoration of Islam to a place of dominance in the world, a battle as old as the Crusades. Despite differences in approach that drove wedges between ISIS and al-Qaida and between both groups and al-Shabab, the organizations shared an apocalyptic view of the battle between the Islamic world and the West that easily allowed the Somalis to switch their

© JOSEPH WEBER

The Dar Al-Farooq Islamic Center in Bloomington, a Minneapolis suburb, was one of the places where the Minneapolis men who plotted to join ISIS met, discussing plans between basketball matches. The center was bombed in 2017 by a small Illinois militia group.

focus to ISIS. ISIS, moreover, had stolen the global limelight from al-Qaida with its territorial expansions in Syria and beyond and its pursuit of a caliphate, a united Islamic state whose leader would take up the mantle of the Prophet Muhammad. In fact, the term "caliph" is derived from the Arabic term for "successor," and was last used by Ottoman Turks until their empire dissolved and the caliphate was abolished in 1924. The armed followers of Abu Bakr al-Baghdadi, the ISIS leader killed in October 2019, had declared him the new caliph in June 2014.[1]

The shadow cast by the first wave of men who left to join al-Shabab, moreover, seemed long and deep for some Somalis in Minneapolis. Stories of young men leaving to go "back home" were common themes for discussion, according to grand jury testimony by one of the men who stood trial for attempting to join ISIS, Abdirahman Yasin Daud.

"It's been a topic since like I was like in grade school, to be honest," Daud, then twenty-one years old, told a grand jury on January 22, 2015, in testimony later made public. "You know, it's been a topic when it comes to like the situation in, you know, back home, the situation you know, the ISIS situation. So, it's always been a topic in the community to be honest, so—and it's—everyone, like the whole city, it's either everyone is paranoid, everyone is like scared of each other."

Nonetheless, it was mystifying and infuriating to the parents of some—though perhaps not all—of the Somalis drawn to ISIS that their children would go that route, as became clear in the criminal trial in Minneapolis that three of the would-be ISIS recruits would undergo in 2016. The parents had raised their boys to be Muslims, but not to be fanatics, and most of the parents publicly abhorred the idea of their sons becoming terrorists or members of what was essentially a death cult, a group that extolled martyrdom even as it murdered innocents.

For some academics and psychology experts who studied cults decades before ISIS, however, strong parallels exist between the appeal the Islamist group and others like it had for young Muslims and the allure other cults held for earlier generations of Americans.[2] Scores of such groups exerted a pull on mostly young people from the 1960s on. Sung Myung Moon's Unification Church and Guru Maharaj Ji's Divine Light Mission drew people looking for spiritual fulfillment and ways of life that would bring happiness and, maybe, change the world. Similarly, the Rajneesh Meditation Centers attracted seekers, some of whom in the 1980s settled in the group's short-lived base in a remote corner of Oregon (where it devolved into violence against outsiders). Even more darkly, suicidal groups such as Jim Jones's Peoples Temple and Europe's Order of the Solar Temple, along with Japan's murderous Aum Shinrikyo group, drew people who sought, however perversely, to usher in some brighter future for themselves and others.

Not all such groups were violent, of course. But, like ISIS, they demanded full commitment and absolute loyalty from their adherents. They also were driven by apocalyptic ideologies and charismatic leaders, cast themselves as outside the mainstream of society or in wholesale opposition to it, and derived their power from idiosyncratic readings of ancient religious traditions. In the cases of these groups, they drew on peculiar interpretations of the texts and traditions of Christianity, Buddhism, or Hinduism. Typically, they also found many of their adherents among adolescents and people in their twenties, though not exclusively so. And generally, the adherents forged powerful bonds of loyalty to one another in an us-against-the-world allegiance, something that was reinforced by the euphoria members got from the sense of community they shared in the group and their united support for its mission.

One expert, Canadian psychiatrist Saul Levine, treated young people who had joined several such groups from about 1969 through the 1980s. He studied fifteen "radical" groups, as he called them, and interviewed some eight hundred members, whom he called "radical departers." As he described them, they left their conventional lives to sign up with the groups, usually to the great surprise of people close to them. Dr. Levine's discussion of them, in his 1984 book, *Radical Departures: Desperate Detours to Growing Up,* is striking in how it could refer to some—though not all—of the Somalis and Somali Americans who sought to join al-Shabab and ISIS.

"In no case was the sudden leave-taking expected by those who knew the youngster best," Dr. Levine wrote of the joiners he observed. "These departures are called 'out of character' by observers and make no sense to them. Indeed, radical departers, despite the fact that they showed no underlying pathology in the years before their joining, appear to have taken leave of their senses."[3]

Certainly, Sadiyo Omar, the mother of Abdi Mohamud Nur, appeared stunned when her then twenty-year-old son slipped out of Minneapolis and made his way to Syria in mid-2014, according to an account in the *Star Tribune.* Nur, one of the group of thirteen of which Bashir was part, had graduated from Southwest High School, where he was well known for his skills on the basketball team, Assistant US Attorney Julie E. Allyn told me.[4] Later, Nur enrolled in Normandale Community College, saying he planned to become a lawyer. His mother, with whom he shared a small apartment, described him as a responsible son, one who gave her no sign that he intended to join ISIS.[5]

But there were some signs of trouble that others close to Nur could see. Nur had begun acting differently in the months before he left, after he started attending a mosque in Bloomington, Minnesota, which borders Minneapolis on the south. He was described as becoming "reserved and unsocial," according to a report by the Voice of America, whose correspondents had interviewed Nur's sister, Ifrah. It's possible that Nur came under the influence of a mysterious Egyptian man who by the summer of 2014 had so alarmed officials at the mosque, the Dar Al-Farooq Islamic Center, that they banned him from the building and called police. He was suspected of recruiting young men for ISIS.[6]

That spring, as reported by the *New York Times,* Nur's Twitter posts had become filled with militant comments, such as a quote from Anwar al-Awlaki, the American recruiter for al-Qaida, that he posted in late March that said: "We are fighting for truth and justice and you (americans/westerners) are fighting for oppression and worldly gain." In early April, he praised Islamic terrorists, posting: "If the sky would be proud of the existence of the stars, the land should be proud of the existence of the Mujahideen."[7]

Such social media postings, however, may have been lost on Nur's parents.

Federal authorities say that the immigrant parents of the Somali men from Minnesota were largely oblivious to such communications among their children. The earliest hard indication of Nur's intention to travel appeared in a text message to his sister, Ifrah, on the day after his departure for Turkey, a stop on the way to ISIS. He told her he wanted to "join the jihad in Syria in search of paradise."[8]

Ifrah reported him as missing and the family sought the FBI's help in trying to get him back, but he eluded authorities. Later, Ifrah tearfully testified in the May–June 2016 trial of Bashir and Nur's friends that she tried to persuade Nur in text messages to return home. But she told jurors that "he believes if he died in Syria he would take his family members to heaven. . . . That's why he's saying: 'I'm doing this for us all.'"[9]

A series of text messages, which attorney Allyn shared with the jurors, reflects both the distress of Nur's family at his departure and the religious convictions that motivated him. "Why would u leave me u promised me," Ifrah told him. Nur's response: "I know but will see eachother [sic] in afterlife inshallah. Know that I love you ifrah And doing this for us all . . . Only allah knows how much I love you guys im doing this for us ifrah and im not coming back. My heart is with allah. . . . And everybody dies but I want the best death ifrah. . . ." Even Ifrah's suggestion that their mother had almost suffered a heart attack did not persuade him to return.[10] US officials believe that Nur is dead.

In treating cult recruits, Dr. Levine found that many joiners were not, in fact, breaking entirely with their past in signing up with their new groups. If anything, they were taking to extremes the lessons they had learned in the moderate religious instruction their parents had provided for them. In a sense, by joining extreme groups, they were living up to the expectations they thought their parents had of them, rather than rebelling. "They believed they were doing good for society," Dr. Levine explained. "They were living up to their parents' ideals: 'I'm doing exactly what you, mom and dad, taught me.'"[11]

Like many adolescents, the joiners he dealt with struggled to build their identities, but they also labored more than most to remedy what Dr. Levine saw as an inner sense of desolation. As he described it, one key difference between joiners and others, though, was that they could not see a satisfying future for themselves before they joined the groups—a blind spot that some of the Minneapolis would-be recruits may also have shared.[12] In short, the groups filled deep spiritual holes the young people felt, much as ISIS seemed to do with the Minnesota recruits and would-be recruits.

To understand the motivations of the Minnesotans drawn to ISIS, consider the forces that have drawn others to sign up with so-called New Religious Movements, whether violent or not. For young people still trying to find their footing in life, such groups seemed to offer an escape from ordinary humdrum existence, a chance to act in some heroic fashion (however perversely interpreted), and simple explanations for how the world works. James R. Lewis of the University of Tromso, in his 2012 book, *Cults: A Reference and Guide,* wrote that the black-and-white thinking and narrowness of cult ideologies are liberating to some devotees, bringing "clarity and stability." Lewis also contended that people joined alternative religions "for the same sorts of reasons one would join any other religion, namely fellowship, a satisfying belief system, and so forth."[13]

Still, Rodney Stark and William Sims Bainbridge, a pair of noted religion scholars, in their 1985 book, *The Future of Religion: Secularization, Revival, and Cult Formation,* pointed to factors that might prompt people to join cults that operate outside the mainstream. "First, persons experiencing great strain and deprivation might join in a desperate search for solutions to their severe problems," they wrote. "Second, social isolates or small, encapsulated groups, unconnected to the conventional social order, might be free to join because they are beyond the social reach of those who might want to punish them."[14]

Stark and Bainbridge also pointed to the careful targeting cultists apply when looking for recruits. In this light, the young Minnesota Somali Americans appear to have been ideally suited for recruitment. The scholars noted that "many individual cults recruit from very narrow strata or from small, homogenous categories of citizens. . . . [Such] recruitment takes place primarily through development of new social bonds linking members with prospective recruits or through activation of existing interpersonal bonds. . . . And persons tend to have and to form enduring social relationships with persons very much like themselves."

More recently, conservative pundit Jonah Goldberg reflected on the vulnerabilities many have to recruitment in his 2018 book, *Suicide of the West.* "Scholars studying such diverse phenomena as Islamic terrorism, white supremacy, street gangs, and cults have found that the key recruitment tool is always the same: the promise of meaning and belonging. Human beings are hardwired to want to belong, to be part of a cause larger than themselves, and to be valued for their contribution to that cause. Young people with scant social capital—i.e., dysfunctional families, unresponsive schools and communities, etc.—are the most susceptible to such appeals precisely because they have few alternative sources of meaning and belonging."

Those stuck in poverty and the undereducated aren't the only ones susceptible to such appeals, Goldberg added. "We all are," he argued. "Many of the 9/11 terrorists were well educated. Osama bin Laden was rich. Modernity itself leaves many cold if they don't have the resources or opportunity to find healthy sources of meaning and belonging."[15]

The World Organization for Resource Development, a nonprofit educational group based in Montgomery Village, Maryland, pointed to five broad categories of risk factors for radicalization. They included: ideology, beliefs, and values—including "us vs. them" worldviews, justification of violence, and perceiving certain cultures or nation-states as threatening; psychological factors such as a desire for purpose or adventure and concern for individual or group security—which may be exacerbated by issues such as previous trauma, posttraumatic stress disorder (PTSD), or mental illness; political grievances related to human rights abuses, limited political and civil liberties, corruption, and foreign occupation; economic factors such as unemployment, relative poverty, and financial incentives from membership; and sociological motivators such as alienation, struggling cultural adaptation, marginalization, discrimination, and kinship ties.[16]

Recruits into troublesome groups or extremist groups of various sorts—ranging from gangs to jihadists to white supremacists—look to such organizations to fill crucial personal needs, Kevin D. Lowry, retired chief US probation and pretrial services officer for the federal court in Minnesota, told me. Lowry, who handled many of the Minnesota cases of terrorism recruitment, has studied the motivations of recruits. These motivations, he said, include identity, meaning or purpose, belonging, and status and significance. Recruits find fulfillment of those essential needs in their groups, Lowry said.[17]

Canadian researchers who questioned 118 Somali immigrants, aged sixteen to thirty, in the Toronto area pointed to the "coolness" factor of joining jihad. Nearly a third of the respondents who explained why people would join al-Shabab "invoked the glory/pride theme, often remarking that al-Shabaab recruits style themselves as pious and glorious religious warriors." One twenty-one-year-old man said heroism is a major theme in Islam, and fighters are looked up to, much like samurai. A twenty-two-year-old man, in part echoing Bashir, said, "They wanna feel like they're a martyr and they wanna feel like the stories during the Prophet's time when there was something worth fighting for, when you were being attacked you know? And you were defending yourself, you know?"[18]

Zakaria Amara, a Jordanian-born Palestinian imprisoned for life in Canada after being convicted in the so-called "Toronto 18" terrorism plot of 2006, was twenty when he pleaded guilty to being one of the ringleaders planning shootings and truck bombings in Canada. In a March 1, 2019, piece for the prison newspaper *insidetime*, he wrote of his early feelings of worthlessness and alienation in Canada, Cyprus, Saudi Arabia, and Jordan and how radicalization in response to the US invasion of Iraq in 2003 fit in with his desperation for acceptance by his peers as a teenager.

"How does it feel to be radical? You feel worthy, righteous, and heroic. You see yourself as a savior of your people," Amara wrote. "Your mind is obsessed with the injustices they are suffering from and that's all you wish to talk about. You see the world in strictly black and white terms. Deep inside, you suspect that there may be other colours, which subconsciously drives you to engage in constant re-enforcement of your beliefs. It is said that those who are the most dogmatic are usually the least certain. A vivid depiction of this internal struggle is that of a boy who is perpetually fortifying the walls of a sandcastle he built too close to the waves."[19]

Studies in the nature of adolescence have suggested that people in their teens and early twenties are especially susceptible to extremist views and recruitment simply as a matter of brain chemistry. Recent insights have led some judges to deal differently with adolescent offenders. As the website for the Center for Law, Brain and Behavior at Massachusetts General Hospital put it:

> Scientists know that the adolescent brain is still developing, that it is highly subject to reward- and peer-influence, and that its rate of development varies widely across the population. . . . With its ability to examine the workings of the teenage brain, neuroscience is improving our understanding of adolescents, and potentially, juvenile offenders. Through their window into the brain, neuroscientists understand, for example, that adolescents mature at markedly varied rates. The presumed trajectory of brain development, demonstrated in existing "bright line" age cut offs for voting, military service, and drinking, however, is not reflective of this variability in brain maturity.

Neuroimaging research suggests that heightened vulnerability to rewards drives risky behavior for adolescents, according to the center. "They can often recognize risks, but incomplete development of brain mechanisms related to modulation of impulsive behavior reduces their tendency to heed those risks," the researchers reported.[20]

Furthermore, adolescents tend to make quick and impulsive decisions that are often short-sighted because their prefrontal cortices—which are associated with making decisions—are still developing, Leah Somerville, an associate professor of psychology at Harvard affiliated with the center, told me. They tend not to look forward to assess the effects their actions might have far into the future.

They tend, too, to want to seek the approval of like-minded peers, which may explain why adolescents may be drawn to gangs or extremist groups. "This is [the] time of life when peers can be highly influential in decision-making, and adolescents are very motivated to find approval from peers," Dr. Somerville said.

Development rates vary widely among adolescents, the psychologist added. The legal system's definition of adulthood at eighteen, she suggested, is problematic, since for some people adolescent development could stretch well into the twenties and even beyond. "Nothing magical happens at eighteen," Dr. Somerville said, noting that some experts now refer to an "emerging adulthood" that for some lasts from perhaps seventeen to twenty-one years old.[21]

Certainly, in 2014, adulthood for Bashir's friends seemed far off. But adventure, even deadly adventure, seemed just around the bend. Some chafed at their boring and unheroic lives in Minnesota and had long wanted to leave for more exciting places. For Bashir and his dozen friends, the adventure, the opportunity for heroism—and the unsettling reality of death—soon seemed within reach. They began their plotting, meeting on basketball courts, in a school and in other spots in the Minneapolis area, as they tried to make their way to ISIS. It would be a journey some of them would not survive, while others would be stymied in a Hollywood-style sting orchestrated by the FBI. For his part, Bashir would face an agonizing personal choice with life-changing consequence for him and his friends.[22]

CHAPTER EIGHT

A Special Case

Passion for the cause varied among the thirteen plotters. But one of the men, Guled Ali Omar, had been long committed to it. Like Bashir, he had family ties that drew him closer to terrorism. Unlike Bashir, he toted a lot of personal baggage.

Omar, who attended Minneapolis Community and Technical College with Bashir and, earlier, had known him at the Minnesota Transition School, was a special case. Omar's oldest brother, Ahmed Ali "Mustafa" Omar, had left Minneapolis in 2007 to join al-Shabab in Somalia when Guled was thirteen. Prosecutors charged that Guled tried to join his brother there in 2012, only to be stopped at the airport by customs officials. The younger Omar also communicated with the ISIS fighters in Syria, using contact information that Bashir said he wheedled out of Bashir's brother. Bashir had used the contact information to communicate with his cousins.

Soon after word spread about Mohallim's departure for Syria in the spring of 2014, Guled Omar and several others among the thirteen friends gathered to complain that Mohallim had beaten them to the country, according to Bashir. Omar leaned on Bashir particularly. Eager to build connections to get to Syria, Omar "was really pushing me," Bashir told me. He called Omar the "mastermind" of the various schemes the friends cooked up to make their way to Syria.

With its pleasant amenities and sports facilities, Brackett Park seemed an unlikely spot for men to plot to join terrorists in distant Syria. But some of the Minneapolis men bore only contempt for American culture and were eager to find the Islamic Utopia promised in ISIS propaganda.

For his part, Omar in court testimony pointed to Bashir and another friend, Abdullahi "Bones" Yusuf, as driving forces. He claimed Bashir encouraged the group to join his cousins in Syria. Omar quoted Bashir as saying in April 2014: "Maybe Allah left me behind for a reason. . . . I think God left me behind for a reason and that's probably to be sitting here with you guys today."[1]

But surreptitious recordings of conversations among the men and testimony by some who turned state's evidence thrust Omar into the heart of the conspiracy, the one around whom it all revolved. He shared details about his earlier attempts to try to leave the United States, for instance, gave at least one man money for a passport, referred the men to books about jihad, cajoled them into signing on to the plot by issuing ultimatums, and stayed in contact with ISIS fighters—all as noted by government attorneys in a sentencing statement about him.

Furthermore, even Omar's testimony in court showed how Bashir was distressed—anything but celebratory—when his beloved cousin Mohallim left for Syria. As Omar relayed the events, some of the friends were playing basketball in Minneapolis's Brackett Park when the Bashir brothers, Abdirahman and Hamsa, came by. They "looked weird, they looked different," Omar said. "You know, I could feel that something was wrong. Everybody kind of knew that something was wrong. So after they—like when my team was out I went up to them and asked them, 'Hey, man, is everything all right? What's going on? Are you okay?' He's like, Yeah, yeah, I'm good. This is Abdirahman Bashir. . . . So he told me nothing was going on, nothing happened."

Soon after shooting a few more hoops, Omar testified, Abdirahman's brother took him to the side and said their cousin had "left." Omar's response: "What do you mean your cousin left?" Then Hamsa said, according to Omar: "He went to Syria. He said Hanad Mohallim went to Syria. And I was like, 'What do you mean he went to Syria?' It didn't make sense to me at that moment. And so he said, 'He went there and he's going to go and fight for the sake of God and he's going to go there and he's protecting people and he's going to go—and at the end of the day he's going there for the sake of God.'"[2]

To be sure, Bashir and his friends were getting contrary messages at that time, too. They watched videos by Islamic scholars who derided ISIS and criticized Western recruits rushing to join it as naifs dazzled by the idea of toting weapons, wearing camouflage clothing, and acting like soldiers. The would-be martyrs, the critics said, knew little of Islam and didn't even pray as required.

Half of Bashir's friends would heed such messages, while the others—"the radical kids"—would scorn any religious leader who spoke against ISIS as a paid "mouthpiece of the West," Bashir recalled. For his part, Bashir remained conflicted, searching the internet for evidence of whether the critical scholars were genuine. Even Bashir admitted, however, that the pictures he saw online of "Western kids" in fighting gear "looked cool."

The pressure on Bashir grew. By May 2014, Mohallim was using encrypted messaging services such as SureSpot to reach out to Bashir and urge him and his brother to join him and their other cousins in Syria. When Bashir would argue with Mohallim about news reports of atrocities by ISIS, Mohallim would counter that such reports were propaganda engineered by anti-ISIS forces. "Anything I was skeptical about . . . I would send it to him and he would tell me like, 'no, it's not true, I'm over here,'" Bashir remembered. "That's when I really started getting radical and I started believing in the cause of ISIS."

Bashir and his friends ramped up their plans to join ISIS. They schemed about it in between basketball matches in the Dar Al-Farooq Islamic Center in Bloomington, a mosque with a gym attached that had become a favorite of one in the circle, Abdi Mohamud Nur. Fearing that they might be on no-fly lists, a few made plans to get out of the United States by car, figuring they could get fake passports in Mexico and then fly on to Syria—taking a page from the way Cabdullaahi Ahmed Faarax, the al-Shabab recruit, had traveled to Somalia by way of Mexico from Minnesota in 2009. Prosecutors later would charge that Guled Omar and Yusuf Jama, an older friend who could rent a car, plotted with Bashir to drive to San Diego to make such a move.

But the California-to-Mexico-to-Syria plan was spoiled when Omar's mother and another brother, Mohamed Ali Omar, on May 24, 2014, confronted the young men in the street near Omar's house and barred him from going. The men were caught up in conflicting lies—with Bashir claiming they planned a leisure trip to San Diego and Omar telling his family he was going to Texas to visit a sister. At one point, Omar's sister even jumped into the backseat of the rental car Bashir was driving to thwart him. After some phone calls, Bashir's father joined the group in a family-to-family meeting, calming down the angry Omar family members, according to testimony Bashir gave in court. Ultimately, Omar was barred from going and the trip plan died. Though he was attending college and had worked as a security guard, the younger Omar deferred to his mother and the big brother, who later was described in court as "intimidating."

Indeed, Mohamed Ali Omar, Guled Omar's brother, was later jailed after threatening FBI agents who sought to question his brother—a crime for which Mohamed Ali Omar was convicted. Reflecting the violent world the Omar brothers lived in, Mohamed Ali Omar had also been shot ten times by a Somali gang, Judge Michael J. Davis said in court, and he carried a pistol to protect himself from others who carried weapons in the dangerous circles he moved in in Minnesota.[3]

Federal authorities involved in the 2016 trial of Guled Ali Omar and two friends on charges of attempting to join ISIS and conspiring to do so saw the then twenty-two-year-old man as the most "hard-core" of the group, as one lawyer involved in the case described him. By his own words in surreptitious recordings, Omar at one point acknowledged (or bragged): "My parents think I'm hard-core al-Shabab." After Omar was convicted, Assistant US Attorney Andrew R. Winter, in arguing on November 16, 2016, for a forty-year sentence for Omar, labeled him "not redeemable."

Winter pointed to scheming that led several of the men in the group of thirteen to make their way to Syria, saying Omar "drew people into the conspiracy. He drew Abdullahi in. He drew Abdi Nur in. He drew Hanad Musse in. He drew Hamza Ahmed in. He drew Yusuf Jama in. As the Court is well aware, Jama and Nur are likely dead. He even says, on two separate occasions, 'We almost got Abdullahi out,' and he's referring to the May attempt, and then in reference to the November attempts, he admits he told him, 'We can work something out. Three weeks is not enough time for us to plan.'"[4]

Winter was scathing in his final assessment of Omar, as the court's transcripts demonstrate. Using the term ISIL (the Islamic State of Iraq and the Levant) for ISIS, the prosecutor said:

> Make no mistake, the government views this defendant as extraordinarily danger-ous. He not only talked about how the kuffar [non-Muslims] are going to get it, America's time is coming, he had a plan for it and he was going to get over to Syria and then he was going to provide the routing information so his ISIL brothers could come back and, as he says, do crazy damage here. It is a great opportunity. . . . At the end of the day, we have a man, he is not a boy, he is not a kid, who presents a very, very unique case.

Winter argued that Omar lied repeatedly, claimed racial and social victimization, and offered false contrition. "You can't fix manipulative. You can't fix deceitful. And you can't fix Guled Omar," the prosecutor argued. "Not in a manner that's consistent with public safety. Ultimately, this defendant has blood on his hands, Your Honor. He's got blood on his hands from people he's helped get overseas who are dead."[5]

But Omar was capable of being charming. He could exude self-confidence and was quick to flash a warm smile. Omar cut a charismatic figure, as Judge Davis noted from the bench. Indeed, Omar's ability to make people follow him had persuaded others in the group to choose him for a time as their "emir," or leader, as they planned their moves to get to ISIS. "Because of the defendant's long association with terrorist organizations, his brother, al-Shabab, he was in a unique position to apply lessons learned from those individuals, apply them in this conspiracy. Guled Omar's base of knowledge spread throughout the conspiracy, throughout the cell, this terrorist cell, like a cancer. He was like a well that people kept going to get information, to get advice, and he kept [doling] it out," Winter said. The lawyer added that Omar was even willing to use his father—disabled and in a wheelchair—by planning to accompany the man to Somalia as a personal aide, so he could then "ditch him and go to Syria to join ISIL."[6]

Omar's relationship with his father was, at best, distant. When Omar took to the witness stand on May 26, 2016, to explain his background and actions to a jury—in what proved to be a misguided bid to try to win the panel over—he said his father had been shot three times in Somalia as the family fled and made its way to a refugee camp in neighboring Kenya. He said his father suffered from psychological problems and lost a leg, a handicap that gave the family priority in moving to the United States in the early 1990s.

The family, including Omar and five of his siblings, immigrated under the auspices of a church that brought them to Dallas, Texas, when Omar was about two years old. A year or so later, the family moved again, to Minnesota. Sometime after the move north, Omar's father left the family, moving for a while to Ethiopia, though Omar said he often visited Minnesota. The family grew to include nine daughters and five sons. But Omar also said he saw his father rarely, saying in the spring of 2016 that he didn't know where he lived and that he had last seen him in the fall of 2014 at a sister's wedding.[7]

As Omar described his life, under friendly questioning by defense attorney Glenn P. Bruder, he painted a picture that in many ways was ordinary. He loved sports, playing soccer for South High School in his junior year, and he played football and basketball with friends regularly. He graduated from South in 2013 and enrolled at Minneapolis Community Technical College. He wanted to play basketball for the school in his senior year but couldn't because he took a job. He worked as a security guard the following year, patrolling apartment and condominium complexes and a methadone clinic. And he picked up extra money working as a personal care aide to an autistic nephew. All the while, he continued to play sports in his free time, especially basketball, which he played often. He captained at least one basketball team. He also spent time in several mosques, especially one near his home at the Karmel Mall, a popular Somali shopping center in Minneapolis.

Under his lawyer's prodding, Omar discussed his religious life, noting his obligations as a Sunni Muslim. Followers of the Prophet, he said, must pray five times daily, fast during one month of each year, give to charity, and make a pilgrimage to Mecca if possible. They gather to offer prayers in groups on Fridays, when Muslims generally stayed together all day, he said. Admitting he wasn't a scholar, he nonetheless sketched out the differences between Sunni and Shiite Muslims, noting that the split dated back to the days of the Prophet Muhammad ("peace be upon him," Omar added), and had to do with differing views of the line of succession.

But Omar also outlined troubling sides to his life. His family lived in Section 8 subsidized housing and, at one point, was ordered by the landlord to move out, he said. For income, he said, the family depended on his job and that of his mother, someone for whom life was a constant struggle, in part because of memories of warfare. "My mom at times, even up until my arrest, would wake up in nightmares sometimes screaming," Omar testified. "I would have to go down there, wake her up, recite some passages from the Quran on her, calm her down."

Omar also admitted that he liked to smoke marijuana and take various drugs, including Percocet and Xanax—even though he noted that such drugs fell afoul of Islam. For that matter, listening to rap music—a favorite hobby of his—was also contrary to Islam, as he understood it. While he testified that he had a lot of friends, he said none were non-Muslim, aside from people he knew at school. He didn't go to the homes of non-Muslims and would not invite them to his house. As Omar testified: "Well, it's kind of hard to explain, but outside of school, like, it was kind of awkward for me to ask my non-Muslim friends if I could go over to their house and I thought they would feel awkward if they had to come to my house because of so much differences in our culture and food and the way our parents act and the way they dress. So it's kind of like a forbidden topic."

Omar was more expansive about his sense of isolation and some of the traumas he experienced while growing up in phone interviews from jail with Minneapolis Public Radio correspondent Laura Yuen. He said he was abused while growing up, suffering from whippings from age nine to eleven—though Yuen reported it was not clear who beat him. When he was in high school, Omar took to using marijuana and other drugs, adding cocaine to the list. He was an outcast, ridiculed by other students for the way he dressed and even how he smelled, he told Yuen. Indeed, even as they took on some of the rebellious practices of their fellow students, many Somali young people in Minnesota complained of not being accepted by non-Somalis, including African Americans.

But, as he got older, Omar did find his way into a group of Somali friends—the group of thirteen young men—who bonded in part over their revulsion at how Muslims were being treated in Syria. As the friends watched ISIS propaganda videos, the messages had their effect on Omar. "When I hear these videos, all this propaganda, and it's telling you who a real man is—that this is what the companions of the Prophet would do—you want to be such a better person," he told Yuen. "You feel something's wrong with you constantly that you have to do something so big."[8]

After sympathetic questioning by his lawyer, Omar underwent a withering cross-examination by the prosecution in which he was forced to acknowledge repeated episodes of detailed plotting that Bashir caught on tape. Once confident, even cocky, on the stand, he shriveled into sullenness under the weight of evidence—mostly his own words—that the government threw at him.

Later, in pleading for mercy at his sentencing, Omar argued he regretted the path he had set out on. Weeping at times, he apologized to the US government, saying the United States had "shown my family and my mother nothing but greatness." He apologized to Judge Davis for his comments on the recordings that revealed his and his friends' plotting—more than forty hours of transcribed recordings—saying he was "disgraced by every single word that came out of my mouth." He said he thought hard over the prior nineteen months about what he had done, adding: "I've made a decision that I don't want to continue on the path that I once was on. That was a ugly path. It was a horrible path. And I never want to return to it whether—whichever way that you decide to sentence me."

Omar claimed to grasp the weight of his crimes. "I understand the seriousness of what I have been convicted of, and I understand that I may not be able to go home any time soon," he told the judge. "But, Your Honor, a book I've read by Wendell Berry, the book that's called *What Are People For?*, and this quote stuck out to me, and I'd like to share it with you. 'The past is our definition. We may strive with good reason to escape it, or to escape what is bad in it. But we will escape it only by adding something better to it.'[9] I have been motivated by this quote, Your Honor." Waxing still more literary, he cited Malcolm X, whom he described as one of his favorite writers and people in history: "He says there's no better thing than adversity. Every defeat, every heartbreak, every loss contains its own seeds, its own lesson on how to improve your performance the next time."

Omar suggested he was a victim of ISIS's seductions. "Your Honor, I don't like to blame anyone or—for—for what I am standing in front of you for, but ISIL and its—its propaganda did take advantage of me. I was vulnerable at times. I was lost many times," Omar said. "But because of—because of me having no sense of belonging, because I had no one to speak to besides my mother and I didn't want her to put through any more pain than the pain that she was going through, I was sucked in by their—by their propaganda."

Bruder asked for leniency. He contended that Omar was not "inherently evil," despite being convicted of offering material support to a terrorist group and plotting to commit murder abroad. After many long meetings with Omar and his family, the lawyer said he knew Omar better than most of his clients, saying he was "respectful, polite and at times engaging." But he acknowledged that the guilty verdict established that he was, "at best, a wanna-be terrorist who was prevented from becoming an actual one only by the intervention of U.S. law enforcement agencies."

Bruder suggested that Omar's interest in joining ISIS sprang from his alienation and traumatic personal background. The lawyer said: "Guled never really felt like he fit in, either in Islamic society, at his mosque, or in western society. You heard his testimony at trial, and you heard that although he had friends at school, not one of them ever visited his home, nor was he ever invited to theirs. The PSR [pre-sentence report] indicates that Guled felt inadequate and powerless. That's not atypical of first generation Somali youth. The PSR recounts the abuse and the violence that Guled experienced growing up, violence that was actually shocking even to a veteran probation officer."

The Omar he sought to portray to the jury was swayed by terrorist propaganda videos, like the others. But Bruder argued that Omar was a source of strength for his family and was "caring and compassionate," even as he and his friends were probably fairly characterized as members of a terrorist cell. The lawyer insisted that Omar, like the others, was an "average participant." Contrary to ISIS guidance urging would-be terrorists to keep their own counsel and trust no one, Bruder said Omar boasted often, and sometimes in public places, of his commitment to the conspiracy to get to Syria. The lawyer said: "One wonders why somebody would do that. Why would he make these kind of boastful comments? I think the answer is pretty clear: he's struggling for some sense of acclaim and respect from his co-defendants."

Bruder asked the judge to sentence Omar to fifteen years, a term that would let him "leave this courtroom with some sense of hope for his future." If the judge, instead, accepted the government's request for forty years, Bruder noted, "he will realistically have no future. He'll be a man close to collecting Social Security."[10] What would the judge do? Would he credit Omar's claims of repentance as sincere or as manipulative? Would he look on the two-year-old schemes of a then twenty-year-old as little more than adolescent bravado or as part of a pattern designed to mimic or even join cause with a brother who was already a committed terrorist?

CHAPTER NINE

Peer to Peer

How did Omar wind up seeing the world as he did? How did his friends fall for the terrorist cant? As their plotting proceeded in mid-2014, some of his would-be jihadist friends failed in their efforts to get to Syria while others succeeded—some sending back messages that enticed the others with promises of heroism and claims about the Islamic Utopia they got to.

One friend, Abdullahi Yusuf, then an eighteen-year-old high school student, was thwarted on May 28, 2014, when he tried to board a plane in Minneapolis for Istanbul. A suspicious passport official had tipped the FBI off about Yusuf, and agents were able to stop him before he could leave.[1]

But another friend—Abdi Mohamud Nur, the twenty-year-old student at Normandale Community College—managed the following day to fly from Minneapolis and make his way to Syria. After a third friend, Yusuf Jama, was set back on his plan to travel to Syria by way of San Diego with Bashir and Omar, Jama then took a Greyhound bus to New York City. On June 9, 2014, he flew from John F. Kennedy International Airport to Turkey, and soon after he made his way to Syria.

The flurry of activity did not appear to have been directly inspired or directed by any outsiders, other than Bashir's friends and relatives who were part of ISIS. It was a matter of "peer-to-peer" radicalization, Bashir told me, a case of "telling each other to go, we should all go."

Bashir echoed the observation of Andrew M. Luger, then the US attorney in Minnesota. Luger's comment: "What this case shows is that the person radicalizing your son, your brother, your friend, may not be a stranger. . . . It may be their best friend, right here in town."[2] Bashir's case showed that the recruiters could be beloved cousins or close friends—making it especially tough for outsiders to deter such recruitments.

That spring, Bashir and his friends wanted to move quickly in part because they were worried that the FBI, working with Luger's office, was tracking them. In fact, the bureau did have them, especially Bashir, in its sights. Agents had checked the cameras at the Minneapolis airport after Mohallim left, and they saw Bashir behind the wheel as he dropped his cousin off. "They were onto all of us," Bashir said.

Even as they made plans in the spring of 2014 for the group to make its way to Turkey and then to link up with Bashir's cousin Mohallim to get to Syria, Bashir and his friends would feel "the heat" of suspicion from the FBI and Luger's office. Bashir did wind up on May 28, 2014, flying to San Diego, traveling there in a bid to get a copy of his birth certificate after his mother had taken it away for fear that he might try to travel to Syria. He wanted the document in order to get a passport and headed to San Diego to await instructions from his friend McCain who had gotten to Syria. While he unsuccessfully tried to contact McCain, Bashir stayed with relatives for a tense month.

"It was really heat everywhere," Bashir recalled. Friends in San Diego were even talking about a group of Minneapolis men who were trying to make their way to ISIS. He called friends in Minnesota, including one who told him "the FBI are on our ass now." He later learned he was being watched at the time.

Meanwhile, in Syria and Iraq, ISIS was making big gains, which further emboldened the Minnesota men. The terrorist group in June 2014 took over the Iraqi city of Mosul and declared the establishment of its caliphate, its Islamic state, in territory it conquered in Syria and Iraq. It anointed its leader, Abu Bakr al-Baghdadi, as the leader of all Muslims. The Minnesota friends excitedly watched videos ISIS generated to tout its gains, thrilled even by the most violent of the videos—or at least seeming to be thrilled as they talked of them.

Privately, Bashir said he felt uneasy about some of the videos—he later singled out one from early 2015 where a Jordanian pilot is burned alive, saying that the Quran taught that burning people was not the province of man, but only of God.

But as he talked with his friends in Minnesota in 2014, he kept any reservations he had about the group's beheadings and crucifixions in the videos to himself.

Indeed, the tug of the slickly produced ISIS videos was strong. Citing religious arguments, the propagandists argued that it was mandatory for Muslims to come and support the caliphate. The message, as Bashir summarized it: "We know how you feel—depressed—all that sin you are in. Come over here, man. It's amazing." The propagandists posted images of families celebrating Eid al-Fitr, the Islamic holiday marking the end of Ramadan. The videos featured such delights as Ferris wheels, aiming to counter the idea that all life there was a war zone.

"It looked like Disneyland over there," Bashir recalled, echoing a video that featured another Minneapolis-area man, Troy M. Kastigar, after he joined al-Shabab in Somalia in 2008. Al-Shabab posted that video, "The Path to Paradise: From the Twin Cities to the Land of the Two Migrations" in 2013, and in it Kastigar claimed he was in "the real Disneyland." Kastigar, whom Bashir had once met briefly in San Diego, was a close friend of McCain, Bashir's family friend. Kastigar, who had converted to Islam and married a Somali woman, was killed in Mogadishu in 2009, and the video included images of his corpse, celebrating his martyrdom.[3]

For some young Muslims, the appeal of the caliphate and the seductions of the videos, easily available online, were spreading. Thousands of people—mostly young men—from all over the world rushed to join the cause, as Bashir and his friends saw in news accounts from CNN and elsewhere. In Minneapolis, the lure was spreading to an even younger set of Somali American boys. Bashir heard from fourteen-, fifteen-, and sixteen-year-olds at Heritage Academy that summer who were eager to make their way to ISIS. Like Bashir's friends who had seen or known slightly older men who had joined al-Shabab, the young teens were looking up to Bashir's group as role models.

Others in the Somali community in the Twin Cities area were taken with the idea of joining ISIS, too: In late 2013 or early 2014, another Minneapolis resident, Abdirahmaan Muhumed—who was also known as Abdifatah Ahmed—had also made his way to Syria, where authorities said he died, at age thirty-four, in an August 2014 battle.[4] A year later, in July 2015, an eighteen-year-old Normandale Community College engineering student, Abdelhamid Al-Madioum, slipped away from his family as they vacationed in Morocco to join ISIS, according to a *Star Tribune* report. Citing unsealed court filings, the newspaper reported that Al-Madioum had laid out his departure plans in a detailed flow chart describing money transfers and a "rehearsed backstop story" in case authorities questioned him en route. His family contacted the FBI for help.[5] Al-Madioum surfaced in September 2019 in a prison in northeastern Syria, but as of October 2019, his fate was unknown.[6]

While Bashir and his all-male group of friends fantasized about joining the "brothers" in jihad, and other men from Minnesota found their way to Syria, some women were also making similar plans or finding other ways to back the cause. They didn't want to be left out, even if the men of ISIS saw them more as supporters on the home front and mothers to the next generations of fighters.

CHAPTER TEN

A Woman's Place?

I n mid-August 2014, a twenty-year-old St. Paul woman, Yusra Ismail, slipped away on a stolen passport, according to U.S. authorities, and sent word back that she had made her way to "Sham," the Levant.[1] Two weeks after Ismail disappeared, relatives told a reporter for the *Star Tribune* that they believed she had been targeted by Islamist recruiters and said they gave the FBI the names of people who may have tried to influence her. They said Ismail was deeply religious. Though unemployed, she planned to attend St. Paul College to become a nurse.[2] Her fate, in early 2020, was unknown.

Women occupied a peculiar place in ISIS and in terrorist recruitment efforts. They were greatly outnumbered in Syria by male fighters, which made them all the more desirable to online recruiters who sought them as wives for the jihadists, as "jihadi brides" as much of the media characterized them. Indeed, the recruiters turned to dating sites, including islamicmarriage.com, in attempts to solicit women, according to a report by Voice of America.[3]

One jihadist, identifying himself as Abujohndaniel, pleaded for a mate in May 2017. "I need a righteous practicing Muslim lady who wants to do Hijrah [immigrate] here inshallah," he said on the site. The VOA report identified him as New Zealander Mark John Taylor, noting he had converted to Islam, had divorced, and in the spring of 2017, he was in Raqqa, the ISIS caliphate's capital. Taylor, nicknamed the "bumbling jihadi" after his tweets identified the locations of ISIS fighters, was also designated a "Specially Designated Global Terrorist" by American authorities for calling on supporters to attack targets in Australia and New Zealand.[4] The designation barred Americans from financial dealings with him.[5] Taylor, forty-six in early 2019, told journalists for the Australian Broadcasting Corporation that he had fled the Islamic State in December 2018 and surrendered to Kurdish forces because life had become too difficult with ISIS. He also said he regretted being unable to afford a Yazidi female slave.[6]

For their part, some women also sought jihadist partners. One such woman was ModestMuslimah, said to be a twenty-six-year-old Somali American woman in Minneapolis. She said on her profile on the site: "I hope one day to go into Jihad and fight side by side with my brothers and sisters in Islam."[7]

VOA reported that in 2014 and 2015 some militants used their own niche matchmaking site on Twitter to form connections—and to recruit and groom. "Jihad Matchmaker" was used by the then seventeen-year-old Samya Dirie, who was of Somali descent, and then fifteen-year-old Yusra Hussien, who traveled together to Syria from England in September 2014.[8]

The women recruited by ISIS were deterred from combat, as dictated by the group's ideology, but instead were counted on as spouses and mothers or to serve as behind-the-front-lines medical caregivers, according to researchers Erin Marie Saltman and Melanie Smith. In "'Til Martydom Do Us Part': Gender and the ISIS Phenomenon," a 2015 report published by the London-based Institute for Strategic Dialogue, Saltman and Smith challenged the "jihadi bride" language used by much of the media as "one-dimensional" and "reductionist," arguing that the women's motivations were far broader than seeking a jihadist husband—even as several women they cited saw that role as central for them.[9] The researchers pointed to "push" factors, including feelings of social and/or cultural isolation (including questioning one's identity and uncertainty about belonging in the West); a feeling that the world Muslim community is being violently persecuted; and anger, sadness, and/or frustration over a lack of international help against persecution.[10] They also identified as "pull" factors the idealistic goals of religious duty and building a Utopian caliphate, a sense of belonging and sisterhood, and romanticization of the experience.[11]

Among the cases that Saltman and Smith detailed was a pair of British twins of Somali descent, Salma and Zahra Halane, who at sixteen in mid-2014, made their way to Syria. The pair, nicknamed the "Terror Twins," appear to have been radicalized—if only by example—by an elder brother, then twenty-one-year-old Ahmed Ibrahim Mohammed Halane, who was believed to have left England in 2013 to join ISIS. Ahmed had moved to England with his parents from Denmark when he was nine years old. The father of the trio ran a Quranic school, and the family was described as "very religious."[12] They lived in Manchester, an area of England that one tabloid media outlet referred to as a "hotbed of terror" because more than a dozen jihadis from there either died fighting for ISIS or were jailed for trying to join it between 2013 and 2017.[13]

Zahra Halane's loathing of the West, as described by the researchers, came across clearly in her Twitter posts from Syria. In September 2014, for instance, she celebrated the 9/11 attack on New York's Twin Towers, calling it the "Happiest day of my life." She "reveled" in atrocities committed by ISIS in Syria and elsewhere, the researchers reported, praising the attacks on *Charlie Hebdo*'s Paris offices.

Both twins were married soon after arriving in Syria and widowed within a few months in December 2014. When their husbands were killed, they marked their deaths with tweets wishing that Allah would accept the men. Zahra said she hoped to join her martyred nineteen-year-old Afghan British husband "very sooooon." Salma in a tweet said she was "honoured to be chosen" to have a martyred husband. The twins then went online as recruiters, urging other Western Muslim women to make "hijra," to migrate to Syria.[14] As of early 2020, the twins' fates were unknown.

Less than a year before the Halane twins traveled to Syria, a Somali Norwegian pair of sisters, the Juma girls, had made their way there after apparently being radicalized. Ayan, nineteen in late 2013, and Leila, then sixteen, seem to have adopted terrorist views at a mosque in Oslo and then slipped away from their family in October that year. Their father, Sadiq, traveled to the country in a desperate bid to bring them home, only to be beaten and to return unsuccessful. As of late 2016, the girls were married, had children, and were living in a collective in Raqqa with Norwegian, British, and Swedish couples, according to Britain's *Sunday Times,* which ran excerpts from a book about the father's search by popular writer Asne Seierstad. Ayan texted her brother, saying: "We did this 100% for Allah's sake. Not for any boyfriends or anyone else. So fear Allah and do not listen to the lies of the *kuffar,* aka the media." Their fates, in early 2020, were unknown.[15]

The gruesome fate of some women recruits may have deterred others from joining. Austrian Samra Kesinovic, seventeen, was reportedly used as a sex slave for new fighters and then beaten to death in 2014, only a few months after slipping away from her parents in Vienna to make her way to Syria with a fifteen-year-old friend, Sabina Selimovic.[16] The girls had been called "jihad poster girls" by the Austrian media after they appeared in online photos wearing burkas and toting assault weapons. But Kesinovic, an ethnic Bosnian who may have been enamored of a Bosnian cleric, had tried to flee in October 2014 after both girls told friends they were sickened by the brutality they saw.[17] Selimovic was believed to have been killed in the course of fighting.

Still, the lure of ISIS was especially strong for younger women. Two Somali sisters, then aged seventeen and fifteen, and a then sixteen-year-old Sudanese friend, all from Arapahoe County near Denver, Colorado, tried to make their way to Syria in October 2014 to answer the call of jihadists and recruiters they followed online. The girls, whose names were withheld by authorities and journalists because they were minors, had followed jihadists from around the world, including the United Kingdom, Canada, the Netherlands, and Syria, according to the *Insite Blog on Terrorism and Extremism.*[18]

The *Insite Blog* reported that one of the Colorado girls was in regular contact with a shady recruiter who went by the Twitter name of Umm Waqqas. Britain's Channel 4 News in April 2015 identified that recruiter as Rawdah Abdisalaam, a Somali who was believed to have lived in the Seattle area, was in her mid-twenties, and who had studied journalism. Despite her radicalization, Abdisalaam had shown many signs herself of being Americanized, which may have helped her connect with American online followers. Along with messages urging some 8,000 Twitter followers to take up jihad, for instance, she tweeted about her love of pizza and the Denver Broncos. She would also tug at her followers with language similar to the phrases Bashir's cousins in ISIS used: as reported by the Middle East Media Research Institute (MEMRI), on January 28, 2015, Abdisalaam tweeted, "The caravan waits for no one, either you hasten to catch it or you watch it pass you by not knowing if you will ever be able to catch up."[19]

MEMRI reported that Abdisalaam was mentioned as a key contact for women in the ISIS e-book *Hijra* [migration] *to the Islamic State—What To Packup, Who To Contact, Where To Go, Stories.* Coincidentally, her online followers also included Bashir's family friend McCain, according to *Insite Blog.* It was reported that Abdisalaam traveled to Syria in 2014 and was believed to operate out of Raqqa, though that has not been confirmed. Her status in early 2020 was unknown. (Much is unclear about Umm Waqqas. MEMRI noted she had claimed online to be Dutch. Further, it was reported that Abdisalaam may not have been the sole user of the Twitter handle Umm Waqqas).[20]

Federal authorities in Colorado learned of the Denver-area girls' departure after they failed to show up for school on October 17, 2014, Greg Holloway, an assistant US attorney in Denver, told me.[21] Their distraught parents had called the Arapahoe County Sheriff's Office at around dinnertime that night, after finding the girls, their passports, and about $2,000 missing.[22] Soon, the FBI got involved, putting out an alert on their passports. German authorities stopped the trio in Frankfurt, a transit point on the way to Turkey and Syria, and sent the girls back.

The girls had felt socially excluded in their predominantly white suburban school, even though they were not the only Muslim students there, according to Holloway. Further, their immigrant parents were not intimately involved in their teenage American lives, and were particularly ignorant of the online world they immersed themselves in, one centered on the fantasy paradise ISIS propagandists described in the Islamic State. (The father of the Somali girls was sixty-eight at the time.) The girls saw a "romanticized version of the caliphate," Holloway said.

Remarkably, ISIS's slickly produced videos exerted such power over both young men and women recruits that they didn't bridle at the brutality of beheadings and crucifixions that, by the fall of 2014, certainly, were common knowledge in the West. They were broadcast online and run, in edited form, on newscasts. One, showing the bloody, beheaded corpse of journalist James Foley, was released in August 2014, for instance. Another, released the following month, showed the beheading of another American journalist, Steven Sotloff.[23]

"It's astonishing to me that it would resonate with anyone," said Holloway. But he noted that many members of the public, especially young people, have been desensitized to violence. Other analysts, moreover, have noted that the ISIS videos were so well crafted that, after the scenes of devastation and killings in airstrikes, viewers who identified with the victims would look on the brutal executions as justice delivered.

The parents of the Denver-area girls were unaware of their computer and phone-viewing habits. It was a sibling who found social media posts that revealed their contacts and hinted at their plans. *The Denver Post* quoted the father of one of the girls saying he did not know that his daughter had been radicalized, and he said that it wasn't until his son saw the teen's Twitter posts that he recognized her intentions. "I believe Twitter is a bad place for kids," the father told the newspaper. "It's a really dangerous place." Officials in the Cherry Creek School District, the well-regarded and well-funded district where the girls went to school, said they didn't know about their travels until other students clued them in about the tweets. Officials called the girls victims of online predators.[24]

While Holloway declined to discuss the details of how the judicial system handled the Denver-area girls' cases because they were minors, he said members of the public could feel assured that they will be long monitored. He noted that there were legal consequences to them for their actions and that state juvenile courts exist to rehabilitate young offenders and to protect both them and the public.

Despite efforts some Islamist religious leaders claimed to make to keep women out of combat, women fighters died in battle in Syria, sometimes while working with radical groups other than ISIS. As George Washington University's Program on Extremism reported, the first American fatality was believed to be Nicole Lynn Mansfield, a thirty-three-year-old convert to Islam from Flint, Michigan. She made her way to Syria in 2013 and was killed there battling Syrian government forces in May 2013. The government forces said Mansfield was working with Jabhat al-Nusra, but another group, Ahrar al-Sham, claimed her as a member, according to the extremism program's February 2018 report, *The Travelers: American Jihadists in Syria and Iraq.*[25]

Just how many Western women, including those of Somali descent, made their way to Syria is not clear. Saltman and Smith's report pegged the total at about 550 in 2014, adding that about 4,000 men had done so by then as well. The number of fighters, overwhelmingly men, was believed to be undercounted, however, and the figure rose to 30,000 by the fall of 2015, according to intelligence estimates cited by the *New York Times.*[26] In all, more than 40,000 foreign fighters from 110 countries made their way to Syria before and after the declaration of the caliphate in June 2014, according to "Beyond the Caliphate: Foreign Fighters and the Threat of Returnees," an October 2017 report published by the Soufan Center.[27] The Soufan Center tallied the most recent number of women who moved from abroad to the so-called Islamic State at about 2,250.[28]

After its territory was hammered down to a sliver of land in Baghouz, Syria, by March 2019, many of the women fled and were apprehended by Syrian Defense Forces. Some remained defiant. Journalist Isabel Coles, reporting for the *Wall Street Journal,* quoted a twenty-year-old widow in custody as saying: "The caliph told us to leave . . . We await victory to return to the land of the caliphate." Defending the horrific violence practiced against enemies of the Islamic State and apostates, a twenty-eight-year-old woman insisted: "They only beheaded the oppressors—I see nothing wrong with that. . . . It [the caliphate] is over in the eyes of others, but not in our hearts." And a twenty-seven-year-old breastfeeding an infant said: "I will raise him according to the way of the Islamic State. . . . Despite everything—the hunger and the bombardment—we felt at ease." Refusing food offered by her captors, the mother said: "I would rather die of hunger than ask them for food. . . . This is the beginning of the launch of a new caliphate. . . . You will see."[29]

CHAPTER ELEVEN

Brotherhood

Women were peripheral for Bashir and his group in 2014, when many of the men were in their late teens. Some indulged fantasies of pairing up in blessed marriages with similarly idealistic young women, reflecting tales of perfect relationships they heard of from friends in Syria. But mostly they seemed to focus on their chances for heroism with "the brothers," a term they repeatedly used to refer to those fighting the battle for Islam. Like other adolescents, too, they seemed more important to one another than the adults in their world were to them.

As his enthusiasm for the cause grew in 2014, Bashir got into more strident debates with his father. They were "head-butting," he recalled. The imagery with which ISIS filled the online world seemed more compelling than his father's theological objections. Videos of ISIS supporters distributing food to poor people and building homes for families put a friendly face on the Islamic State. "I was hard-headed. 'Nope, I don't care, this is right and you're wrong, Dad,'" he recalled himself thinking. "We used to debate all the time."

Hanging out with his friends and feeling the power of brotherhood, too, was far more persuasive for Bashir than the arguments his father mustered. The young male-bonding, coupled with the amateurishness of the group, was striking, however.

None of the young men knew anything about battlefield weapons, for instance, so to get a sense of what could be in store for them, in the summer of 2014 they started going to a paintball-shooting park. There, they would shout "Allahu Akbar" ("God is greater" or "God is greatest") as they fired on one another. Some got in trouble with the manager, as they broke safety rules and unnerved other guests, some of whom complained. They drew notice, too, from the FBI, whose agents gathered records of who went on the shooting sprees and who followed some of the men. The details of their shooting sprees—on two or three separate occasions, according to Bashir—later became evidence in court of their serious intent to take up real arms. The paintball games echoed episodes of other would-be terrorists, more than a decade before, who had trained themselves in such games in Virginia.[1]

Bashir and his friends followed social media, too, where blogs described the delightful life in the caliphate and counseled would-be recruits on how to make their way there. The friends, many of whom took jobs together at a UPS facility that summer, reinforced one another's beliefs. They bolstered one another with more videos, including some in which the Sunni ISIS fighters systematically lined up and shot unarmed Shia who, they said, had been involved in horrors against innocents. They heard from the friend in Syria, Abdi Mohamud Nur, who shared images of himself as he downed smoothies in a shop and spoke of how wonderful life there was. "The entire summer was like that," Bashir recalled.

But the friends knew the FBI was not far away. Bashir was summoned to appear in August before a grand jury that was looking into efforts by Somalis to join ISIS. He was questioned about contacts with his cousins and the interests of some of his friends, including Guled Ali Omar. As he later admitted in court, he lied repeatedly to protect them. Soon after, the FBI blocked him from getting back the job he had the prior summer cleaning planes at the Minneapolis airport; he learned of that when he applied and came in to talk to his boss, only to find two agents eager to talk to him. The conversation didn't go well, as Bashir protested that he had told the truth to the grand jury and claimed the men were discriminating against him as a Somali.

The FBI "heat"—as they called it—and the conflicting messages only hardened the views of Bashir and his friends. They avoided mosques where imams would preach against ISIS, deriding them as "puppets" of the West. They shunned "moderate kids" among their friends. Such apologists for the West were "coconuts," hard-headed and empty inside or, perhaps, brown on the outside and white inside, they told one another. They saw themselves in "us against the world" terms, as a hardy band of Muslims who with their brothers in ISIS were facing apocalyptic battles that would precede the Day of Judgment, a staple of ISIS theology.[2] "We were preparing to go, getting money and passports," Bashir said, an effort that included clandestine nighttime planning sessions at a Minneapolis "dugsi," an Islamic school to which one of Bashir's friends had a key.

The role that certain Minneapolis-area mosques and at least one publicly funded "alternative" school played in the radicalization of the young Somali Americans is unclear, but such institutions amounted to a troublesome common denominator among some of the would-be jihadists. They used the facilities as meeting places. But some had also been educated in them.

According to court records, Bashir and at least seven others among the thirteen who plotted to make their way to Syria had for varying lengths of time attended Heritage Academy of Science and Technology, a "contract alternative" school in Minneapolis that catered to Somalis from grades 6 to 12.[3] While government investigators never produced evidence that pro-jihadist doctrines were being espoused in the mosques or the school, the environments did isolate the men from the larger Minnesota community during their impressionable high school years.

Some critics contend that self-segregated environments, such as Heritage Academy, are unhealthy. They fly in the face of the American ideal of public schools that push people of varying backgrounds together, forcing them to rub shoulders and, perhaps, to learn better to tolerate and accept one another. For decades, diverse public schools have helped immigrants of various ethnic origins to assimilate into American society, as well as equipping them intellectually to climb the social ladder, to move up from often impoverished childhoods.

Diverse schools, with integrated classes and after-school activities such as sports teams that include members of many ethnic groups, have been central to creating the American melting pot. Such schools have helped immigrants from far-flung cultures to hammer out distinct American identities even if they were blended ones, such as those of Italian Americans, Irish Americans, African Americans, or any number of others.

By contrast, the sense of separateness that Heritage and the mosques strengthened in the thirteen men who plotted to join ISIS may have worked against their forming such an American identity. Some professionals who dealt with the men pointed to a confusion of identity they felt—not knowing whether they were Somali, American, or something in between—and the insularity of these institutions may have played into that uncertainty.

Heritage, in particular, long sat on a hot seat. Minneapolis Public Schools funded the school by contract after members of the Somali community set it up in 2008, though the school was led independently by its own board. "It's a perfect example of a failure of leadership because the Somalis at some point asked for their own school and the school district gave it to them," an official for a Minnesota group familiar with the school district told me. "It doesn't work. . . . You don't have a public school that's just one ethnicity."[4]

Troublingly for the district, for students and parents, Heritage came under scrutiny by the FBI in the spring of 2014, according to court papers.[5] Officials at the Minneapolis Passport Office in late April had tipped the bureau off that Abdullahi Yusuf, then an eighteen-year-old student at Heritage, had applied for an expedited passport, claiming he wanted to travel to Turkey. A staffer in the office had grown suspicious because Yusuf could not name the hotel he planned to stay in, had no connections to Turkey, and had not gotten money from his parents for the trip.

FBI agents tailing Yusuf on May 5, 2014, watched his father drop him off at Heritage and then saw him skip out to a nearby mosque and then take off for the passport office to get his passport. A couple weeks later, on May 28, 2014, Yusuf's father again dropped him off at the school, but Yusuf again left early and, this time, made his way to the Minneapolis–St. Paul International Airport. FBI agents there stopped him from flying, and it emerged in interviews with him and his parents that he had been hiding his plans from his family. Yusuf pleaded guilty the following February to charges of conspiring to provide material support to a terrorist organization by trying to join ISIS in Syria—becoming one of six of the thirteen men in the conspiracy who would offer guilty pleas and avoid trial.

By being immersed in all things Somali at home, at mosques and in school—instead of becoming more acculturated into American life—young Somalis such as Yusuf may have suffered from damaging social isolation. They in effect were ghettoized, living in social and cultural echo chambers that may have made them more susceptible to the seductive messages of terrorist recruiters, according to Kenneth Ubong Udoibok, an attorney for Adnan Farah, another of the thirteen men. "Based on my experience as an immigrant, this country can be a very, very lonesome place, despite all the freedoms and diversity we have," Udoibok, who came to the United States from Nigeria at age twenty-one, told me.[6]

Udoibok, who could relate to the thirteen men because of his African background, himself was almost recruited as a child into joining Biafran rebels in their fight against the Nigerian government. It took the intercession of his grandfather to keep him away from the fighters who wanted him in their ranks. He knows, he said, how susceptible young people can be to recruiters who share the cultural backgrounds of those they try to seduce. Udoibok's personal experience figured into his representation of Adnan Farah, the attorney said. Farah had attended a diverse public high school—Minneapolis South—but transferred to Heritage. While there, Farah "developed a heightened Somali identity and the Americanness was diminished," Udoibok said. "At Heritage, he dressed differently—he was encouraged to wear the garb that was pleasing to his parents and the adults. He changed."

Udoibok pointed to the men's immersion in Somali life in America as a disadvantage in their assimilation. By contrast, he had no Nigerian community to bury himself in when he moved to Wisconsin in 1982 to attend college. That forced him, he said, to Americanize. Groups that form enclaves, as the Somalis have, make assimilation difficult for themselves. "Is it possible for you to be a full American and also be a Somali Muslim?" he asked. "American society makes it difficult."

Udoibok, who also is a Christian Pentecostal minister, drew a distinction between Heritage Academy and parochial schools such as the Catholic schools he and his children have attended. In such schools, there is often some ethnic diversity even as they teach a particular type of Christianity. Heritage, by contrast, he likened to a seminary, a much more culturally and religiously homogeneous place.

The parents of at least one of the men involved in the plans to join ISIS, Zacharia Abdurahman, had split opinions on whether Heritage was a good place for him. His mother, Ayan, pressed for him to attend there, while his father, Yusuf, opposed it, according to the young man's attorney, Jon M. Hopeman.[7] Ayan, who also relied heavily on her son as she raised six other children after getting a divorce from Yusuf, spoke little English and focused mostly on her home life, including preserving Somali traditions, while supporting her family by driving a school bus part-time. By contrast, Yusuf worked as a translator for Head Start because he spoke several languages, and for years helped Somali newcomers integrate into American life. He also was a controversial figure in the Minneapolis Somali world, for a time publishing a newspaper that at times criticized religious leaders he disagreed with and sharing his nontraditional views on local television news programs.

"That is a segregated school," Yusuf Abdurahman told me over lunch in a Somali restaurant.[8] "I don't want my kids going to a place where there is only one people, one ideology. I want my kids to grow up [with] variety, people with different backgrounds." Moreover, he was troubled by what he called the indoctrination his son and other children at Heritage got there from religious leaders from the Abubakar as-Saddique

Mosque who he said were connected with the school. The same mosque had been linked to the recruitments of the earlier generation of al-Shabab recruits.

The conflicting influences appeared to have torn at his son Zacharia Abdu-rahman. As reported by attorney Hopeman, Zacharia seemed in many respects as American as any other young man from Minneapolis—a teenager fond of ham-burgers, basketball, and hanging out with his friends—but he also had distinctly Somali qualities. His mother counted on him to help at home from the time he was fourteen. Later, he helped at home while studying computer science in community college and working at night as a security guard (including a short stint at a battered women's shelter). He had long studied the Quran and had taken up studying some Arabic. He had a girlfriend who wore the veil, the hijab, and the two had a chaste relationship. "They didn't touch each other," said Hopeman. "He arranged to marry her by contacting her family in Africa."

The cultural isolation at Heritage may have deprived students there, particularly the would-be ISIS recruits, of an alternative that underprivileged young people have long had. Military recruiters, permitted to visit other public schools in the district, did not pay calls at Heritage, according to Hopeman. Whether that was by school policy or whether recruiters did not see such visits to a small, mostly Muslim school as worthwhile isn't clear. (Minneapolis Public Schools, through a spokesman, declined to discuss the question.) Either way, impressionable young students were denied the chance to see different role models who could have opened career and personal routes far different from the treacherous paths some of them sought, tragically, to take.

Much of the school community was cool toward authority figures in mid-2015, though—especially those in law enforcement. The school's principal at the time, Abdirashid Abdi, invited then US Attorney Andrew M. Luger to speak to parents, faculty members, and students shortly after April 19, 2015, when his office had six of the thirteen men involved in the plan to join ISIS arrested and made the charges against them public. Luger went to the school on June 3, when emotions were still running high among friends and relatives of the men, according to Angella LaTour, director of community affairs for the US Attorney's Office. He got a "mixed bag" of a reception, LaTour told me. He was applauded for some of his remarks about outreach efforts, such as after-school mentorships and support for sports programs. But he also faced heated criticism from friends of the arrested men, some of whom were popular in the community. "Some questions were not friendly, but were very emotional," LaTour said.[9]

Indeed, some community members were angry at Abdi for inviting Luger. Within weeks of his appearance, the school's board opted to not renew Abdi's contract, setting in motion the fall 2015 takeover of the school by officials at Minneapolis Public Schools. Heritage was beset by disputes among its board members, parents, and staff, according to a report in the *Star Tribune*. So the school system cancelled Heritage's contract and took it over, with then MPS Interim Superintendent Michael Goar saying the district needed to step in after some parents expressed concerns over safety and the disarray within the school's board.[10] The board filed suit against the takeover and problems persisted: in January 2016, students staged a walkout, claiming the school's non-Somali principal was not heeding their worries. They were angry that a Heritage graduate, hired as an assistant coach in 2014, was fired, according to a report by Minnesota Public Radio.[11]

Enrollment at the school was reported to be dropping amid the tumult. But some parents—keen to preserve their children's Somali identity—stuck by the school: "My children are American children, but they are Somali American children. I want my children to know their language, their heritage," one mother quoted by a Minneapolis TV station, Fox 9, said.[12]

Bridging the gap between cultures is challenging for Minneapolis school authorities, even though many of the Somali American children were born in the United States. At home, parents expect their children to behave as Somalis, while in a diverse public school they act as other American students do. Furthermore, new arrivals must acclimate to a foreign culture. Since 2008, a nonprofit, the Somali American Parent Association (SAPA), has trained parents, students, and school staff in ways for all parties in the Minnesota schools to get along better. The group, which in 2015 collected about $533,000 in public agency grants and donations for its activities, reported that it provided tutoring and after-school activities from 287 students that year, talked with 220 community members and service providers about health issues, and "advocated for and trained" 256 people new to the school system as well as fifty-seven educators and administrators in the Twin Cities, according to its Form 990 tax-exempt organization filing.[13]

SAPA was founded and run by Mohamed Mohamud, who epitomized the sorts of acculturation struggles that Somalis can wrestle with. The Somali refugee in 1997 got a job in one of the Minneapolis elementary schools as a parent liaison, in a program in which MPS hired bilingual Somalis to act as links among students, staff, and parents. Mohamud, who later earned a master's degree and taught at a Minneapolis high school, was personally hit with family tragedy and disappointment in the educational system, according to a report in the *Star Tribune*. Mohamud was widowed and left to raise two sons on his own, journalist Mila Koumpilova reported. One boy "acted out" at his public high school, while his younger brother earned failing grades, dropped out of high school, and had problems with the law; the boy's troubles propelled Mohamud to create SAPA. His older son, at age twenty-three in late 2014, traveled to Somalia in a bid to better understand his roots and identity, but he was shot to death after arguing with a soldier there, Koumpilova reported. [14]

For some Somali American students, the public schools fell short of unvarnished success. Many of the thirteen young men who sought to join ISIS attended public high schools, either all the way through or before transferring to Heritage. A few attended well-funded suburban public schools. Somali American students in some of these diverse public schools have run into problems with other students, including black American students who sometimes didn't accept them.

Fights broke out. One notorious brawl at Minneapolis South High School in February 2013 began as a cafeteria food fight and escalated into a battle involving two hundred to three hundred students, where students kicked one another and threw bottles and were maced by police. Three students and a staff member were taken to a hospital after the melee, the *Star Tribune* reported. In its online account, the newspaper included a video of two Somali American students discussing the fracas with reporters; coincidentally, both later wound up among the thirteen who plotted to join ISIS: Guled Ali Omar and Udoibok's client, Adnan Farah. Farah, who later transferred from South to Heritage, said on the video that his culture did not allow him to let a girl be beaten up, so he had to get involved. [15]

In the years following the 2013 fight, Minneapolis's South High School sought to bring students together, according to Mary McKinley, executive director of Heartland Democracy Center, a Minnesota nonprofit that aids immigrants and young people in trouble, in part through programs in the schools. [16] Her clients included the would-be ISIS recruit Abdullahi Yusuf, who had attended both Heritage and suburban Burnsville High School. Yusuf repudiated his earlier beliefs, turned state's evidence, and testified in the May–June 2016 trial against his friends, Guled Ali Omar, Abdirahman Yasin Daud, and Mohamed Abdihamid Farah. [17] At South High School, McKinley said staffers have worked to create a more cohesive environment, addressing such issues as segregation, racism, social justice, and economic and academic disparities. "From all reports, it is a place most students and parents really love," McKinley said. [18]

For their part, officials running Heritage Academy in recent years seemed to be making efforts to better acculturate students there and familiarize them with post-graduation opportunities. They brought in AchieveMpls, a nonprofit that helps students map out professional and academic paths, to open a career and college center at the school. Such efforts may have helped boost the graduation rate at the school to 100 percent of its senior class in 2018 after the four-year graduation rate had dipped to just 25 percent in 2016, according to Minneapolis Public Schools.[19] The number of students remained small, however, just twenty-six students graduated in 2018.[20]

Regardless of whether they were diverse large schools or small self-segregated ones, schools overall avoided dealing with ISIS, jihad, and the challenges Muslims face in the West, according to journalist Dina Temple-Raston. She reported that Ahmed Amin, an assistant principal in the Minneapolis system and one of the counselors for Yusuf, referred to a kind of conversational blackout on the topics. Amin, a Somali American, suggested that educators fear being accused of fomenting radicalism and of stigmatizing Muslims. As a result, teens such as Yusuf lead "unexamined" lives that can make them easy prey for radical propagandists, and they seek their own answers.[21]

Amin, in an April 2019 interview with me, unapologetically advocated for Somali youngsters to adopt American ways—or, at least, positive ones, such as pursuing education and dressing to fit in, professionally and personally. Somali American girls at his school routinely get on the bus from home in traditional clothing, covered from head to toe, he said, only to duck into the bathroom at school to change into yoga pants. "They want to be American, to be mainstream," he said.

This often puts the children—and, sometimes, school administrators—at odds with the parents. "The kid is like, 'I want to be American. I want to fit in,'" Amin said. "And then you have parents who are pretty much like, 'No, that's not allowed.' . . . The parents absolutely refuse to acculturate and to adapt. They are very traditional and don't want to change." Clothing was less of an issue with boys, but they found their own ways to Americanize, sometimes negatively by joining gangs.

Amin, a Somali American whose father was educated in economics in England and who served in the Somali government as a technocrat, came to the United States with his family in 1996. The family had fled Somalia and lived modestly for about four years in Ethiopia, awaiting a visa. After they got to the United States, when Amin was growing up as a teenager in Minnesota, Amin's father encouraged him and his siblings to mingle with people of all backgrounds—Cambodians, Liberians,

Mexicans, a gay couple down the block. His father, who worked in the public schools as a liaison to Somali families, encouraged assimilation. That was fairly easy because the family was not religious. Amin considers himself both Somali and American.

Amin, who was educated in public schools in Minneapolis and at the University of Minnesota, counseled his students to develop their own identities, which likely would involve a blend of their traditions—and could mark departures from their parents' expectations. "There's not just one way to be Somali or one way to be Somali American," he said. "There are millions of ways to be Somali American."

Amin was sympathetic to Somali parents fearful of their children becoming involved in gangs, crime, drugs, and other problems that plague inner-city youngsters, who sought out a homogenous environment such as that at the Heritage school. But he argued that retreating into "affinity groups," whether by ethnicity or gender, is not the best answer for young people.[22]

CHAPTER TWELVE

The Caravan Beckons Again

Among most of Bashir's friends, the radical propagandists had set in deep hooks during their high school years and soon after. In the second half of 2014, efforts by Bashir and his friends to join ISIS picked up steam. Eager to take up the cause, Bashir even quit college in his second year, the 2014–15 academic year. "What was the point of school?" he asked.

Others among his friends appeared to be in school solely to get financial aid. They would use the money to travel, a crime for which some of his friends were later charged. Court papers detailed the transactions in which the college students borrowed money and used it to buy airplane tickets.[1] Omar, for instance, had tried to bankroll his ill-fated trip to San Diego with Bashir and Jama in May 2014 with cash from his student loans at Minneapolis Community and Technical College, only to have his family take the funds, according to Bashir's testimony.

As the summer of 2014 moved into the fall, the men tried to cement their plans. Some thought they would wait until January, when their families would use money from tax returns to travel to Africa to see family members still there. They would travel with their families and then slip away to get to Syria. Others said they would make arrangements to study in Egypt, using that as a pretext to make their way to the caliphate.

"Everybody had their own plans," Bashir said, even as he acknowledged that some parents were "on high alert" about the possibility of their sons trying to join ISIS. Worried, some parents had locked away their sons' passports to prevent them from following the two recent émigrés, Abdi Mohamud Nur and Yusuf Jama, as well as Bashir's cousins and McCain.

The friends moved forward with their plans even as word spread, in late September 2014, that McCain had been killed in Syria in late August, becoming one of the first American jihadists known to die fighting for ISIS.[2] Deaths such as that of McCain and the influences of people close to him, however, would soon chip away at Bashir's fervor.

An uncle of Bashir's from San Diego came to visit, and he and Bashir's father, bolstered by Bashir's anti-ISIS cousin, Abdihafid Maxamed, spent a good bit of the fall arguing with him about Syria and the terrorist group. Was it true jihad? Was ISIS a force for good? Was Bashir's interest in going just a matter of wanting to join his cousins there? "Three people are basically in my ear," he recalled. His father and uncle were relentless in their criticism: "All these kids, they don't know what the heck they're doing, they think they're scholars now . . . misinterpreting verses," Bashir remembered them saying.

Bashir and his relatives argued, even as a threat from the outside arose that, for some of the men, would hasten the travel plans. Abdullahi Yusuf, one of the friends who had been grabbed by the FBI as he tried to board a plane in May, heard from his lawyer that he would likely soon be arrested, something the lawyer may have surmised from his official contacts. So the young men gathered and talked of getting a van, driving to Mexico, and finding a way from there to Syria. "We were all scared, trying to get him out of there," Bashir said.

The men needed money—a problem, since theft was not a big part of their histories (their police records showed mostly minor scrapes, including a few traffic violations and one charge for fighting). As they plotted, they pointed to ISIS materials that counseled them that it was okay to steal from the "kuffar," non-Muslims, in a country with which you are at war. They thought of ripping off laptops from people in cafes, of faking car accidents to get access to pain pills they could sell. Some, of course, had college financial aid money. Bashir, who had been spending his free time mostly away from the group, with his uncle, told his friends to count him in, to make sure he had a seat if they moved ahead with the van plan.

By the end of October or early November 2014, Bashir got another nudge. His beloved cousin in Syria, Hanad Mohallim, called him. Mohallim, who was joined on the call by his other cousin Hersi Kariye and by Abdi Mohamud Nur, told him again how great life was in the caliphate and how he had heard that a group was leaving soon from Minnesota.

"Don't let the caravan leave you this time," Mohallim told him, repeating the familiar refrain, tugging at Bashir's yearning to belong. Feeling desperate, Bashir hurried to a mosque the friends attended and learned that the men were considering different routes and that some had set a departure date of November 8, 2014, for themselves. One friend urged him to get his passport on an expedited basis, even if that meant risking attention from the FBI.[3]

Rushing their plans, four of the men traveled on Greyhound buses to New York City in a bid to fly from John F. Kennedy International Airport, as Yusuf Jama had done the prior June. The FBI prevented them all from flying, however, nabbing one, Hamza Naj Ahmed, on November 8 on board a plane slated to leave for Istanbul, and grabbing the three others—Mohamed Abdihamid Farah, Zacharia Abdurahman, and Hanad Musse—at their gates as they awaited flights to their way stations on the road to Syria. The bureau allowed the men to return to Minnesota and, lacking enough evidence to bring charges at that time, held off on arresting them. Agents kept the men under close watch, however, as they built a case.

The men's efforts to travel suggested that some of their parents, by then, had a troublesome sense of their intentions. Mohamed Abdihamid Farah, one of the four, took the trip after fighting over his passport with his parents, who angrily barred his younger brother, Adnan Farah, from traveling. The parents apparently felt they couldn't stop Mohamed, then about twenty-one, from doing what he wanted to do.

Both Farah brothers wound up being charged for their efforts to join ISIS. Adnan pleaded guilty while Mohamed later was convicted after a trial. Dramatically, their mother, Ayan, fainted in court when Adnan opted to change his original plea to guilty, delaying the proceedings. Adnan had reportedly wanted to plead guilty earlier but was deterred by an imam who pressed both men to stand trial, according to an Associated Press account.[4]

At about the same time that the foursome headed to New York by bus, Guled Ali Omar also tried to travel, going to the Minneapolis airport with a ticket to fly, round-trip, to San Diego, on November 6. The FBI stopped him before he could board the plane. His name may have been on a no-fly list, possibly because he had attempted in 2012 to travel to Somalia to join his brother in al-Shabab, as evidence turned up by prosecutors demonstrated. Omar claimed he was going to San Diego for a week to see a girl he had met online and had no intention of traveling elsewhere, adding that he was slated to serve later in November as a reciter in his sister's wedding, an honor in which he would chant part of the Quran.

Undercutting his claims and suggesting that he had merely crafted a cover story, however, he admitted that he did not have a hotel reservation in San Diego. Furthermore, he was carrying his passport, though he insisted that was simply for identification. He made the attempt to fly, even though he said he, a sister, and a friend in their car were followed to the Minneapolis airport by ten cars with tinted windows. "I tried because I was 100 percent—110 percent sure I wasn't hiding anything," he later testified. "I didn't want the FBI to follow me and then think that I was hiding something because once I seen them following me I was going to abort my California trip."[5]

While several of the men were involved in what seems, in hindsight, like playing cops and robbers with federal authorities, the plans to fight for ISIS were soon to get deadly serious—and painfully real—for Bashir. He received sad news that shook his world and was to change his attitude about the Syrian misadventure for good; he received word that all four of his cousins were killed in a November 18, 2014, airstrike in Kobani, Syria, only weeks after he spoke with two of them.

The news devastated him, even though for some of his friends, the prospect of dying in Syria—in the abstract—seemed to make ISIS more appealing. When they spoke among themselves of going, several talked giddily of how they might quickly become "shahids," martyrs in the cause of jihad. That exalted status would guarantee "jannah," Paradise, not only for them but also for their families, they believed.

But to Bashir, to whom family turned out to be more important than being one of "the brothers," the deaths of his beloved cousins were not matters of martyrdom to be celebrated. They were just agonizing, irretrievable personal losses. "That really traumatized me, my little brother, everybody," he said. "I started reconsidering a lot of things."

Bashir pleaded with his parents to send him away, perhaps to Africa, saying that he had gotten himself into a big mess. But his parents didn't trust him to not make his way to Syria. He talked with his dad again about what was really happening in Syria. His dad told him that Kobani was not even militarily significant but that the ISIS leaders had based a number of Somali Americans and many other Westerners there, where they proved to be little more than fodder for airstrikes.

CHAPTER THIRTEEN

The Glory of the Shahid

The willingness—indeed, eagerness—of fighters for ISIS to die for their cause has mystified most of the civilized world. While soldiers in most countries go to great lengths to avoid dying or having their colleagues killed, ISIS fighters seemed to rush to embrace their own deaths and, of course, those of others. Several of Bashir's friends said they craved such deaths.

Suicide bombing, moreover, is a weapon ISIS fighters used enthusiastically, celebrating their deaths in advance with videos, even as the Quran forbids suicide.[1] Islam draws distinctions, though, and ISIS's religious thinkers (as well as those in al-Qaida and other Islamist terror groups) used one such distinction to define a fighter's death in a suicide bombing to be an act of martyrdom and, as such, noble self-sacrifice for a cause.

Thus, the now dead al-Qaida leader Osama bin Laden orchestrated and later celebrated the suicide attacks of 9/11 in the United States.[2] Nearly three decades earlier, in 1983, suicide attacks had gained legitimacy in Islamist circles with an assault by Hezbollah on a Marine compound in Beirut that killed 241 people.[3] Similarly, suicide attacks by Palestinians on Israelis have accelerated since the intifada of 2000 and, as described by Middle East expert Haim Malka, have gained widespread acceptance in the Arab world as legitimate resistance.[4] Perhaps the most inflammatory recent endorsement of such suicide attacks came from Hamas leader Ismail Haniyeh, who in 2014, said in a speech broadcast on Al-Aqsa TV: "We love death like our enemies love life. We love martyrdom, the way in which [Hamas] leaders died."[5]

Despite the widespread view in most countries that war is something one tries to survive, the idea of dying nobly for a cause or a nation may be as old as warfare. Trojan leader Hector, in Homer's *Illiad* (eighth century BCE), proclaims:

> Death is the worst; a fate which all must try;
> And for our country, 'tis a bliss to die.
> The gallant man, though slain in fight he be,
> Yet leaves his nation safe, his children free;
> Entails a debt on all the grateful state;
> His own brave friends shall glory in his fate;
> His wife live honour'd, all his race succeed,
> And late posterity enjoy the deed![6]

The ancient Spartan poet Tyrtaeus, in the seventh century BCE, also celebrated such deaths, writing: "It is a beautiful thing for a man to fall in the front line and die fighting for the fatherland."[7]

More to the point on suicidal efforts, in the Russo-Japanese War in the early 1900s, Westerners were stunned by the willingness of Japanese soldiers to rush to attack superior forces in battle, with one writing of their "uncanny wild bravery . . . which sets the value of the individual at nought," a quality said to be rooted in the samurai tradition.[8] And more recently, in World War II, Americans were appalled by several thousand suicidal assaults on military objectives by kamikaze pilots eager to die for their emperor,[9] and by Japanese banzai charges at stronger military forces and the doctrine that urged such soldiers to kill themselves rather than be taken prisoner.[10]

And yet, there were crucial differences in the so-called martyrdom attacks by terrorists operating for Hamas, ISIS, and similar groups. For one, the attacks were aimed at civilians, requiring the groups to redefine their enemies as all Israelis, all Americans, or more broadly, all nonbelievers in Islam, regardless of whether the targets were involved in military activities or not. That way, the attackers appeared able to rationalize what would otherwise be considered murder, which is also forbidden by Islam.[11] Moreover, the attackers embraced the notion that great rewards for their actions await them in the afterlife, including the promise of seventy-two virgins and 80,000 servants for male suicide attackers and eternal life in Paradise with a husband for females.[12] The terrorist groups also promised supernatural rewards for the families of the attackers as well as an enduring good reputation for the attackers in the communities they leave behind—something that may have been especially persuasive to adolescents for whom social standing is everything.[13] Groups such as ISIS celebrated the deaths of their "martyrs" with videos praising them, while the Palestinian Authority and the Palestine Liberation Organization cheered those who died killing Israelis and gave their families cash payments.[14]

Stunningly, suicide attacks continued, even as Kurdish and Arab militias backed by the United States put ISIS on the run in Syria and neighboring Iraq. ISIS fighters were driven out of such bastions as their de facto capital, Raqqa, in October 2017, and Iraqi Prime Minister Haider al-Abadi on December 9, 2017, declared the battle against ISIS over in Iraq.[15]

But such routs likely will not mean the end of the group's influence over terrorists now scattered across the world, or the threat posed by independent operators.[16] The Chicago Project on Security & Threats (CPOST) at the University of Chicago recorded 5,430 suicide attacks in more than forty countries between 1974 and the middle of 2016, of which a fifth—some 1,028—took place in 2015 and 2016 alone (based on preliminary figures as of October 2016). Those recent attacks, killing 10,728 people and wounding 20,444, occurred mostly in war-wracked Iraq, Afghanistan, Syria, and Somalia, though a handful of headline-grabbing assaults occurred in the West, in France and Germany, according to CPOST.[17]

Organizers of the suicide attacks seem to have had varied aims, depending on the group and the location. Attacks in Iraq, Afghanistan, Syria, and Somalia may have been tactical, a matter of weakening enemies or pursuing territory. Outside of such countries, in the West, the attacks seemed intended to unsettle Westerners, to make them want to sever ties with Muslim lands or to provoke a military response. ISIS leaders long wanted to draw Western soldiers into Syria for an epic battle in the town of Dabiq, a fight that a British Broadcasting Corporation report said features in Islamic prophecies "as the site of an end-times showdown between Muslims and their 'Roman' enemies," with "Roman" said to be the ancient equivalent of non-Muslim Westerners.[18] The town was so important in the apocalyptic theology of ISIS leaders that they named their Western-oriented magazine for it.[19] Frustrating those leaders, however, ISIS lost its hold on the town in October 2016 and renamed the magazine "Rumiyah," said to refer to Rome.[20]

The motivations of the individual "martyrs" have been more complex and difficult to understand. Early research on suicide bombers suggested they were sane, often religious people inspired by altruism and, perhaps, the self-interest of promised eternal rewards and a fierce sense of loyalty to a group—and that still is the mainstream view among experts who have studied suicide bombers and terrorists. As journalist David Brooks wrote in *The Atlantic* in June 2002: "Suicide bombings are initiated by tightly run organizations that recruit, indoctrinate, train, and reward the bombers. Those organizations do not seek depressed or mentally unstable people for their missions."[21] More recently, though, some studies have suggested the bombers are mentally disturbed, maladjusted, or at best, isolated individuals susceptible to manipulation. Focusing on Mohammad Youssef Abdulazeez, a Kuwaiti-born man who was raised in the United States and who killed five people at a military recruitment center in Chattanooga in 2015 and then died in a gunfight with police, criminal justice professor Adam Lankford wrote in *Scientific American* that many martyrs and failed would-be martyrs displayed symptoms of mental illness. "Until suicide attackers are widely seen for the desperate, traumatized, and mentally ill people they really are—instead of 'psychologically normal' altruists—America will continue to suffer Islamic mass shooters who seek glory and heavenly rewards through death," Lankford argued.[22] Abdulazeez, for instance, was said to use drugs, be depressed, and have grown up in a violent and broken home.[23]

Lankford pointed to research by Israeli counter-terrorism expert Ariel Merari, a psychologist, and others who studied failed Palestinian suicide attackers. "Members of this group had a significantly lower level of ego strength than the organizers of martyrdom attacks," Merari's group reported in the journal *Terrorism and Political Violence* in 2009. "Most of the would-be martyrs displayed a dependent and avoidant personality style, a profile that made them more amenable to group, leader, and public influence. Others were assessed as having an impulsive and emotionally unstable style. Some of the would-be martyrs but none of the control and organizers groups' participants displayed sub-clinical suicidal tendencies," as well as depression.[24] Lankford also cited an essay about female suicide attackers in several countries by Stockton College psychologist David Lester that pointed to "feelings of depression, hopelessness and purposelessness" among the women, particularly among those who had lost husbands (including so-called Black Widows) and who had suffered various types of abuse.[25]

The question of whether individuals in terrorist groups operate rationally—whether as "martyrs" in suicide attacks or as organizers pursuing the group's larger goals—is a thorny one. Experts on cults pointed to the religious—and therefore non-rational or irrational—motivations of some of the most murderous organizations of the last century. Understanding ISIS as such an apocalyptic death cult—one that relishes and celebrates such brutal techniques as crucifixions, beheadings, beatings and the bombings of innocents—is helpful in trying to understand its seemingly irrational collective and individual actions.

Outsiders who dismiss ISIS's end-of-the-world ideology and its extreme views of Islam may conclude that the organization, its leaders, and its murderous suicide bombers are simply irrational fanatics or criminals who invoke religious doctrines just to maintain power. But, as William McCants observed: "Violence and gore work." History is replete with state-building based on terror and death-dealing, ranging from the Mongols of the thirteenth century to the Saud family and its Wahhabi allies at various times between 1744 and 1926 to the Taliban in Afghanistan in the 1990s, the Brookings Institution fellow argued. Moreover, even as the ISIS leaders have been selective in their use of theology to arouse their foot soldiers, they know Islam thoroughly and find plenty of justification in the texts to rationalize their tactics. "The caliph has a Ph.D. in the study of the Qur'an, and his top scholars are conversant in the ahadith [the words and deeds attributed to the Prophet by his followers] and the ways medieval scholars interpreted it," McCants wrote. "There are many stupid thugs in the Islamic State, but these guys are not among them."[26]

With the enthusiasm and naivete of youth, several of Bashir's friends said repeatedly that they looked forward to dying for the cause. They envied and celebrated those who did so. Indeed, as we shall see, the lawyer for one even argued that martyrdom—not joining ISIS—was his goal. For Bashir, however, death was not something to be celebrated, at least not when it hit close to home. It would mark the beginning of a fateful change of heart for him.

CHAPTER FOURTEEN

Breaking Down

As they approached the end of 2014, Bashir and his friends soon saw even more bloody news. In Syria, the body count was climbing among men from the Minneapolis-area Somali community. Yusuf Jama, one of the thirteen in the circle who had made his way to the country in June 2014, died there, as his family learned in December 2014. That family had been already touched by terrorist tragedy because Jama's elder half-brother, Mohamed Osman, known as "Bashi," had earlier joined al-Shabab and died in a battle in Kenya.

Bashir's friends, moreover, had been affected because one of the leaders of the group, Guled Ali Omar, in 2012 had driven Osman and another Minneapolis man, Omar Ali "Khalif" Farah, to the airport. Omar had helped them on their way to sign on with al-Shabab, according to prosecutors.

While Bashir grieved for his cousins in late 2014, he got another subpoena to testify before a grand jury in Minneapolis. Again, in December, he appeared, and again, he lied repeatedly. "I didn't want to get anybody in trouble," he said, admitting that he knew he was putting himself "in a deeper hole." But Bashir felt he was "shifting" from radicalism, driven from it by his cousins' deaths and his father's arguments. Emotional and weeping even before the grand jury, nonetheless, he still didn't want to betray his friends.

But the FBI agents tasked with recruiting informants in the case—special agents Carson P. Green and Daniel P. Higgins—saw an opening after Bashir's emotional appearance before the grand jury. Tearfully, he told them afterwards that he wanted to obey the laws of his country, that he felt he was an American, and that he knew what he was doing was wrong, Green recalled.[1]

At that point, Bashir's resistance broke down. Green, a former Army officer with the incongruously friendly demeanor of a school counselor, took a warm tone toward him, saying the bureau could help him get his airport job back. All he had to do was talk with agents. Bashir thought the agent was going to give him his life back.

At the same time, Bashir began spending more time with his "moderate" cousin, Abdihamid Maxamed. He stayed with Maxamed often, watching videos of scholars who derided ISIS and, in a learned manner based in the Quran, destroyed its arguments. The beheadings by ISIS of journalist James Foley and others, in August of 2014, now seemed wrong to Bashir. Mutilation was forbidden in Islam, he learned.

Because he was out of work, was no longer going to school and had lost his cousins, his friends were worried and tried to reach out to him. "I was getting off the radical phase, and Guled Omar and them were getting mad," Bashir recalled. Omar and other friends came to his house. They tried to tell him his cousins were martyrs, but their arguments fell flat. "I used to hate it," he said. "Stop talking to me about my cousins. It's still new, fresh. I don't want to think about it."

By contrast, the engaging tone that FBI agents took struck a chord with him. The agents said the bureau had tried to get Mohallim back when his mother searched desperately for him. Their message, as Bashir remembered it: "We know, man. We tried to get Hanad back, we tried to get him from Turkey. It didn't work out. It's just not fair, man. He was a little kid; they just tricked him." Bashir thought, "Wow, these guys really care. They care about me."

Gingerly, in January 2015, he talked with the agents. They sympathized with Bashir about his dead cousins and let him talk of them. At first, Bashir resisted implicating his Minnesota friends, telling the FBI agents their trips were probably just vacations—even as the agents scoffed about vacations the men claimed to be headed for in such spots as Bulgaria in the winter. The agents said they were not interested in prosecuting his friends, but rather in getting to the recruiters they believed were soliciting them. They did, however, point to Omar as such a recruiter. Still protective of his friends, Bashir played down even Omar's leading role in the planning, saying he was just a fellow MCTC student, but he said he felt at that moment that the FBI knew what was up.

Bashir asked his father for advice, and his father told him to tell the agents everything. Bashir decided to cooperate with the bureau. Persistence and a soft approach by the agents, together with a strong parental hand, turned the tide for him. Not least of all, too, he knew that he was at risk for prosecution himself, as the FBI had long followed his activities among the thirteen plotters.

Even as Bashir opted, in February 2015, to cooperate with the FBI and inform on his friends, those friends' hopes to get to Syria still burned bright. They were stoked by learning that another Minnesota friend, Mohamed Amiin Ali "Rose" Roble, had made it there. Roble had traveled to China the prior fall and, in time, made his way to Syria through Turkey.

In a peculiar twist, Roble may have funded his trip with some $68,400 he was entitled to get because of a bizarre accident that made big headlines in Minneapolis a decade earlier. He would get the money when he turned eighteen, a few weeks before his departure, as part of an insurance settlement. As detailed by Associated Press reporter Amy Forliti, Roble had been hurt in 2007 when he was ten years old and a school bus that he and four siblings were riding on fell thirty feet in a Minneapolis bridge collapse. Despite physical and psychological injuries, Roble felt God spared him for a reason, according to a therapist's note.[2] Roble's uncle, Abdi Mohamud Nur, a year or two older than Roble, had left Minneapolis to join the fighting in Syria in May 2014. That gave Roble the high purpose he sought in life. It also set up his death: US officials believe Roble was killed in Syria.

Despite his decision, Bashir was torn about how much to cooperate with the FBI. Fearing he would get in trouble, he balked at first about admitting how much he had been plotting to join ISIS. "I was terrified," he recalled. "I thought I was going to get in trouble and I was going to jail."

While he told the FBI that his friends were planning anew to travel, perhaps by getting fake passports, he also discouraged his friends from "being hot, being radical online," and he told them to avoid him. He warned one that FBI agents were questioning him. His friend, in turn, warned him that the agents were "tricky guys" whom he should avoid. The prospect of prosecution, however, hung heavily over Bashir. His thought: "Damn, I got to work with them before I get arrested."

Bashir had long been ambivalent, of course, swinging between feeling driven to join ISIS (and his cousins) in Syria and rejecting the group over brutality that to him seemed un-Islamic. Even when he was in college, studying law enforcement in 2013–14, he was of two minds. "I was a nineteen-year-old kid. I was very confused," he said. "Half, I was thinking about ISIS and stuff. Half, I was still becoming a cop."

Together with his cousin, Maxamed, he had even signed up for a spot as a community service officer in a program in Minneapolis that allows law-enforcement students to work twenty to thirty hours each week for the city police department toward a chance to become police officers. Enticed by his friends and relatives to take steps to go to Syria, however, Bashir failed to follow through and join the program.

Cooperating with the FBI and acting as an undercover informant for the bureau, in early 2015, proved difficult, though. For one thing, younger teens who hung around Bashir and his friends, including friends of Bashir's younger brother Hamsa, posed a threat. Some ten to fifteen younger Somalis, in their early teens—"little kids, radical," Bashir said—hung around the older men involved in the plans to join ISIS. Bashir struggled to keep the boys at arm's length, not letting them in on the schemes.

When the boys talked of making their way to Syria, Bashir discouraged them. He didn't want the younger teens risking their lives, but he also had to keep up a radical façade for his friends—something the younger teens could compromise. "Some of them would go back to Guled Omar and be like, 'hey man, Cali . . . he changed, man,'" Bashir said. "My excuse to them was I was trying to not be hot . . . to be low-key, be low-profile."

While he got used to his undercover role, it took time. Even when he finally agreed to wear a recording device for the bureau, he was reluctant at first. He feared his friends would somehow find it. In time, though, he started recording, logging scores of hours of conversations with his friends. Bashir, infelicitously codenamed "Rover" by the FBI, had cast aside his radical views and taken a liking to the FBI agents.

The appeal that ISIS had for the younger boys took a toll on him, too. Bashir felt partly responsible for the pro-ISIS ideas that one of his younger brothers, Hamsa, and his friends were adopting. He even showed one a video that his father had shared with him of American missile strikes and the havoc they wrought, saying that was what the boy had coming if he tried to join ISIS. He steered the boy away from the group. "I felt I had done wrong, and I had to stop it," Bashir said. Only then, he felt, could he avoid repeating a cycle that had begun in Minneapolis when Omar's older brother and others had left to join al-Shabab, which in turn inspired Omar and his other friends to try to sign on with ISIS.

Even as his ideas were changing—something he kept from his friends—others in the group saw him as useful for getting out of the United States and on the way to Syria. He knew San Diego, for instance, and could help them maneuver around, perhaps making connections on the way to Mexico, from which they hoped to fly overseas.

The men had spoken of getting fake passports to ease the way, so Bashir's FBI handlers came up with a plan. They would set up a sting in which an undercover contact in San Diego would provide the documents and would spirit the men off to Mexico and then on to Syria and the ranks of ISIS. They made plans for Bashir and his friends to head out in April 2015.

One by one, however, several of the men dropped out of the plan to go by way of a car trip to San Diego. Omar, for instance, wanted to wait until winter and go with a small group. Others tried to make their own arrangements, eager to move sooner, fearing they could be arrested. Hamza Naj Ahmed, one of the four men who had tried to leave the prior November on buses bound for New York City, had by then been arrested, making others want to move (and sowing some mistrust in the group). One friend wanted to follow the advice of an earlier recruit to al-Shabab from Minnesota whom some in the group looked to online for guidance, Mohamed Abdullahi Hassan (known as "Miski"). Miski had counseled taking other routes to Syria, such as through Dubai.

Still another friend quit the scheme when his father learned of his plans. In the end, Bashir and just two friends opted to go to San Diego. The friends were Mohamed Abdihamid Farah, who had tried to leave by bus the prior fall, and Abdirahman Yasin Daud. The trio hit the road on April 17, 2015, driving continuously and stopping only occasionally to grab an hour or so of sleep. They traded driving responsibilities and steeled themselves by listening en route to recordings of Anwar al-Awlaki.[3] Daud and Farah made clear, in conversations with Bashir later entered into evidence at their trial, that they were committed to the trip and to joining ISIS. Daud even spoke with an Islamic State member who told him how to get to Syria once he had left Mexico for Turkey.

Daud, who had immigrated to the United States with his family as a child, had assured grand jurors in an appearance just a few months before, in January 2015, that he regarded the United States as home. He had never sought citizenship, however, as others in his family had. And in talking with his friends, he said: "I can't believe I'm driving out of the land of the kuffar. I'm going to spit on the—I'm going to spit on America, wallahi, at the border crossing.[4] May Allah's curse be upon you."

As the men discussed possibly being ordered by an ISIS leader to return to the United States, Farah balked at first. Then, as suggested by prosecutor John

F. Docherty in his closing statement in the May–June 2016 trial, Farah added an ominous threat. "I'm done with America. Imma burn my ID," Farah said in the recording. Then, the man who had laughed at scenes of violence in videos, added: "If he tells me to come back, I'm going to have fun."[5]

CHAPTER FIFTEEN

A Very Real Threat

The possibility of attacks in the United States was not an idle one. Some, involving Somalis, had already happened. One of the Minnesota men's online guides, former Minnesotan Mohamed Abdullahi "Miski" Hassan, for instance, was among the ISIS recruiters who inspired a pair of gunmen who on May 3, 2015, were killed in a shootout with police outside the Curtis Culwell Center in Garland, Texas.

The center was hosting a contest for cartoon images of the Prophet Muhammad, an effort regarded as blasphemous by Muslims. According to a report in *The New York Times,* Miski on April 23, 2015, urged his followers on Twitter to attack the contest site. He referred to the murderous January 2015 assault on the offices of *Charlie Hebdo,* a satirical Paris newspaper that had run cartoon images of the Prophet. Miski tweeted: "The brothers from the Charlie hebdo attack did their part. It's time for brothers in the #US to do their part."

The New York Times reported that Elton Simpson, one of the Garland gunmen, retweeted Miski's message and asked him to message him privately. Then, after Simpson and his partner, Nadir Soofi, were killed, Miski tweeted a series of posts, calling Simpson "Mutawakil," meaning "one who has faith." Miski said: "I'm gonna miss Mutawakil" and "He was truly a man of wisdom. I'm gonna miss his greeting every morning on twitter."[1]

Miski in December 2015 was arrested by the Somali National Intelligence and Security Agency. He claimed in a phone interview with Voice of America that he quit al-Shabab in 2013 and that he escaped a November 2015 raid on his home by the group.[2] Assistant US Attorney Kovats described Miski as "the most notorious defendant" that the US Attorney's Office in Minnesota charged.[3]

Closer to home, in St. Cloud, Minnesota, a twenty-year-old Somali man stabbed ten people in the Crossroads Center Mall on September 17, 2016. Until June of that year, Dahir Adan had worked part-time as a security guard at an appliance factory and was wearing his uniform when he attacked shoppers, according to a report in the *Washington Post*. He also had been studying information systems at St. Cloud State University, though he had not enrolled for the fall term.

Adan referred to Allah during the attacks and asked one shopper if he was a Muslim, according to police. A news agency tied to Islamic State claimed Adan was a soldier of the state and had responded to calls "to target citizens of countries belonging to the crusader coalition." Adan was shot dead by an off-duty police officer.[4]

Then, two months after the St. Cloud attack, on November 28, 2016, a Somali student at Ohio State University, Abdul Razak Ali Artan, drove his car into a group of students on the Columbus campus, got out, and started stabbing them. He injured eleven people, and two others were hurt as he was shot and killed by a university police officer. Artan had immigrated to the United States only two years before after living in Pakistan for seven years, according to a *National Review* account. Moments before his assault, the magazine reported, Artan had posted comments on his Facebook page saying he had hit a "boiling point," referred to "lone wolf attacks," and cited Anwar al-Awlaki. "I am sick and tired of seeing [Muslims] killed & tortured EVERYWHERE," Artan wrote. "I can't take it anymore.... America! Stop interfering with other countries ... [if] you want us Muslims to stop carrying [out] lone wolf attacks. .... Let me ask you this question if the Muhammed peace and blessings upon him and his Sanaba[5] [companions] were here today wouldn't the western media call them terrorists? To conclude by Allah, I am willing to use a billion infidels in retribution."[6]

Nearly a year later, on the night of September 30, 2017, a Somali in Edmonton, Canada, hit a police officer with his car, jumped out, and stabbed him before fleeing, according to police. A few hours later, the assailant was pulled over while driving a U-Haul truck and took off, running down four pedestrians before overturning the truck.[7] Police found an Islamic State flag in the car of the man, Abdulahi Hasan Sharif, thirty, Reuters reported. The Royal Canadian Mounted Police had investigated Sharif two years before for promoting extremism but did not have sufficient evidence to bring charges.[8] CBC News reported that Sharif had been detained in San Diego in 2011 and ordered deported but, in 2012, he crossed the border into Canada and obtained refugee status.[9]

Thanks to luck and astute policing, a Somali from Ohio, Abdirahman Sheik Mohamud, did not get the chance to carry out plans to attack targets in the United States. As recounted in "The Travelers," the George Washington University extremism project's report on terrorists, Mohamud went to Syria in April 2014 to join Jabhat al-Nusra, another Islamist group fighting there. He was following the lead of his half-brother, Abdifatah Aden, who had made the journey in August 2013. Aden, at twenty-seven, was killed in battle in June 2014,[10] the same month that Mohamud, then twenty-three, returned to the United States after being trained in explosives and firearms and instructed by a cleric to stage an attack at home.

The authors of "The Travelers" suggested his target may have been a federal prison in Texas that held Aafia Siddiqui, an MIT-trained neuroscientist from Pakistan who joined al-Qaida and was convicted of attempting to murder American soldiers in Afghanistan. There is evidence that Mohamud also considered targeting police or military personnel in the United States.

Seven months after returning to Ohio, in February 2015, Mohamud was pulled over by a police officer in Columbus for a routine traffic stop. When he gave the officer Aden's driver's license, the police arrested him. He was indicted and, in August 2015, pleaded guilty to charges of providing material support to terrorists and lying to the FBI. In January 2018, he was sentenced to twenty-two years in prison.[11]

As military forces moved to shatter ISIS in 2017, al-Qaida was the group that proved appealing to a young Somali woman from Minnesota, Tnuza Jamal Hassan. Hassan, a student at St. Catherine University in St. Paul, tried to make her way to Afghanistan in September 2017, only to make it as far as Dubai where she was stopped for lack of a visa, according to an Associated Press account. She told FBI investigators that she intended to marry a fighter and might even have been willing to wear a suicide vest for the Islamist cause. Later, in December 2017, authorities barred her from traveling to Ethiopia with her mother. Reportedly, she was carrying her sister's identification and a coat and boots, which would have been useful in Afghanistan but unnecessary in Ethiopia, located near the equator.

Determined to make her mark for the cause, Hassan then ran away from home and her family, on January 10, 2018, reported her missing. Seven days later, she set a series of small fires on the private Catholic university campus, including one in a dormitory housing a day care center tending to thirty-three children, authorities charged in a federal grand jury indictment handed up in February 2018. Hassan told investigators she had expected the buildings to burn down, and "she hoped people would get killed," Assistant US Attorney Andrew R. Winter said in court, according to the AP report. He said Hassan, nineteen at the time, was "self-radicalized" and had become focused on jihad.[12] After being arrested, she told investigators, "You guys are lucky I don't know how to build a bomb because I would have done that," the *Pioneer Press* reported.[13]

Federal authorities had been aware of Hassan since the spring of 2017. At the end of March, three students at St. Catherine University told school officials about a letter they had gotten from an unknown person that urged them to "join the jihad in fighting," and the university turned the letter over to authorities who quietly launched a probe.[14] It turned out that Hassan had sent the letter to a couple of fellow students, reportedly her roommates, urging them in it to join al-Qaida, the Taliban, or al-Shabab, according to the federal indictment. She was indicted for trying to provide material support for a terrorist group, for lying to FBI agents by denying she wrote or delivered the letter, and for setting fire to a campus building used in interstate and foreign commerce.[15]

Authorities in Ramsey County, Minnesota, also charged Hassan with first-degree arson. Quoting a criminal complaint in her case, the *Pioneer Press* reported that Hassan had "been reading about the U.S. military destroying schools in Iraq or Afghanistan and she felt that she should do exactly the same thing." According to the news account, the complaint said: "Hassan said this was the same thing that happened in 'Muslim land' and nobody cares if they get hurt, so why not do this?"[16] As of late 2019, Hassan was undergoing psychiatric care, delaying the legal actions against her.

CHAPTER SIXTEEN

Straight Out of Hollywood

The sting operation the FBI developed in San Diego would leave no doubt that the Minnesota plotters were not just talkers. It would provide concrete evidence—efforts even more convincing than bus trips to planes in New York City—that demonstrated the men's plans to make their way to ISIS were real.

After much planning that was caught on tape from a wire that Bashir wore, Abdirahman Yasin Daud and Mohamed Abdihamid Farah joined him on a car trip to San Diego. Only moments after Bashir and his two friends arrived in a warehouse not far from the Mexican border on the morning of April 19, 2015, the scenario played out, with huge consequences for all the men.

The video, screened for the jury at the May–June 2016 trial of Bashir's fellow travelers, seemed straight out of a movie studio. The trio examined fake passports ostensibly made by an undercover agent, who had gone by the name of Miguel, then money changed hands. At that point, heavily armed police charged in, tossing flash-bang grenades to stun the would-be ISIS recruits. The police subdued the men and put them into custody, taking Bashir off separately on the pretext that he had been injured.

But was it entrapment? Clearly, the men were caught in a law enforcement sting.

But would they have gone to Syria, had it been the real thing? Did they intend to join ISIS, and did the trap merely prove that? Such questions would prove crucial at the trial. Moreover, how did the affair affect Bashir, who had betrayed his friends and the cause they had all seemingly embraced?

After the sting operation, life grew challenging for Bashir and his family. Media reports noted an informant was involved, and when charges were lodged against Daud and Farah, it became clear that Bashir was the informant. "All of San Diego and Minnesota, Minneapolis, everybody was saying I entrapped kids—they were innocent and I entrapped them," Bashir recalled. "Everybody was isolating me, staying away from me, even my own family members—my cousins, [saying] 'hey, don't hang out with Abdirahman,' in San Diego." Bashir and his immediate family were threatened after police closed in on others remaining among the original thirteen men.

To keep him safe, the FBI kept Bashir in San Diego through the end of the spring and the summer of 2015. His family from Minnesota visited, easing the isolation he felt. He worked each day with agents to transcribe months of recorded conversations.

He was paid well for his work, with the agency racking up bills topping $119,000 in cash and lodging payments to him over time, up to $4,000 a month at times—far more than the $12 an hour he had earned in jobs before, as defense lawyers caustically noted in court. Daud's attorney, Bruce D. Nestor, labeled Bashir "a paid true believer." But it's misleading to suggest that all was bounty going into Bashir's pocket: as prosecutor John F. Docherty said in his closing statement on May 31, 2016, the sum included hotel payments and the cost of a used car, not merely straight cash outlays. Authorities had to move Bashir to San Diego for his own safety when he was threatened in Minneapolis.

Furthermore, the isolation wore heavily on Bashir. At one point, in August 2015, he called 911 because he was suffering anxiety attacks, as he testified later in trial. Under the strain, he wound up being admitted to the Scripps Highland Hospital in San Diego. Bashir also admitted to smoking marijuana at night in that period to ease his nerves and loneliness.

His consolation in that tough time came from the FBI agents. As they worked through some one hundred hours of recordings—transcribing more than forty hours' worth that included conversations that were a hodgepodge of English, Arabic, and Somali, as well as American street slang—the agents and Bashir developed a close rapport. Special Agent Carson P. Green called Bashir "bud" or "bro" in text messages and, according to testimony in the case, had bought Bashir some 731 meals. The men grew so close that Bashir asked Green if he could list him as a reference someday for a job in a police force, perhaps in San Diego or Minneapolis.

Indeed, Green told me Bashir would be a great asset to any police force that hired him. He knew the system from a unique perspective, the agent said. He also praised Bashir's diligence and hard work in the many hours they spent together over months as Bashir helped develop the materials that proved so damning to the conspirators. Unhesitatingly, Green put the chances of Bashir ever taking up the radical path again at zero.[1]

After returning to Minneapolis in September of 2015, Bashir worked steadily for the FBI until the time of the trial of his friends, the following May and June, transcribing conversations during the day and then attending college courses—which the bureau paid for—at night. All along, Bashir and his immediate relatives felt a cold shoulder from some in the Somali community who regarded him as a traitor and betrayer of his friends. Bashir's father and sister even were fired from their jobs at a Somali day care facility, he said. For his part, Bashir coped by living in an FBI-provided apartment and avoiding areas where Somalis congregated.

In the Somali community and among some of its supporters, the claim of entrapment by the FBI and by Bashir was common. Defenders of the would-be ISIS recruits Abdirahman Yasin Daud, Mohamed Abdihamid Farah, and Guled Ali Omar echoed it, as the three men stood trial together in a single proceeding that stretched from May 9, 2016, until June 3, 2016. For instance, Sadik Warfa,[2] a community activist who often translated for relatives of the three at press conferences, said, in a video published in late 2016 by Vocativ: "This paid informant, the community feels, played a big role, leading these young men to do things maybe they don't want to do it. . . . I can say 90 percent of the community feel that these young men, they were entrapped."

In the same video, Rashid Daud, a brother of one of the men, Abdirahman Yasin Daud, hit on the theme. He took aim at Bashir, saying: "This man popped out of nowhere, he telling me he came up with a whole new idea, a whole idea about a way out, a easy way out, a easy way to go on jihad, you know. I don't know, man, it just . . . never had that idea before until a person, Mr. Bashir, came and I believe that if Mr. Bashir never came into this role my brother wouldn't be where he is today and would be here today with us."[3]

Demonstrators outside the courthouse, including some protesters who were not Somali, at times carried placards making the same claim. As attorneys made closing statements in the trial of the three men on May 31, 2016, demonstrators carried placards saying: "STOP Entrapping Somali Youth," "FREE entrapped youth," and "STOP FBI ENTRAPMENT."[4]

Lawyers for the trio similarly argued that the government was luring their clients into the scheme through Bashir and the promised fake passports in San Diego. "You got to remember, his job is to get as many people ensnared/entrapped in this," Murad H. Mohammad, the lawyer for Mohamed Abdihamid Farah, argued in his closing statement. The only way the men would be able to leave for Syria, the lawyer added, "was because of the FBI supplied pipeline to the passports. Without that, these kids never would have gone anywhere. That's what entrapment is." The defense lawyers contended that their clients would not have committed the crimes they were accused of if not for enticement by the informant and the FBI.

Mohammad also sought to make a novel, somewhat hairsplitting argument in defense of Mohamed Abdihamid Farah. While Farah did intend to travel to Syria, according to his lawyer, he didn't plan to join ISIS (or ISIL, as the lawyer called it). Farah's plan, Mohammad argued, was "to die as a martyr, uncomfortable as that may seem." The lawyer underscored the point: "My argument to you, very simply put, is that Mohamed Farah did not go or attempt to go to Syria to join ISIL. He went there to find a path to martyrdom. And, as much as you may not like that, it's not illegal, it's not impermissible, it's not a violation of US laws to die for a cause that you believe in."

Farah did not get to Syria, of course, though the sting proved he tried. And Mohammad's argument did not persuade the jury. The lawyer's handling of the case also irked Farah's father, Abdihamid Farah Yusuf, who complained about the lawyer to Judge Davis later. Farah's brother, Adnan, had broken ranks with his brother and become one of the half dozen men who pleaded guilty to terrorism-related charges, but Farah decided to fight. Farah's lawyer, in fact, had sought to withdraw from the case shortly before the trial, after his lead lawyer, P. Chinedu Nwaneri, pulled out in a flap over an imam on his team, but the judge refused to let him do so.[5]

Despite claims by the government's critics, though, the evidence was over-whelming that all thirteen of the men schemed for more than a year to join ISIS. The actions they took and, later, their own recorded words proved that they were committed to joining the group long before the trio became enmeshed in the sting. The men met repeatedly and made many plans well before Bashir's change of heart in February 2015, when he reluctantly decided to cooperate with FBI agents and record his friends.

Furthermore, as noted earlier, several of the men went beyond mere talk to take action to get to Syria. Long before the San Diego sting, three of the thirteen found their way to Syria and to ISIS, for instance: Bashir's cousin Hanad Mohallim left the United States on March 9, 2014, Abdi Mohamud Nur left on May 29, 2014, and Yusuf Jama left on June 9, 2014. Guled Ali Omar and Bashir, who at that point very much intended to join ISIS, tried on May 24, 2014 to drive to California, the way station to Mexico and beyond, only to be stymied by Omar's family. (Bashir actually was a late addition to that driving plan, which at first included Omar, Yusuf Jama, and Daud, though Daud was dropped when he didn't have travel documents).

Another in the group, Abdullahi Yusuf, tried four days later, on May 28, 2014, to fly out of Minneapolis but was stopped by the FBI. Then, a few months later, in early November 2014, four others—Hamza Ahmed, Zacharia Abdurahman, Mohamed Abdihamid Farah, and Hanad Musse—left Minnesota by bus, planning to fly overseas from John F. Kennedy International Airport, as Jama had done. They might have succeeded, if the FBI had not stopped them at the airport, even pulling Hamza Ahmed off a plane. Abdullahi Yusuf, moreover, had been arrested in November.

Then the recordings, of course, were damning—especially for Guled Ali Omar, the former leader, or emir, of the group. One of the more revealing recordings, transcribed as Exhibit 198 in the trial of Omar, Daud, and Mohamed Abdihamid Farah, was a March 2015 conversation among Bashir, Guled Ali Omar, and one of the men who pleaded guilty, Hanad Mustafe Musse. In it, Omar recapped the planning for Bashir, who had been out of the loop while grieving for his dead cousins the prior fall. Omar spoke warmly of friends, apparently in Syria, who seemed to be thriving—despite some discomforts.

Omar told, for instance, of Abdi Mohamud Nur, saying he was sick from the dirty food he had to eat. "When you're in the city everything is amazing it's lovely," Omar said. "He said the problem is when you go out to the battle." Omar spoke of another friend, Mohamed Amiin Ali "Rose" Roble, who seemed to taunt him for not being with them in Syria. "I talked to him, bro. He called," Omar said. "He's laughing at me, 'Oh, you a punk ass nigga.' He's like, 'Bro, ya'll still there.'" Omar said Roble—who had gotten cash when he was eighteen from his insurance settlement for the 2007 Minneapolis bridge collapse—brought $20,000 with him and "bought all the brothers over there a new car," and paid for two marriages for another friend.

Omar sought to reassure Hanad Musse about the plan to go to Syria by way of Mexico: "You don't need a way to get out of here. We have a way to get out of here. We just don't have . . . the exact person," seemingly referring to a guide to lend a hand in Mexico. Further, he said: "We need to be 100 percent sure. A nigga with a name and number that can say yes to that guy and I'm a do it. Once we get that, willahi, billahi, tillahi, that's when . . . who stays back and whoever goes from there.[6] That's goin' be, goin' be a 110 percent . . . get to Spain, get to Spain. Once we get to Spain, we can get all that . . . train all the way to Sham [the Islamic State]. It will take three days and fifteen hours. And if we take a plane from Spain to Turkey, it's five hours."

Omar also told Musse how he would need to change his appearance, as others who had made the trip did. "Yeah, so you gotta shape up. Bald up. Go bald. Everything gotta change. There this one guy at . . . brother . . . that his name is Shirwa from Virginia. When he left, they put his face everywhere. Every country . . . and they still couldn't find him. Before he left, he had like long hair, beard, big beard, shaved all off. Everything."

And Omar wistfully bemoaned the fact that earlier ISIS recruits had beaten the thirteen men to the punch, already becoming glorified martyrs, or shahids (spelled "shaheeds" in the court documents): "Some of his friends are dead, shaheeds, dead, shuhada. The guys that he came on the mission at the same time as, some of them are shuhada. . . . It's all it is, bro, life. . . . We got passed, people we were around all the time."

Omar also spoke of visiting a mosque, repeating the conversation he had there with the brother of one man who had been killed and another who was still fighting: "Bro, Yusuf became a shaheed!," the young man told Omar. "I was like damn . . . and he's like, 'Ahmed's fighting for the sake of Allah.' What happened to you, bro? Wallahi, he said that to me, literally. I was like, I was like 'those guys were better than me. Your brothers were way better than me.' . . . He's like, 'No, bro, it's okay. Me and you are gonna go together, inshallah.'"

Omar also sounded eager to leave the United States. "Damn. Wallahi, you don't even know how much I'm sick of this place, bro," he told Bashir. "We gotta just, we gotta stop saying, just talking, and come up with real shit. That's our problem. When you come together we talk. [We talk nonsense. We laugh.] Nobody ever, you never do legit shit."

Omar sketched out the various schemes the men had in prior months for leaving to get to Syria. Musse, for instance, had intended to go with his mother to Kenya, and "he was gonna leave from there. And that would have been an amazing plan for him, because me and him could have easily met up in Africa." Omar had planned similarly to travel with a parent, intending to leave in December 2014, when his father planned to visit Africa. Omar's father would get a doctor's note saying his father needed him to tend him. "So he was going to do that for me, so I was going to definitely make it through," Omar said. Others in the group wanted to go earlier and by different routes—including through Canada. But all the plans fell apart by Omar's account.

For Daud, too, any claim of entrapment also rang hollow. By Omar's account in the March 2015 recording, Daud had come up with his own scheme the prior fall to steal passports from friends and, on November 8, 2014, to leave for Syria with another in the group, Adnan Farah, through California. As Omar described it, when Omar confronted Adnan Farah about the plan, Farah said: "Yo, to be honest, I didn't even make this plan. Daud made this plan and told me about it and told me to go along with it."

At the time, the men were squabbling about when to leave, with some, such as Omar, worried that moves by some of the men would bring pressure on those who wanted to pick a different time. Omar's comment: "We're like, 'Yo, it's not gonna work out and if these niggas try to leave we're gonna. It's gonna be tight on us. If they get caught up, it's gonna be tight on us. We're not gonna get to leave.'"

For his part, Daud, in his own words, made it clear after his conviction that there was no entrapment. In his statement to Davis on November 16, 2016, moments before he was sentenced, Daud said: "I want to send a final message to everyone sitting here and to my community. Your Honor, I want them to know that I'm certainly not being persecuted for my faith and that I was certainly not entrapped. No one lured me into doing any of these crimes. I intended to travel to Syria, Your Honor, with the sole purpose of joining a terrorist organization. I was not going there, Your Honor, to pass out medical kits or food to the people who I believed at the time would be innocent. I was not—and I want to make certain that that's not my purpose. That was, you know, something I, you know, made myself to believe. I was going there strictly to fight and kill on behalf of the Islamic State and ISIL, Your Honor. And I did everything I could, although it—looking back, it—it's not who I like to believe I am, but I lied and I deceived everyone to achieve those goals, Your Honor."

Similarly, after his conviction and minutes before his sentencing, Mohamed Abdihamid Farah appeared to take responsibility for his actions. He told Judge Davis that before the plans to join ISIS he was adrift in his life, "feeling purposeless and without a direction," not even certain about why he was in school. Then Farah added: "And throughout that time, for a period, I seen the tragedy of Sham or the Levant, and in the midst of that chaos, I seen a group that proclaimed themselves to be a caliphate for all Muslims and I was enticed by it. I felt like that was the direction that I—or that was the place intended for me. So I found myself a solution, basically, to all of my problems, a place to go with a righteous cause and a place to cure my sense of incompletion that I thought at the time. So I left—or I tried to leave—and I lied and I deceived and I committed illegal crimes, and I've done all that, Your Honor, and I stand before you today admitting my wrongdoings. I admit my mistakes."

They jury handed down guilty verdicts in the cases of Daud, Farah, and Omar in June 2016, and then it fell to Davis to sentence the three. He also needed to sentence the other six men who had opted to plead guilty, including a couple who had testified against their friends in the trio's trial. Davis waited until the fall of that year to send the nine off to their different fates.

CHAPTER SEVENTEEN

The Backlash

Bashir's work as an informant drove a wedge between him and much of the Somali community in Minneapolis, as well as in San Diego, his hometown. Not only had he worked with the federal government against his friends, but critics in Somali circles saw him as betraying all Somali Americans. When he and I met several times afterward to talk about the events, he advised against us meeting in any locations frequented by Somalis because, he said, there was still a lot of resentment. Even in mid-2017, years after the events, Bashir said he occasionally ran into Somali young men on the street who, he said, taunted or challenged him, pulling out their phones to photograph him as they badgered him.

The circle-the-wagons, defend-your-community-against-the-world approach that this reflects has been a major obstacle for federal law enforcers. While some Somalis and their organizations have urged cooperation with authorities, some instead have viewed the FBI and the US Attorney's Office in Minneapolis as enemies determined to harass, ensnare, and imprison young Somalis rather than to protect the community at large, including Somalis. While some rallied to support Somalis who were accused of crimes—literally rallying outside the federal courthouse at times—and mounted fundraising efforts to pay for their defenses or help their families, few supported those who helped the law enforcers as they sought to ferret out likely recruits or backers of terrorist groups.

The issue came into bold relief in the spring of 2017 when a Somali woman from Minneapolis, Amina Mohamud Esse, was sentenced for her role in an international online fundraising effort that routed funds to al-Shabab, the Somalia-based group. Esse, who was forty-three at the time of her sentencing, had cooperated with federal investigators and testified against a couple other women convicted in a case brought in Virginia. She had been pressed by an abusive husband into contributing about $850 to the terrorist group in 2011 and 2012, according to her attorney, Robert Sicoli, but after her fall 2014 arrest, she worked with investigators to gather evidence against the other women.[1]

Two Somalis—Muna Osman Jama of Reston, Virginia, and Hinda Osman Dhirane of Kent, Washington—collected money from other women and sent it to financiers of al-Shabab in Somalia and Kenya, which they referred to respectively as the "Hargeisa side" and the "Nairobi side," according to federal prosecutors. The pair also organized a "Group of Fifteen" that included women from Somalia, Kenya, Egypt, the Netherlands, Sweden, the United Kingdom, and Canada, as well as Minneapolis, which met regularly in a private internet chatroom that Jama set up to organize and track monthly payments of money, according to court papers.

Money slated for the "Hargeisa side" financed al-Shabab military operations in the Golis Mountains in northern Somalia, while funds for the "Nairobi side" supported a pair of al-Shabab safe houses, according to the prosecutors. One of the safe houses was used to store weapons and prepare for attacks, while the other was used to treat wounded al-Shabab fighters.[2] The money totaled in the thousands of dollars.[3]

As a March 2017 US Justice Department press release reported, the government's case turned on recorded telephone calls and other communications among the "Group of Fifteen." These recordings revealed how close the women were to al-Shabab leaders. According to legal papers in the case, the group took part in discussions that included lectures by Sheikh Hassan Hussein, a Somali cleric in Nairobi who was accused of providing religious justifications for al-Shabab's assaults and who reportedly endorsed ISIS.[4] The recordings of the women also demonstrated their callousness in the face of attacks on innocents. Jama and Dhirane were recorded laughing as the September 2013 assault at the Westgate Mall in Nairobi unfolded. Dhirane and a co-conspirator were also taped laughing at the Boston

Marathon Bombing in April 2013. Convicted of supporting terrorists, Jama and Dhirane were sentenced to twelve and eleven years, respectively, in federal prison.

Amina Mohamud Esse's cooperation in gathering evidence against the online fundraising group was crucial to winning the convictions, Assistant US Attorney Charles J. Kovats Jr. told me.[5] But Kovats was appalled at the lack of support for Esse among Somalis in Minnesota, noting that some had packed the courtroom to support would-be ISIS recruits in their trials and raise funds for their families. "Look who's here today," Kovats was quoted as saying in an account of Esse's sentencing day by Associated Press reporter Amy Forliti. Pointing to the gallery, he said, "Look at the community support for the defendant who did everything right. . . . There is no one here." Only an uncle of Esse's turned up for her sentencing. Esse was sentenced to five years of probation.[6]

Women in several places across the United States had helped Minnesotans who had joined al-Shabab. Nima Ali Yusuf, a San Diego woman, admitted to sending $1,450 to al-Shabab fighters. Court papers also disclosed that she had arranged conference calls between at least one al-Shabab supporter in Minnesota and the group's fighters from the state. Yusuf pleaded guilty to conspiring to provide material support to a foreign terrorist organization and, in December 2012, was sentenced to eight years in federal prison and three years of supervised release.

Yusuf, twenty-six at the time of her sentencing, tearfully apologized for her actions, according to an Associated Press account. The news service reported that Yusuf and her family fled Somalia to a refugee camp in Kenya when she was four years old and returned when she was a teen. She told the judge in a letter that she had been gang-raped by soldiers when she was thirteen, two years before the family was granted asylum in the United States. "I am and will always be thankful to this country for the help my family was given. There's nothing but sorrow in my heart for causing this problem and cost to the government," Yusuf wrote the judge.

Prosecutor Sabrina Feve described Yusuf at the time of her involvement with the fighters as an insecure woman "whose extremist beliefs made her feel better by making her feel part of something big." Feve wrote the judge that "she clearly relished her proximity to the fighters and the reflected glory she felt when describing their exploits and tribulations to her friends."[7]

Other Somali women, in Minnesota, had also raised money to support the terrorist group. In 2008 and 2009, two women from Rochester, a city about eighty-seven miles southeast of Minneapolis, raised at least $8,600 for al-Shabab by collecting money door-to-door in Minneapolis and Rochester, as well as elsewhere in the

United States and Canada, according to the federal indictment handed down in their case.[8] The women—Hawo Mohamed Hassan and Amina Farah Ali—were convicted in 2011 of aiding terrorists and, in 2013, were sentenced. Hassan, sixty-six at the time of her sentencing, received ten years, while Ali, then thirty-six, got twenty years.

Citing religious reasons, Ali had refused to stand for Judge Davis during the opening two days of her trial, breaking ranks with her codefendant. Dressed in a black hijab, Ali told Davis: "It's just a matter of faith for me to not stand for anyone. I am willing to do anything and everything other than . . . to compromise my faith. . . . As far as the other people who have the same faith as me, if they stand up for the jury or for anyone else, that's their rights. When I am before God, God will charge me individually, and they will be charged individually."[9]

Davis held Ali in contempt for twenty instances of refusing to stand during the two days and sentenced her to a total of one hundred days in jail. After two nights in jail, Ali relented and agreed to stand.[10] Later, the judge dropped the jail time, while keeping the contempt citations in place.[11] Somalis rallied outside the federal courthouse to support the women, with one saying Ali "deserves the Nobel Prize because she is a great human being." A woman in a green hijab waved a sign saying, "FREE HAWA! FREE AMINA! They Are Our HEROS. They are HUMANITARIANS!"[12]

Somalis seemed split on how to look on the government's efforts. This cleavage showed up most starkly in the 2016 trial of Bashir's friends, where the men's defenders claimed the FBI, through Bashir, lured them into actions they would otherwise not have taken—a claim in the cases that the jury members, all of whom were non-Somali, rejected. Protesters outside court proceedings in Minneapolis—groups that included both Somalis and non-Somali Minnesotans—toted signs saying "Stop FBI Entrapment" and "Stop Targeting Somalis!"[13]

Still, parents of some who joined ISIS turned to the FBI for help in trying to bring them back. The mother of Hanad Mohallim, Bashir's cousin, for instance, pleaded with the bureau in March 2014 to help get him back after he left for Syria. The bureau could do little, however, and Mohallim ultimately died there. Similarly, Abdi Mohamud Nur's family sought FBI help. Most of the other parents of Bashir's friends who pleaded guilty urged their sons to cooperate with the authorities, even if that meant turning on the three friends who stood trial.

But, at the trial, opponents of those who pleaded sometimes lashed out at relatives of cooperators, leading Judge Davis to warn that he would eject anyone in the gallery who disrupted the proceedings. On one trial day I attended, for instance, two women loudly argued in the hall outside the courtroom, and the dispute led a police officer to wrestle one belligerent young woman to the floor and then out of the courthouse.

Because of the splits, the atmosphere was often tense in the courthouse, especially on the thirteenth floor, where Davis held court. When defendants who had turned state's evidence testified, some Somalis packed the public gallery to glare at them, creating almost palpable tension in the courtroom. When Ifrah Nur, Abdi Mohamud Nur's sister, took the stand, she did so reluctantly and, under questioning, offered little detail to flesh out the anguished pleas that she had made in her text messages to her brother as she begged him in 2014 to return. And when Bashir, escorted by law enforcement, walked to the courthouse after testifying, young men tracked him—taunting him by pointing up from the street—on his way through Minneapolis's overhead skyway system.

At one point, one of Guled Ali Omar's brothers, Khadar Ali Omar, tried to bring a six-inch long pair of scissors into the courthouse. He also was observed photographing elevators in the building on a cellphone and, when confronted, he gave security officials a different phone. Davis banned him from the courthouse. Another spectator was caught trying to tamper with a courthouse elevator. Indeed, Assistant US Attorney Julie E. Allyn, a veteran of violent criminal prosecutions in Minnesota, told me she had never seen such overt efforts to intimidate witnesses.[14]

The legal actions against the Somali men infuriated friends of theirs who threatened the lives of court officials. Soon after most of the men were arrested, in April 2015, a friend of some of them, Mahamad Abukar Said, took to Twitter. The *Star Tribune* reported that Said in various tweets said, "Ima whack that us attorney general. The Feds are getting two choices. Either they gon free mybros or they gon have a massacre happen then they gone take me too. Ill kill for these guys if they don't free my brothers." Later that fall, Said pleaded guilty to a misdemeanor charge of assault in a plea deal with federal prosecutors. Another friend of some of the men, Khaalid Adam Abdulkadir, in December 2015 tweeted after another of the men was arrested: "More brother get locked up the cops body they will find on the floor body's dropping fast #kill them FBI and fuck as judge" and "Fuck them F.B.I. I'm kill them FEDS for take my brothers," according to court papers. Earlier, in January 2015, Abdulkadir had exchanged Twitter messages with "Miski," the al-Shabab recruiter, about how he could get to Syria, and in May 2015 he messaged Abdi Mohamud Nur, an ISIS fighter from Minnesota, about wanting to "chill with u soon as possible." Abdulkadir pleaded guilty to attempting to intimidate Judge Davis.

Outside the courtroom, government efforts to deter terrorist recruitment were fostering splits in the Somali community. The federal government in 2014 developed a pilot program called Countering Violent Extremism (CVE) in which it promised funding to initiatives in Boston, Los Angeles, and Minneapolis that sought to create programming to give vulnerable people alternatives to the online enticements of ISIS. Because the program in Minnesota was administered by the US Attorney's Office—which also investigated and prosecuted would-be recruits—some Somalis were suspicious of it. They saw it as chiefly a means for developing informants and for keeping the Somali community under a watchful eye.

"Despite overwhelming evidence that American Muslims are committed to the national good, the U.S. government still frames its relationship with American Muslims through a securitized lens. Such an approach stigmatizes the whole community," a Muslim civil right advocacy group, the Council on American-Islamic Relations, said in an early 2015 statement. "To be effective, any conversation related to CVE should include a discussion of overbroad surveillance by the NSA and FBI, use of informants in places of worship and other community gathering places without evidence of wrongdoing, and other problematic law enforcement tactics."[15]

Officials in the US Attorney's Office knew all about the concern, of course. They sought in many community meetings to explain the separation between law enforcement and community support in the program, which they branded locally as Building Community Resilience (BCR). They publicly stated it was not a surveillance program, with then US Attorney Andrew M. Luger going so far in May 2015 as to sign a memo of understanding that was also signed by a dozen local Somali leaders to make the point clear.

"The BCR is a crime prevention pilot program that focuses on addressing the root causes of radicalization to violence, by providing resources to prevent young people from seeking to become involved in criminal activity, provide community-based support and increase engagement between government stakeholders, law enforcement and the Somali Minnesotan community," the memo of understanding said. "BCR will NOT be used as a tool to conduct surveillance on the Somali Minnesotan community or to building intelligence databases about participants of the various programs under the BCR umbrella. BCR is led by the Somali Minnesotan community to increase support and resources to enhance opportunities for Somali Minnesotans."[16]

Several Minnesota groups in 2016 accepted seed money under the program, using federal and state dollars and local private money. Among these, according to a *Star Tribune* report, were the Africa Reconciliation and Development Organization, which received $25,000 for youth sports, arts, and education programs; the Confederation of Somali Community, which received $100,000 for employment training and school achievement; Shanta Link, which received $35,000 for youth mental health services; Somali American Parent Association, which received $85,000 to promote school achievement, family resiliency, and cultural integration; Ummah Project, which received $35,000 to train youth mediators and restorative justice facilitators; and West Bank Athletic Club, which received $25,000 for youth sports and parent events.[17]

Later, however, the program ran into trouble as many Muslims took umbrage at incoming President Trump's repeated slights of immigrants and Muslims, including criticisms he leveled at Somalis. For instance, shortly before the presidential election in November 2016, Trump visited Minneapolis and told supporters that Somali migration into the state was "a disaster" for Minnesota.[18] His election prompted some former supporters and beneficiaries of the CVE program to rethink their participation. Ka Joog, a Minnesota nonprofit, in February 2017 turned down nearly $500,000 that officials of the outgoing Obama Administration announced for it only days before Trump's inauguration on January 20, 2017. Ka Joog issued a statement on its Facebook site, saying: "As an organization trying to bring change, we feel like this process has been hindered by The Trump administration to instill fear, uncertainty and anti-Muslim sentiments. . . . As Minnesotans, we are deeply troubled by our nation's new administration and their policies which promote hate, fear, uncertainty and even worse; an unofficial war on Muslim-Americans and Immigrants."[19]

Ka Joog executive director Mohamed Farah told Minnesota CBS affiliate WCCO that rejecting the nearly half-million dollar award was difficult but necessary. "I think the president is against who we are and he has shown that," Farah said. "I know it's a lot of money but it all comes down to principle. They are promoting a cancerous ideology that is promoting divisions and we don't want to be a part of that."[20] Perhaps not coincidentally, Farah was running for a seat on the Minneapolis City Council at the time, though he lost that race in the fall of 2017.

Nonetheless, Farah's rejection of the CVE funds was especially stinging because only two years before Farah had been part of a Minnesota delegation to President Barak Obama's White House that endorsed the CVE effort. Furthermore, Ka Joog in 2016 worked in partnership with SAPA, sharing in that organization's $85,000 grant, according to the US Attorney's Office.[21] Farah had then said: "At Ka Joog, we are committed to working with our community and government partners to break the cycle of recruiting and radicalization. We view this pilot program as a unique opportunity to engage our youth in positive programs. Providing more opportunities, more outlets and more connections for our Somali youth will help break the cycle that has drawn too many of our friends and relatives to a life of terror."[22]

Another group in Minnesota that was instrumental in distributing the BCR funds for the US Attorney's Office in the early stages of the program also repudiated its involvement and apologized for it. The group, Youthprise, had come under pressure from activists opposed to the CVE efforts. "Though the money we granted went exclusively to organizations that do positive youth development in the Somali community, we now recognize that CVE as an initiative is problematic and divisive to the communities we wanted to serve," Youthprise leaders said in a May 2017 statement. "While we wanted to use our position as an intermediary to pass the funding through to positive youth programs and we support the organizations we funded, we also acknowledge that CVE hurt many members of the community and disrupted community cohesion. We are sorry for the role we played in causing hurt and harm to community members, especially youth. Many believe the framework of CVE perpetuates dangerous stereotypes about the Somali community in Minnesota, and casts suspicion on Muslim communities across the United States, negatively impacting Muslim youth."

Youthprise leaders added a broadside against efforts that focus on the Somali community, including the type of surveillance by federal authorities that uncovered the would-be ISIS recruits. The statement said: "Youthprise denounces the surveillance of youth. We do not support labeling young people as inherently criminal. We do not support efforts that prey on vulnerable communities. We will continue to work with youth, community members and other organizations to dismantle narratives that criminalize and stigmatize the Somali community. We see islamophobia and the stigmatization of Somali youth as connected to the systemic racism that young people of color face across the state and our country."[23]

Youthprise's reversal stunned officials in the US Attorney's Office. The CVE program, one official said, was built on models of other grant programs that support efforts to help at-risk youth, including drug-intervention programs and anti-gang efforts. Surveillance is not a part of such programs. In fact, the US Attorney's Office and Youthprise had a deal, a signed agreement in 2016, that was aimed at alleviating concerns about mixing law enforcement and community support; according to Angella LaTour, the agreement expressly said the goals and intent of the BCR were to increase resources and support for Somali Minnesotans and not for law enforcement purposes. Echoing language from the memorandum of understanding with Somali American leaders, the pact said the activities governed by the agreement and Youthprise's role in those activities were not intended to conduct surveillance of participants in the various programs under the BCR umbrella.

As it happened, though, the highly publicized rejection of the money by Ka Joog likely was more symbolic than real. The Trump Administration may have been disinclined to send such groups any money. Indeed, the CVE program by the spring of 2017 appeared dead for any future new awards. The Trump White House, in its proposed budget in May 2017, cut $50 million in previously planned funding for the program and froze $10 million that had been allocated earlier, Reuters reported.[24] Then, in June, the US Department of Homeland Security shifted the $10 million in earlier allocations to favor more law enforcement efforts.[25] In Minnesota, for instance, the Hennepin County Sheriff's Office was slated to receive $347,600 for "training and engagement."[26]

The Trump Administration did boost the amount of money set aside for one Minnesota nonprofit, Heartland Democracy Center, to $423,340 over two years from the initially awarded $165,000. The administration said the money was for "developing resilience," although Heartland executive director Mary McKinley told me that Heartland does no deradicalization training and did not single out Muslim communities or Somalis for special efforts.[27] Heartland operates more broadly, promoting civic engagement through programming for young people in school, with a particular focus on immigrant and distressed communities.

The group helped counsel one of the six young Somali men who pleaded guilty to charges relating to trying to join ISIS, Abdullahi Yusuf, before he was sentenced in the fall of 2016. Yusuf had turned state's evidence and testified against his friends. Heartland planned to use its CVE allocation to partner on pilots, evaluation, and programming with other groups, including a few that serve the Somali community, according to McKinley.[28]

Thanks, perhaps, to tumult in the change between the Obama and Trump administrations, organizations that earlier were told they would get grants got no information between the presidential inauguration in January and late June 2017, the leader of one such organization complained.[29] Some groups that had accepted funding wound up getting none, while the awards for others—such as Heartland—were raised. Early in the Trump Administration, some officials appeared to want to narrow the focus of the efforts to preventing Islamic terrorism. Indeed, administration officials reportedly considered changing the CVE program's name to "Countering Islamic Extremism."[30] But, as of December 2017, the Department of Homeland Security was still using the CVE term, and its updated Terrorism Prevention Partnerships website noted: "Violent extremist threats come from a range of groups and individuals, including domestic terrorists and homegrown violent extremists in the United States, as well as international terrorist groups like al-Qaeda and ISIL." Nonetheless, the partnerships effort appeared to be unfunded in late 2017 and, as of early 2019, officials in Minneapolis said the program was dead there.

Part of the problem with CVE programming is measuring success. As an October 2016 report by the National Security Critical Issues Task Force put it: "It remains difficult to correlate outputs to demonstrate the success of CVE programs to policymakers. As CVE focuses on prevention, success is a 'non-event.' Also, most prevention models are only loosely tied to CVE because the primary and secondary levels of prevention affect other social programs along with CVE. Without meaningful data or metrics, it is difficult to justify funding and political support for CVE."[31]

Like the CVE program in the United States, similar efforts abroad have been plagued by complaints that, because they single out Muslim groups, they make young Muslims feel stigmatized. The Prevent program in the United Kingdom, which dates back to 2003, alienated the young people it sought to deter from terrorism, Harun Khan, then deputy head of the Muslim Council of Britain, told the British Broadcasting Corporation. "Most young people are seeing [Prevent] as a target on them and the institutions they associate with," Khan said.

Further, Muslims in Birmingham were angered when program funds were used to install cameras—albeit publicly visible CCTV cameras, not covert spy cameras—in their community. As a 2014 analysis by BBC correspondent Dominic Casciani noted, "So the real problem with Prevent is this: every time officials try to win trust, they are met with the accusation that they are treating Muslims as a 'suspect community.'"[32] The Prevent program's name had become "toxic," with British Muslims feeling "picked on," mayor of Greater Manchester Andy Burnham said after a suicide bomber killed twenty-two people and himself in a May 2017 attack at the Manchester Arena, *The Telegraph* reported.[33]

The Prevent program came under harsh criticism from the Open Society Foundations, a nonprofit group founded and led by philanthropist George Soros. The group's October 2016 report, "Eroding Trust," said such programs required teachers, psychologists, doctors, nurses, and other caregivers to tell authorities about students and patients who seemed to be at risk for extremism. It warned that such an approach could make the communities feel like they were being surveilled and therefore could backfire.[34]

The Prevent program had defenders, however. After the Manchester Arena attack, Britain's home secretary, Amber Rudd, said the program had helped stop 150 people—including fifty children—from leaving Britain to fight in Syria in the prior year alone. "There's really strong evidence of Prevent initiatives helping families, saving children's lives and stopping radicalization," she said at question time in Parliament, as quoted by *The Telegraph*. "Prevent is saving lives, it is doing good work." The newspaper reported that a senior Whitehall source said eighteen plots had been foiled since 2013 in Britain, including five in the nine weeks after a car attack in March 2017 on Westminster Bridge. But the report noted that it was not known if the Prevent program had contributed to deterring those attacks.

One can only speculate on whether the CVE initiative, piloted in Minneapolis, Boston, and Los Angeles in 2014, or some other early intervention could have helped deter Bashir's friends from terrorism before their arrests the following year. None of them were directed into any CVE-funded programming until after they were well along in the legal proceedings against them, even though some had had many contacts with the FBI and other federal authorities as they investigated the men's plans to join ISIS.

CHAPTER EIGHTEEN

The Judge

B efore taking the bench on one of the early days in the spring 2016 trial of Abdirahman Yasin Daud, Mohamed Abdihamid Farah, and Guled Ali Omar, Judge Michael J. Davis had learned that some Somali spectators were arguing passionately at lunch in the courthouse café. He was determined that the spat between the mother of a cooperating defendant and the mother of a non-cooperator would not spill into the courtroom. The atmosphere in the courthouse had long been tense, marked by nasty exchanges in the hallways and at least one incident of a police officer wrestling an enraged young woman to the floor.

So Davis stepped into the visitor's gallery at the back, towering above the seated hijab-clad Somalis and other onlookers. He extended his hand to one of the older women and then, knowing that Islam discourages contact between unrelated men and women, he pulled back his hand, laid it upon his chest and smiled broadly, as if in apology. He then grew stern and politely, but with no smile, cautioned the woman and others nearby that he would tolerate no disruption in his courtroom. He strode over to the other side of the gallery and repeated his warning to the other mother.

Davis had learned a lot about Islam and Somali ways over the prior decade, as he presided over all the significant Somali terrorism trials in Minneapolis in that time. The nearly bald and bespectacled judge, who stands 6 feet, 5½ inches tall (befitting a former Macalester College basketball player), had traveled to Muslim countries including Egypt, Saudi Arabia, and Senegal.[1] He had also learned a lot about terrorism. For the trial of Daud, Farah, and Omar, and the proceedings for the six other men who pleaded guilty, he made a special trip to Germany to visit an expert in deradicalization, Daniel Koehler. He later brought Koehler to Minneapolis to assess the rehabilitation potential among some of the men. The judge had learned still more about terrorism as a member of the Foreign Intelligence Surveillance Court, on which he served from 1999 to 2006.[2] The FISA court, nicknamed for the legal Act that created it, reviews government requests for electronic and other surveillance of spies and suspected terrorists.

As he sat on cases ranging from people supporting al-Shabab and ISIS to people taking up weapons to fight for those groups, Davis sought first of all to protect Americans from would-be terrorists. At his sentencing of Mohamed Abdihamid Farah on November 16, 2016, the judge noted that he had traveled the world trying to figure out what to do with people involved with "extremist Jihadist behavior." But nothing in the criminal justice system, he said, "could even come close to trying to rehabilitate someone that has extreme Jihadist ideology," according to the court transcripts. And he told the Somali community that it needed to understand that there was a jihadist cell in its midst. "Its tentacles spread out," Davis said. "Young people went to Syria and died."[3]

Indeed, he suggested that the Somali community was tarnished and victimized by would-be terrorists. In sentencing Farah's friend, Abdirahman Yasin Daud, Davis went out of this way to say that he was not faulting Somalis in Minnesota. He said the "great spirit of the Somali community" is that it survived the civil war in Somalia, something most Americans don't understand. "I do, but the vast majority of Americans don't have the slightest idea of what the Somali Americans have gone through," the judge said.

Would-be terrorists, such as the men involved in the conspiracy to join ISIS, damage the community, he said. Somalis, he added, came to the United States seeking a better life. Noting that the country is a nation of immigrants, he offered a ringing endorsement of diversity and shared his sympathetic view of Islam, saying: "That's why I say the Somali community is so important to our community, just like the Hmong community has been, so has the Liberian community, so has the Russian community, so has the German community. . . . I want to make sure that the Somali community understands that we need that vibrancy, and I will fight anyone that talks about Islam [as] a dirty religion or one of violence. It is not."[4]

Davis, appointed by President Clinton in 1994 as the first African American named to the federal bench in Minnesota, then doubled down. He reiterated his appreciation for immigrants and their enrichment of the United States. "My sentences are not an attack on the Somali community," he said. "They're a vibrant, wonderful community, adding diversity to this state, just as the Liberians and Nigerians and the Hmong and the Russians and the Germans and the Swedes and the people that came from Yugoslavia and even from Europe. My people came here in chains." The United States, he added, is a country ruled by law, and he said the grave threat to it represented by terrorism must be dealt with severely. Referring to the conspiracy of the men before him, he said he needed to "incapacitate this cell."

So he handed down lengthy sentences to the trio (the judge bridled at the term "stiff" in an interview with me, contending that the jail terms were appropriate and that the term suggests otherwise).[5] The jury had convicted all three of charges including conspiracy to murder outside the United States, conspiracy to provide material support to a designated foreign terrorist organization, and attempting to provide material support for a designated foreign terrorist organization.

Davis sent Guled Ali Omar, whom the prosecutors had cast at the center of the thirteen men's moves and schemes, to prison for thirty-five years. Not only were Omar's actions, surreptitiously recorded statements, and admissions in court damning but also his family history troubled the judge: Omar's eldest brother, Ahmed Ali Omar, had joined al-Shabab when Guled was thirteen, and there was evidence that Guled had sought to travel to Nairobi to join the man, who remains at large. Another brother, Mohamed Ali Omar, who was shot repeatedly in what authorities suspected was gang-related violence in Minneapolis, was convicted of interfering with FBI agents investigating Guled. Davis handled Mohamed Ali Omar's case, as well.

The judge gave Abdirahman Yasin Daud and Mohamed Abdihamid Farah, who had traveled to San Diego in the sting operation, each thirty years in prison. Moreover, he ordered that upon their release all three men would be supervised by authorities for life. The men, each twenty-two at the time of sentencing, would be well into middle age before they would see the outside of a federal prison again.[6]

The prison terms he handed down reflected the tough sentencing guidelines established for terrorism crimes, sentences other judges around the country have imposed for similar offenses, and the judge's abhorrence of the jihadist efforts. With those sentences, he also broadcast a loud warning to friends of the thirteen and to others in the Somali community who might try to follow in their footsteps, just as the thirteen had sought to follow in the path trod before them by the al-Shabab recruits and supporters that Davis had dealt with. The judge had sent some of those al-Shabab backers off to similar fates years before, of course. Would-be terrorists who wound up before Davis would be dealt with severely, especially if he believed their claims of repentance to be hollow—as he did in the cases of the ISIS plotters.

His unsparing view, however, surprised some in Minnesota, especially in light of his personal and professional background. One Somali activist at the opening of the trial told me that he and others in the Somali community had hoped that Davis, as a black man who understood the social forces arrayed against young black men, would be more inclined to mercy.

Indeed, the judge had been a staunch advocate for African American issues. In 2013, for instance, he played a key role in the Dred Scott Project, an effort to educate high school students and others about the notorious 1857 US Supreme Court decision that said African Americans could not become US citizens and were not entitled to the rights to sue that such citizens had. The Federal Bar Association in 2016 gave the judge the Sarah T. Hughes Civil Rights Award, recognizing him for his forty-five-year-long "passion for equal access and equal justice for all," in the words of the association's award citation. "His lifelong commitment to and pursuit of equal access and equal justice for all shows through his work with the Legal Rights Center, Neighborhood Justice Center, Hennepin County Public Defender's Office, and throughout his 11 years as a state court judge in Hennepin County. This flame burned bright as the editor-in-chief of the comprehensive and influential Minnesota Supreme Court Racial Bias Task Force report issued in 1993. . . . He has made groundbreaking achievements and sustained a body of work in the area of civil rights, due process, and equal protection."[7]

For much of his early career, the judge worked on the defense side of law, dealing with civil rights issues in particular. After graduating from the University of Minnesota Law School in 1972, he worked in criminal defense and legal rights areas until he was appointed as municipal court judge in Hennepin County, Minnesota, in 1983. He served as a public defender from 1978 through 1983 and as an attorney and commissioner for the Minneapolis Civil Rights Commission from 1977 to 1981.[8] After fourteen years on the federal court, he rose to chief judge in 2008, and soon after, he helped create Minnesota's federal Pro Se Project after finding that people of color and the poor often represented themselves in federal civil litigation, according to a *Star Tribune* report. The project matched clients with volunteer attorneys.[9] Davis assumed senior status in 2015.

In dealing with the six men who pleaded guilty in the ISIS-recruitment cases, the judge wielded a tough hand, as well. But he appeared to draw distinctions among the men based partly on their cooperation and his judgment of their likelihood to slip into terrorism. He sentenced one of the men, Hamza Naj Ahmed, to fifteen years in prison, later cutting it to ten years. He sentenced three—Zacharia Abdurahman, Adnan Abdihamid Farah, and Hanad Mustafe Musse—to ten years in prison each. In dealing with two men who testified against the trio who stood trial, he sent Abdirizak Warsame off for two and a half years in prison and sentenced the least culpable and most cooperative of the group, Abdullahi Yusuf, to time served. Upon their release, moreover, he mandated that each man would be supervised by legal authorities for twenty years.

Scores of relatives and friends of the men attended their sentencings on November 14, 15, and 16, 2016, illustrating how much attention the cases commanded in the Somali community. Thirty of the family members of Hamza Naj Ahmed, for instance, wanted to come into the courtroom, though it could hold just twenty of them. As noted by Ahmed's defense attorney JaneAnne Murray, eighty-five of his relatives, out of nearly one hundred in his extended family, signed a letter of support for the then twenty-one-year-old Ahmed, who two years before had been pulled off a plane bound for Turkey by FBI agents.

Ahmed's lawyer painted a picture of him as a loving and dutiful son to his divorced mother. He had taken on the role of surrogate father to three siblings starting at age fourteen, Murray told the court. Because of his domestic responsibilities, he could not develop an independent identity as a teenager, she said, so he turned to the internet, where he was "a perfect mark for that powerful, voluminous, incredibly well produced propaganda coming out of ISIL." In turn, he tweeted more than 180 photos of orphaned and injured children in Syria victimized by the country's dictator, as well as photos of ISIS fighters. He felt a call to avenge the deaths of the children, Murray said, because he was "fundamentally a caring, dutiful, kind man." After he was yanked off the plane at John F. Kennedy International Airport, he cut ties with his fellow plotters, went back to school and babysitting, and recanted his interest in joining ISIS, even as his friends continued their plotting. Citing a psychiatrist who assessed him for the defense, Murray said he was unlikely to turn back toward terrorism.

But, under questioning by Davis, Ahmed said he planned to become a jihadist with ISIS, willing to kill for the group. If necessary, he would die for it, becoming a martyr and thus assuring places for himself and his family in the highest level of heaven, he said. Further, he acknowledged that he and his fellow plotters celebrated the martyrdom of one of their own who did make it to Syria and was killed, Bashir's cousin Hanad Mohallim.

Ahmed admitted that he had exchanged tweets or talked with a brother, a former Somali gang member, about jihad. The brother, identified in the court transcripts as Sharir, had gone to Ethiopia and, at the time of his sentencing, Ahmed said he didn't know whether he was alive or dead. Ahmed also admitted to watching violent ISIS propaganda videos, such as the particularly gory "Upon the Prophetic Methodology," for hours and hours. Once he had been turned back from his trip, Ahmed also acknowledged not reporting the conspiracy to join ISIS to authorities. Prosecutor Julie E. Allyn described Ahmed as a recruiter who had repeatedly lied to authorities, prompting the fifteen-year sentence that the judge later trimmed to ten years.

Zacharia Abdurahman had also tried to fly out of New York on the way to Syria in November 2014, only to be stopped at the gate by the FBI. During his sentencing, he tried to explain his seduction by ISIS: "And I seen atrocities that was going on. I seen the people being killed. And I also seen the ISIL videos, their fighters and what they propagated, the message, what they stood for. And they stood for, they had a structure that wasn't just any type of organization that was just killing, and this is why they were so deceiving because this organization was different. They emulated the Prophet, peace and blessing be upon you, in a way, because they were going out, they were saying they were righteous men, men that are fighting for the religion, that are protecting the people. They quoted Quranic verses, like where the almighty says permission is given to those who are oppressed—permission to fight is only given to those who are oppressed and who are driven away from their homes because they say our Lord is God. And this had a deep impact on me."

Though he was born and raised in the United States, Abdurahman also said he had felt out of place and harassed in Minnesota as a Muslim. As a high school freshman, he said, he once walked out of a McDonald's in traditional Muslim clothing and a group of strangers spat on him and told him to go back where he came from. This and other incidents, he said, "made me feel like a foreigner in this country." And when he looked at images of the victims in the Syrian war, he said, he felt like the whole world was ignoring their cries. When he connected the dots, as he said, he felt compelled to join ISIS.

One of Abdurahman's lawyers, Marnie Fearon, told the judge that Abdurahman was feeling "most radical" in early 2015 and that if the FBI had not arrested him in April that year "he would be overseas right now and he would likely be dead." After that, she said, her client began a "process" of moving away from ISIS, though she could not say that, as of November 2016, he was no longer committed to the group. The process, Fearon said, included him getting into interfaith dialogues with other inmates in jail and seeing their viewpoints. At the suggestion of his lawyers, he also read such materials as *Radical,* a 2012 book in which Maajid Nawaz, a British-Pakistani, recounts his journeys into and out of violent Islamism.

Nawaz's story, in a more drawn-out and more dramatic fashion, echoes Abdurahman's. As a teenager, Nawaz had been harassed by white racists. As he grew older and more alienated from British society, he wound up joining Hizb ut-Tahrir, a group founded by a Sunni Muslim in 1953 that, like ISIS, sought to unify all Muslims under a caliphate. Later, after being imprisoned for four years in Egypt and after returning to England, Nawaz in time rejected the ideology he had held to for a decade. "It is important to understand that my change of views wasn't an overnight process," Nawaz wrote. "Ideological dogma doesn't work like that: it's not like a tap you can just switch off. So ingrained was HT's cause in my very being, that it would be a process of years for me to work my way out of it."[10]

Abdurahman's lawyers developed a plan for him to be drawn away from radicalism. It included religious instruction by an imam from north Minneapolis and a non-Somali mosque of the sort that deradicalization expert Daniel Koehler recommended as a way to provide a "wider base," albeit one with an Islamic perspective, according to Fearon. Furthermore, the lawyer noted that Abdurahman had influenced two of his friends—Adnan Abdihamid Farah and Hamza Naj Ahmed—to stick with their plans to plead guilty when a member of one of the defense teams, Imam Hassan Jami (also known as Hassan A. Mohamud and Sheikh Xasan Jaamici), tried to persuade them all to renege and go to trial. That imam subsequently left the defense group, leading to a shake-up among the lawyers. The imam had predicted "good things would happen" if the men stood trial, Fearon said, though the men could have faced far longer prison terms.

The Hassan Jami flap added a peculiar sideshow to the legal proceedings. On April 1, 2016, less than six weeks before the trial of Mohamed Abdihamid Farah, Abdiraham Yasin Daud, and Guled Ali Omar opened, Judge Davis permitted lawyer

P. Chinedu Nwaneri to withdraw as Mohamed Farah's main attorney. As MPR News reported, Nwaneri wanted to "stop further distractions in this matter." Nwaneri was being aided in the case by Hassan Jami, a well-known imam from St. Paul, Minnesota, but prosecutors said they had evidence that the imam had taught one of the men, Abdirizak Warsame, "the manner in which to pray on a battlefield where one is engaged in jihad."[11] Warsame later opted to cooperate with the government and plead guilty in the case. For his part, the imam insisted he did not support violent extremism, but he did oppose the government's CVE program.[12]

In seeking leniency for Abdurahman, attorney Fearon's final point was a nod to Abdurahman's parents. At the request of then US Attorney Luger, the couple spoke at a Somali community meeting against the notion that the men had been entrapped, refuting a claim widely believed in the Somali community. The government asked Davis to sentence Abdurahman to fifteen years in prison, but he trimmed the figure by one-third. He noted Abdurahman's cooperation in the Hassan Jami flap and highlighted his parents' help. Davis told the prisoner: "You're getting credit for your parents stepping forward and talking to the community about the types of things that should not occur, their pain and anguish of seeing their son go off to prison for ten years, ten years instead of fifteen."

While Abdurahman's parents helped his case, the parents of two other men—Mohamed Abdihamid Farah and his younger brother, Adnan Abdihamid Farah—appeared to hurt their sons' prospects with Davis. The judge on November 15, 2016, sentenced Adnan to a decade in prison and, the following day, sent Mohamed off for thirty years. When the judge questioned the men's parents during Adnan's sentencing, their mother, Ayan, told him that they loved the United States and were grateful to be here. And their father, Abdihamid Farah Yusuf, told him that the United States was their country and they had no other.

But Yusuf also insisted that his sons had been "misled" by others and complained that the government had not warned him about his boys' plans—though prosecutor Andrew R. Winter noted that the FBI had met with Yusuf three times about his sons' plans. Furthermore, Yusuf was concerned enough about the plans that he took Adnan's passport away. Indeed, in an interview with Minneapolis's KSTP Channel 5 News, Adnan was quoted as saying: "My dad and my mom sat down with me, and they talked to me and they said, 'What are you planning to do?' . . . They said, 'Do you want to join a terrorist organization?'" Adnan said he told them he wanted to go to China, according to the report.[13]

Perhaps hurting his son's chances for leniency, Yusuf got into a testy exchange with the judge. At one point, the judge told the man to let him finish a comment, Yusuf told him to "go ahead," and Davis said, "You don't tell me when to go ahead. Do you understand that?" Yusuf apologized, saying he didn't know the rules, and the judge retorted, "Yes, you do. You know respect, and you respect me." Davis told the man he had saved his son's life by taking his passport. The judge added: "So whatever anger you may have about him being here, he is alive. Do you understand that?" Yusuf said he did and had no anger, though he repeated he felt the boys were misled and that the government had not cooperated with the parents.

In an interview with Vocativ, the Farah brothers' mother, Ayan, denied that anyone in Minneapolis was even interested in joining ISIS. "Never . . . no one," she said. [14] But, under questioning by Davis at his sentencing on November 16, 2016, her son Mohamed acknowledged that his parents knew he wanted to become, as the judge put it, a "warrior for Allah" and a martyr.

Further, the would-be martyr acknowledged that his mother didn't want to lose Adnan, his younger brother. But, the judge said to Mohamed, "you were old enough, you could make your own decisions. She knew that you were brainwashed and you were a jihadi and you were going to do whatever you were going to do?" Farah answered, "Yes." Moreover, according to the judge, Ayan had caught Mohamed watching ISIS videos "when she told you not to watch them." Prosecutor John F. Docherty, furthermore, told the court that the FBI had "fully briefed" the men's parents about their plans, even as the parents denied that their sons were trying to travel to Syria.

Adnan, in fact, had wanted to accompany his brother on the fateful April 2015 car trip to San Diego with Bashir, and Abdirahman Yasin Daud, according to the judge. Adnan didn't join them on what turned into the FBI sting operation because, Judge Davis said, the men feared that he was "mama's boy and mama would be looking for him an hour after he was supposed to be home for dinner." Adnan's attorney, Kenneth Ubong Udoibok, admitted that was true.

Before imposing his sentence on Adnan, the judge fretted that Adnan seemed to have just "one foot out" of supporting terrorism, and he worried that a stiff sentence for his brother, Mohamed, could "just push him right back into extremism." The judge initially said he wanted to delay sentencing Adnan for a few months to see how the family would react to his brother's stiff sentence. After the testy exchange with Yusuf, however, Davis opted to move ahead, though he shaved five years off the potential fifteen years that sentencing guidelines suggested.

Most of the men, in pleading for mercy, struck similar chords. The common tropes among the men, in admitting their guilt, included blaming propaganda for their seduction into terrorism, apologizing to the court and the community, and renouncing ISIS. But the judge, who said he had read ISIS's playbook, was in almost all the cases not persuaded about their sincerity—even with the plotter who agreed first to plead guilty, Hanad Mustafe Musse.[15] Deceiving everyone by staying out of trouble, getting jobs or going to school, and by leading outwardly normal lives until one could get to Syria was a tactic ISIS encouraged. Indeed, the judge invoked the Minnesota group's mantra of "fake it until you make it," a phrase that Mohamed Amiin Ali "Rose" Roble, a Minnesotan who made it to Syria, popularized among the thirteen plotters, according to Musse.

Davis's interrogation of Musse, at his sentencing, made clear the judge's skepticism. Musse admitting lying repeatedly, especially to himself in believing he was seeking to do good by joining ISIS. He said he understood his errors and now urged people to "stay away from terrorism and condemn it."

But the judge faulted Musse for failing to back up his renunciation with action, for failing to help the government break up the jihadi cell he was part of. When Davis asked Musse why he didn't do so, Musse said he would have lost his "community support." Musse said, "They have been supporting me and backing me and making me feel good inside and looking after me, and I thought if I would have done such things that I would have lost them." Davis said the man's comments amounted to "a beautiful statement," but he said Musse had "built a series of lies" while failing to stop "this jihadi behavior" by his friends.

Further, Davis suggested that Musse, by acting outwardly as if all was normal, appeared just to be continuing the deception. The judge said, "If this was a normal case and you came into court and you were dressed in a white shirt and a tie and you had a job and you had never been in trouble, you graduated from high school and you were going to college, you would be the great prospect of not getting a severe sentence first time in court … because those are all the predictive—predictors that we use for someone to succeed. … And so what you've done is you've turned us on our head. You have used what we use as predictors for success to be able to deceive us and do harm to us. Do you understand that?" Musse said he did.

Indeed, Musse, for all his renunciation, refused to cooperate with the government in pursuing his friends. As Prosecutor Winter told the judge, "His mission was to protect his coconspirators who were still pending trial. That was his—that was his mission. He was standing fast with his brothers. And I think that speaks volumes, that says so much more than his guilty plea, it says so much more than what he told you today."

Instead of believing his comments in court, the judge appeared to be swayed by Musse's remarks to his friends, as secretly recorded by the informant, Bashir. Among these, as Winter recounted it, was a threat that Musse made in April 2015, before the car trip Bashir and two others made to San Diego. When Musse quizzed Bashir about the man who would provide the travelers with fake passports, Winter said Musse's comment was: "If it turns out that he's kuffar [non-Muslim], I want that N killed ASAP." Finally, Winter quoted Musse as saying: "If I get caught, I tried my best. I'll face the music. I'll face the consequences. I have no problem with it." The consequence, as delivered by Davis, was a ten-year prison sentence.

The judge proved lenient with two men who did cooperate with the government and testified against their friends. While the sentences differed—thirty months for Abdirizak Mohamed Warsame and time served for Abdullahi Mohamud Yusuf—they were similar because Yusuf had been in custody longer, for nearly twenty-two months at the time of his sentencing, compared with eleven months for Warsame. Yusuf, who had been in a halfway house for part of his detention, in fact, had violated the strict rules Davis laid down by watching television programming about terrorism, and he wound up back behind bars for most his time. Davis in November 2017 ordered Yusuf freed into the custody of his parents.[16] Warsame was scheduled to be released from prison in March 2018, and he was then to go to a halfway house for up to a year. Prosecutors had asked for "downward departures" from the federal sentencing guidelines for the men because of their cooperation with authorities, with US Attorney Luger personally pleading for leniency for them.

"In this case, under strong pressure not to cooperate, defendant Yusuf came forward, admitted his own guilt, and testified truthfully against close friends," Luger said. "While this is difficult in any trial, it was made far more stressful for Mr. Yusuf. Not only was he subjected to community pressure, so was his family who was present in court only to provide support for their son. I sat in the courtroom during his testimony, and we all saw and felt the hostility toward him and his family. Ironically, now the three defendants who went to trial are claiming remorse, stating that they were not entrapped and that they are, in fact, guilty. Their newfound contrition would have spared Yusuf an excruciating trial experience had the contrition come earlier, but it did not. Instead, Yusuf and his family were harassed, but Yusuf withstood the anger and hostility and came through stronger and better."[17]

Yusuf, who had been seventeen at the time he fell in with the would-be ISIS members, had taken part in a novel rehabilitation program conducted by the Heartland Democracy Center in which he read such works as the Rev. Martin Luther

King's "Letter from Birmingham City Jail" and *The Autobiography of Malcolm X,* as well as writings by Native American Sherman Alexie and French philosopher Michel Foucault. Yusuf had also gotten a lot of personal attention from prosecutors and FBI agents, some of whom warmly embraced his gleeful relatives in the hallway outside the courtroom before and after his release.[18]

As journalist Dina Temple-Raston reported in *New York* magazine, the Heartland program opened Yusuf's eyes to a world of literature that resonated with him. The Malcolm X autobiography particularly struck him. "The back of the book was talking about his shift from radical Nation of Islam black extremism and black nationalism to regular Sunni Islam," the reporter quoted Yusuf as saying,. "I'm like, hmmm, this is something in my backyard." Yusuf even recounted the details for Temple-Raston: "It begins with his identity crisis. He didn't know who he was. . . . Malcolm Little was born in Nebraska. He went through a lot of phases in his life, stuff like he got in trouble when he was young and went to prison. But in prison he did something most people don't do—he bettered himself, you know, as a human being. His extremist outlook got changed, and he describes it all in the book."[19]

The story spoke to Yusuf, for whom the reading and discussion program seemed to be an intellectual conversion experience. He also was counseled by his lawyer, federal public defender Manny Atwal, who shared such books with him as *Is Everyone Hanging Out Without Me?* by Mindy Kaling, the Indian writer who discusses life as the child of immigrants, someone caught between cultures. Indeed, Atwal also spoke candidly with him about her own background as an Indian woman and a Sikh raised in Britain.[20] While in custody, Yusuf earned his high school equivalency degree and started seeing himself as an adult with a future. Shortly before the hearing at which Davis released him, the studious-looking Yusuf—who Atwal said was once approached by Abercrombie & Fitch staffers to model for the retailer—told me in a short hallway conversation that he wasn't sure what the future held for him but that serving his community would likely be a part of it.[21]

The Heartland Democracy program, however, appears to have carried less weight with the judge than did a program set up in March 2016 by former chief US probation and pretrial services officer Kevin D. Lowry and his office, at the direction of Chief Judge John R. Tunheim and Judge Davis. The Terrorism Disengagement and Deradicalization Program was the first and, at the time, the only such program for people convicted of terrorism-related crimes. This program included risk-assessment efforts, mentoring and other deradicalization elements, and other social services. Officials used a team approach, involving probation officers, psychologists, substance-abuse counselors where necessary, family counselors and mentors, all of whom were schooled in radicalization and Muslim practices.

"We address the underlying issues of their radicalization and what factors enticed them or initiated them into the group radical materials," said Lowry, who in 2019 was continuing his work on extremist-related matters as a consultant for the Federal Judicial Center, the education and research agency of the federal court system.[22] "There are many narratives in radicalizing materials. It's a battle for hearts and minds, and it's done through narratives that either incite or entice the individual into radicalized ideas or belief systems."

The radicalization process that Islamist terrorists undergo is similar to that of other extremists, such as white supremacists, Lowry said. Whether on the radical right or left, they have grievances against the majority culture, feel threatened by it, often are motivated by Utopian visions of how society should operate, and see violence as a way to get to the promised ideal world. Just as his office had been involved with assessing and attempting to turn around jihadists, so it had been involved with a number of supremacist cases.

Programs aimed at leading recruits away from terrorism—or extremism of various sorts—need to weigh personal factors when evaluating people for reintegration into society, according to terrorism-rehabilitation researcher Daniel Koehler, whose work helped shape Lowry's efforts. Koehler's findings may have figured heavily into the sentences the men got, according to journalist Brendan I. Koerner's January 2017 account in *Wired* magazine. Yusuf, for instance, had reached a "very advanced stage of disengagement and critical reflection," Koehler found.[23] Lowry cautioned, however, that the judge did not rely solely on Koehler's efforts or any other single element in the cases, but looked at many factors. There's no quick fix or magic bullet, Lowry suggested.[24]

Indeed, in imposing a similar sentence on the other man who testified in the cases, Warsame, Davis appeared to reject Koehler's finding that Warsame's professed turn away from radicalism was less convincing. Koehler had said he feared that Warsame would be likely to join a jihadist group if he could.

Compared with sentences other judges imposed on those convicted in terrorism-related crimes around the United States between 2014 and 2016, the terms the six men got were lenient. Attorneys in the Minnesota cases submitted a final report to Davis on November 1, 2016, that reviewed sentencing nationwide for twenty-six cases. On the low end, a judge in Colorado imposed a sentence of four years on Shannon Maureen Conley in January 2015, nine months after law enforcement officers stopped the then nineteen-year-old as she tried to board a flight on the way to Syria. On the high end, a judge in New York imposed a forty-year sentence on Minh Quang Pham, a Vietnamese-born London man who had joined al-Qaida in 2010 at about age twenty-seven and a year later planned to kill himself bombing Heathrow Airport. The sentences for the twenty-six cases averaged about seventeen years.[25]

While federal sentencing guidelines dictated much of Davis's decisions about how much time to give the men who appeared before him, they appear to have been shaped, in part, by his Terrorism Disengagement and Deradicalization Program. The program's aims were to give courts information not otherwise available to them for sentencing purposes, to supervise the defendants closely before and after incarceration in ways that assure they don't revert to terrorism, and to rehabilitate those convicted, as spelled out by John Jay College research fellow Kelly A. Berkell in the *Journal for Deradicalization*.[26] To those ends, Davis enlisted Koehler to evaluate the men before him and to train probation staffers in his assessment techniques.

Davis was connected to Koehler by then Minnesota chief federal probation officer Lowry. In the fall of 2015, Davis and Chief Judge John R. Tunheim had asked him to find an expert in deradicalization. Davis asked defense attorney Atwal, who had defended a couple al-Shabab travelers years before, to join Lowry in Europe to visit with some experts. The pair met Koehler and were impressed by him. On Lowry's recommendation, the judge then visited Germany to meet Koehler himself, and the probation office contracted with Koehler for his expert assistance. The probation officer also tapped into the expertise of Her Majesty's Prison and Probation Service of the United Kingdom to train officers in risk assessment and intervention strategies.

Koehler, who founded and edited the *Journal for Deradicalization,* detailed his methods in a hearing in Minnesota in late September 2016. He weighed the factors that contributed to each defendant's radicalization and led him to ISIS, assessed the degree of radicalization and risk for slipping back into support for terrorism, and recommended mentoring and counseling to deradicalize each man. He pegged the risk for Yusuf, for instance, at medium to low, for Abdurahman and Ahmed at medium to high, and for Warsame at high, Berkell reported.

Koehler acknowledged there was "no 100 percent guarantee that these intervention methods actually work." But he said, "It's better than working blindfolded without any kind of assessment or structure or protocol."

Various elements play a role in the success in redirecting offenders, according to Lowry. Among them may be relationships with FBI agents, close monitoring by the court, and the Koehler-Lowry program. The program offered by Heartland Democracy, the community organization dedicated to building civic engagement in Minnesota, also appeared to have helped Yusuf, mainly through personal relationships he established with people involved in it.

Such a personal touch can make a huge difference with offenders, according to Lowry. "A significant part of this process is the relationships established with offenders that build hope for them and contribute to establishing an identity, meaning, purpose, belonging, and significance," Lowry told me. "Somebody has hope for these people and then, through these relationships, they develop hope for themselves."[27]

But will these or similar programs work with all or even many of the other defendants in Minnesota and elsewhere? Certainly, Davis identified the need, but the comprehensive means for meeting it in similar cases across the country still appear elusive. Researcher Berkell, in her article in the journal Koehler edited, complimented Davis for advancing the state of terrorism jurisprudence in the United States but noted that courts in all fifty states "should be prepared to handle the post-conviction environment in terrorism cases with approaches that reflect state of the art expertise and duly considered policy choices."[28]

Changing hearts and minds is a huge challenge. It took persuasive FBI agents, a father's firm hand, and the traumatic deaths of beloved relatives and friends, as well as the possibility of prosecution, to shift Bashir's views. It also took the ordinary process of leaving adolescence and its passionate, but often mistaken, convictions behind. Bashir, too, had to look beyond the closed Somali American world he and his friends were so deeply immersed in.

CHAPTER NINETEEN

A Closed World?

nsularity in the Somali American community—a sensibility not unlike that other ethnic groups have held when they first arrived in the United States— seemed to play a big role in ISIS's seduction of the men. It closed their minds to media reports, government information, and even the warnings of some within the Somali American orbit. The men preferred to take the word of video seducers, radical imams, and some of their own friends in Syria, dismissing the warnings abounding in broader American society.

Somalis are quite literally clannish, with their first loyalties to members of their historic clans. Beyond that, their language, ways of dress, and of course, religion put them outside the American mainstream. Such tendencies can isolate them, especially when they are reinforced by exclusive school environments or the closed social circles the young men moved in.

Even as many Somalis branch out and take up sometimes high-profile positions in politics and the professions in Minnesota, the inward-focused nature of the community may constrain it, hampering development of a Somali American identity. Plenty of outsiders, too, are all too willing to isolate the community, to refuse to accept it on its terms. Racism and Islamophobia, sometimes stoked by

© JOSEPH WEBER

Few non-Somalis venture into sometimes elaborate multilevel shopping malls in Minneapolis that cater to Somali tastes in food and clothing.

American political leaders, have marked the Somali experience across the United States, including in Minnesota.

Indeed, the world some Somalis occupy can be quite small—but also fascinating to an outsider. Consider the Karmel Mall in Minneapolis, where some of Bashir's friends occasionally met to make their plans. A walk through the mall, called the Suuqa Karmel in Somali, is like a visit to a foreign bazaar.

The bustling four-story Minneapolis shopping complex features small shops, some barely bigger than walk-in closets, and usually staffed by sole woman proprietors, that offer stunningly colorful women's clothing. Rolls of rich, elaborately patterned fabric, suitable for such clothing, fill shelves in some shops. Ornate water pitchers, goblets, and cookware are on offer in various boutiques. Rugs with eye-popping traditional designs are available. Women can get intricate floral designs drawn on their arms with henna dye. And traditional Somali food abounds, with the aromas of goat meat, pasta, and other dishes wafting throughout the mall's two buildings, enticing visitors and the center's two hundred or so vendors alike.[1]

Upstairs, in a corner of the topmost floor, men gather several times a day to pray and to listen to Somali preachers in a mosque. As is traditional, the heart of the mosque is a spacious carpeted room where all but the oldest of worshippers eschew chairs to stand shoulder to shoulder with friends to practice traditional rites of standing and bowing as they pray in unison. Shoes are banned, and areas for washing—the customary practice before joining the group—can be found nearby. Chandeliers brighten the space, helped at times by sunlight shining from outside through stained-glass windows. From here, calls to pray sound on speakers throughout the mall five times a day.[2]

Chatter in Somali can be heard throughout the mall. Women walk about in flowing clothing, their hair and bodies covered in the traditional style, emphasizing modesty. Men usually dress in more conventional Western clothing, slacks and shirts, though some wear cotton skullcaps called koofiyad or long robes. Almost all the visitors are Somalis; I saw few whites there on a couple visits to the mall.

Few of the goods on offer would appeal to non-Somalis. Places such as the Karmel Mall—and another in Minneapolis known as the 24 Somali Mall—differ from the Chinatowns and Little Italies that for decades have graced some American cities. Where non-Chinese and non-Italians often frequent such enclaves in New York, San Francisco, and elsewhere, particularly for the food that has woven itself as much into American culture as McDonald's has, few non-Somalis have reason to visit Minneapolis's Somali suqs.

There are many explanations for why many Americans—and some Somalis themselves—see Somalis as foreign and unassimilated. Unlike Italian Americans and Chinese Americans, who have blended into American culture during the past century (or longer) and through several generations, Somalis are largely new to the United States. Most of those living longest in the country have been here only since the early 1990s, when Somalia collapsed into chaos, and many have come more recently.

Even many teens and twentysomethings now here were born outside the United States, some in refugee camps or Somali enclaves in Kenya, where their families stayed for years before being cleared to travel to America. Moreover, many in the older generation of Somalis can't speak English or do so poorly, and they prefer to live and work among others they can speak with. Even younger Somalis—perhaps no different in this respect from other relatively insular ethnic groups—often prefer to mingle with other Somalis. Religion, too, sets Somalis apart, as they find comfort and company in mosques serving their community—perhaps no differently than the parishioners of Catholic churches that cater to Hispanics or members of synagogues that serve specific Orthodox Jewish subcultures.

For many Somali women, too, clothing sets them apart most conspicuously from other Americans. The flowing dresses and head-coverings that many wear mark them more distinctively than the Western suits, pants, and shirts that Somali men usually wear outside of special events. But the garb is as much religious as cultural, with the women following traditional Islamic dictates on modesty in choosing their clothes.

Some of the traditional clothing, such as the hair-covering scarves and wraps, are part of a relatively recent phenomenon, according to University of Minnesota sociologist Cawo M. Abdi. Abdi, a Somali-born American who did extensive research among Somali women, found that many once-secular Somalis adopted traditional clothing only in recent decades as a way to protect themselves from predatory men when the country slipped into political chaos and many Somalis were forced to flee to unsafe refugee camps.

More recently, Abdi told me in an interview, many younger women have adopted head-coverings as a political and identity statement, a way of saying they are proud to be Muslims even at a time when that's risky because of anti-Islamic bigotry in the United States and elsewhere in the West.[3] Such self-assertions of identity have become widespread among young Muslim women from many countries.

Still, the slow process of Americanization has been under way for years for Somalis, following much the same pattern that marked generations of other new Americans. Children of Somali newcomers—who have been through American schools, up to and including universities—sound and often dress as American as any suburbanite whose family's US roots stretch back into the 1800s or beyond. Some younger people, such as the Minnesota men who sought to join ISIS, sound as American as any inner-city non-Somali African American with similarly deep US roots, even down to the in-group pejorative idioms common among non-Somali African Americans. (The N-word, for instance, was common street-slang in the conversations among the Minnesota men who sought to join ISIS.)

In Minnesota, moreover, Somalis have been making their way in the professions and in public service. Somalis practice medicine and law and teach in the state's universities, high schools, and elementary schools. Somalis run restaurants, civic groups, and health care organizations. Like other Americans, they run shops, drive cabs, and serve in the military.

Five Somali police officers in Minneapolis in 2012 founded the Somali American Police Association, whose membership doubled within a few years.[4] Sadly, one such police officer—Mohamed Noor—made international headlines in

July 2017 for fatally shooting a woman who had called police to report a possible sexual assault near her home. Many in the Somali community rallied to defend the officer, who admitted his mistake—one he said he committed out of fear when the woman approached his police car in the dark. The case, which led to the resignation of Minneapolis's police chief, ended with Noor being found guilty of third-degree murder and second-degree manslaughter and a sentence of 12.5 years in prison.[5]

Somalis have made inroads in politics, too, even as that brought controversy. The most notable is Ilhan Omar, who won a seat in the US Congress in the fall of 2018, becoming the first Somali American in the body. Omar, whose district includes Minneapolis and nearby suburbs, had prevailed in her primary by more than 20,000 votes out of more than 135,000 cast, a record turnout.[6] After she won and was seated in January 2019, the Congress undertook a special vote to accommodate her hijab, the traditional head-covering she favors, voting 234 to 197 for rule changes including permitting head-coverings on the House Floor; members amended a rule that dated back to 1837. Omar marked the vote with a pointed and scrappy tweet: "I thank my colleagues for welcoming me, and I look forward to the day we lift the Muslim ban separating families all over the U.S. from their loved ones."[7]

But Omar, thirty-seven in early 2019, quickly drew flak because of other tweets and comments widely seen as anti-Semitic. Critics pointed to a 2012 tweet in which she said, "Israel has hypnotized the world, may Allah awaken the people and help them see the evil doings of Israel," a tweet she apologized for after taking her Congressional seat, saying she had "unknowingly" invoked an anti-Semitic trope that Jews were covertly tricking the world into supporting Israel. Then, just a few weeks later, she tweeted that backing for Israel in the House was "all about the Benjamins," $100 bills, implying that that American Israel Public Affairs Committee was buying off American politicians, prompting her to again apologize. Soon after, she drew still more heat when she said in a panel discussion: "I want to talk about the political influence in this country that says it is okay for people to push for allegiance to a foreign country. And I want to ask, why is it okay for me to talk about the influence of the NRA, of fossil fuel industries, or Big Pharma, and not talk about a powerful lobby?"[8] After Democratic and Republican leaders alike criticized her remarks, the House of Representatives passed a resolution condemning hate, a measure that equally condemned anti-Semitism and discrimination against Muslims.[9] Omar, who was not singled out for criticism in the resolution, voted for the measure and joined with two other Muslim congressional members in issuing a statement that said: "It's the first time we have voted on a resolution condemning anti-Muslim bigotry in our nation's history."[10]

Apparently trying to set the record straight—without criticizing Palestinians or Israelis—Omar struck her own evenhanded note in a March 17, 2019, commentary in the *Washington Post.* She acknowledged that Jews had a connection to "their historical homeland," but said the area was also the historical homeland of Palestinians who now "live in a state of permanent refugeehood and displacement." She called for a "balanced, inclusive approach" and a two-state solution with internationally recognized borders that allowed Israelis and Palestinians "to have their own sanctuaries and self-determination." Omar noted that the way the United States deals with issues abroad was "deeply personal." She wrote of how she had fled Somalia at age eight and spent the next four years in a refugee camp in Kenya where she said she "experienced and witnessed unspeakable suffering from those who, like me, had lost everything because of war." [11]

Nonetheless, Omar fast became a foil for President Donald J. Trump. He called her "terrible" in remarks to reporters and tweeted out a video critics of the congresswoman made that focused on remarks she made at an event sponsored by the Council on American-Islamic Relations. The congresswoman, making a point about losses of civil liberties, seemed to play down the 9/11 attack on the World Trade Center in New York City, saying "some people did something." Defenders argued that Trump was using Omar's verbal clumsiness to bolster his standing with Islamophobes.[12] Trump continued his attacks on her and three other members of Congress, all progressive women of color, through mid-2019, saying they should go back to their home countries (though only Omar was an immigrant) and triggering chants from followers at one North Carolina rally of "send her back." For her part, Omar responded with an op-ed in the *New York Times* attacking Trump for racism and arguing that the 2020 presidential election would be about the fundamental ideals of equal protection under the law, pluralism, and religious liberty.[13]

Trump kept up the heat on Omar, giving his battle with her an international dimension in mid-August 2019, when he tweeted that Israel would "show great weakness" if it permitted Omar and fellow congresswoman Rashida Tlaib, of Michigan, to visit the country. He said: "They hate Israel & all Jewish people, & there is nothing that can be said or done to change their minds." Within hours of the tweet, Israeli Prime Minister Benjamin Netanyahu reversed his government's earlier approval of the visit, citing the congresswomen's support of the Boycott, Divestment and Sanctions (BDS) drive and an Israeli law that bans active BDS supporters. The women had skipped a bipartisan congressional trip to Israel earlier that month, instead choosing to visit under the auspices of Miftah, a Palestinian group.[14]

Omar's star rose fast in Minnesota, where she was elected in November 2016 to serve in the state's House of Representatives and was named the assistant minority leader in the chamber. Shortly after being elected to the state post, Omar weighed in on the cases of Bashir's friends who pleaded guilty or were convicted of crimes related to trying to join ISIS. In a letter to Judge Davis specifically regarding the conviction of Abdirahman Yasin Daud, but dealing with all nine men who were then awaiting sentencing, she said that imprisoning "20-year-old men for 30 or 40 years, is essentially a life sentence."

She argued that such punitive measures "lack efficacy" and "inevitably create an environment in which extremism can flourish." She contended that "a long-term prison sentence for one who chose violence to combat direct marginalization is a statement that our justice system misunderstands the guilty." Pleading for a "restorative approach" in the sentences the judge was to hand down, Omar wrote: "The most effective penance is making these men ambassadors of reform."[15] Nonetheless, Judge Davis sentenced Daud to thirty years in federal prison.

There's no doubt that Trump's hostility elevated Omar's standing with some on the left in the Democratic Party, but whether her politically mixed district will continue to back her seemed unclear in early 2020. Political observers such as Isaak Osman Rooble of the Somali American National Institute's health advocacy group said she could wind up facing electoral challenges, including possibly one from a longtime opponent, Abdi Warsame. Like Omar, Warsame was born in Somalia, but he was seen as more moderate and so more acceptable to the more middle-of-the-road Democrats in the state's party leadership, Rooble suggested in an interview with me.[16]

Warsame, who earned a college degree in the United Kingdom and came to Minnesota in 2006, in 2013 became the first Somali American elected to the Minneapolis City Council when he defeated a Native American incumbent.[17] In 2017, Warsame narrowly won a pitched reelection battle with another Somali, a former ally and former Minneapolis Board of Education member, Mohamud Noor. Hussein Samatar, a financier who died in 2013, had blazed the path for Somali politicians in the state when he was elected, in 2010, to the Minneapolis Board of Education after serving as an appointed member of the Minneapolis Library Board of Trustees.[18]

Like Omar, Warsame also wrote a letter to Judge Davis in support of Abdirahman Yasin Daud in advance of his sentencing in 2016. Warsame's much shorter note mentioned that he had long known Daud and wanted to "advocate for his future." He urged the judge "to consider the most impactful approach for his rehabilitation and reinstatement to society." Daud, Warsame wrote, was "a young man who has a future ahead of him."[19]

Somalis in Minnesota are notching victories in smaller political entities, as well. Abdikadir "AK" Hassan, who was born in Somalia, grew up in Kenya, and came to Minnesota in 2008, beat out another Somali American, businessman and public radio host Abdi "Gurhan" Mohamed, among a crowded field of other contenders, in a surprisingly contentious race for seats on the Minneapolis Park and Recreation Board. Hassan had served as an outreach officer for a southern Minneapolis district in Minnesota's Democratic Party, formally known as the Democrat-Farmer-Labor Party, and had helped Ilhan Omar get elected to the state House. Another Somali, Fartun Ahmed, won election to the school board in Hopkins, Minnesota, a small suburb west of Minneapolis. She ran in a slate with two non-Somalis.

Indeed, Ahmed may epitomize the American dream as many Somalis are experiencing it or hope to. As reported by the *Lakeshore Weekly News,* she attended a Hopkins High School, finishing in 2009 with a perfect grade point average. She studied at Metropolitan State University, and while an undergraduate, she worked on community efforts put together by Minnesota Congressman Keith Ellison, an African American Muslim, and by former US Attorney Luger. Then, she earned a master's degree in divinity at the University of Chicago and began work on a doctorate in anthropology at the University of Minnesota. She was the first in her family to attend college.[20] In fact, by Ahmed's account, she was the first in her family to graduate from high school, and when her parents enrolled her in elementary school, they could not speak English. Ahmed, who wears a hijab, speaks perfectly uninflected English with a midwestern accent.[21]

Some leading Minnesota non-Somali politicians welcomed Somalis, praising them for enriching the state's culture and economy. Former Minneapolis Mayor Betsy Hodges, for instance, rebuked then candidate Trump in November 2016 after Trump had appeared in Minnesota and said the state's residents had "suffered enough" from accepting Somalis. As reported by *Time,* Trump said: "Here in Minnesota you have seen firsthand the problems caused with faulty refugee vetting, with large numbers of Somali refugees coming into your state, without your knowledge, without your support or approval."[22] Hodges replied on Facebook, lambasting

Trump for an "ignorant tirade" in which he said refugees should not be allowed to "roam our communities." Hodges retorted: "This is America, Donald, and the Somali people of Minnesota and Minneapolis are not *roaming* our communities, they are *building* them." And she added: "Minneapolis is a better, stronger place for having our Somali and East African immigrants and refugees in it. It is a privilege and an honor to be mayor of the city with the largest Somali population in this country. Your ignorance, your hate, your fear just make me remember how lucky we are to have neighbors who are so great."[23]

But, for many of the Somalis living in the United States, loyalties and identities remain divided. Perhaps because so many Somalis have strong ties to a homeland they were forced to leave, many keep one foot in American society and culture and the other in Somali culture, sometimes in the Somali state. For instance, the man elected president of Somalia in 2017 was Mohamed Abdullahi "Farmajo" Mohamed, who had lived, worked, and been educated in New York State. As reported in late 2017 by Amy Forliti of the Associated Press, some 105 of Somalia's 329 Parliament members were then dual citizens of Somalia and elsewhere, according to Sadik Warfa, a Somali from Minnesota who was elected in 2016 to Somalia's Parliament. Forliti reported that twenty-two of those Parliament members hailed from the United States. Further, many businesspeople, including some from Minnesota returned to Somalia to work there or aid the government.[24]

The dual loyalty, felt especially by Somalis who remember a less tumultuous time in their homeland, in some respects is similar to sentiments among immigrant groups who arrived long before in the United States. Many have developed cultural affinity groups, such as the Sons of Italy, German fraternal organizations, or in Minneapolis, the American Swedish Institute. Such groups allow Americans of Italian, German, and Swedish extraction to celebrate their historic cultures and pasts, preserving traditions in food, music, art, and dress, even as the members live most of their workaday lives looking, speaking, and acting like other Americans, smoothly blended into the general population. Members easily walk both roads, even as younger people—several generations down from the original immigrants— may look on their ancestral roots as pleasant, perhaps quaint, but mostly irrelevant to their very American lives.

For many Somalis, including some in their teens and early twenties, the connection with the homeland and its culture is much fresher, though. So they may live more on what British-educated Kenyan Parliament member Yusuf Hassan called the "Somalia island," a sometimes insular existence with few strong links to non-Somalis. Some, particularly those now in their thirties, grew up expecting someday to return to their childhood land, according to Jaylani Hussein of the Council on American-Islamic Relations (CAIR).

Furthermore, some younger people feel a duty to go to Somalia to help their ancestral homeland, even if they were born in the United States—much as the al-Shabab wave of recruits in Minnesota sought to do. Libin Said, who in late 2017 was a premed student at the University of Minnesota, is one example. Born in Georgia to immigrant parents, she came to Minneapolis when she was six years old. She told me she planned to earn a medical degree, work for a time in the United States, and then take her skills to Somalia. "I feel like my home is there, even though I've never been there," said Libin Said, as we sat in the school's bustling student center, where her hijab made her stand out in the crowd.[25]

The dual roads that some young Somalis walk were clear in a conversation I had with Said and two other students in the fall of 2017 at the university. All knew one another through the Somali Student Association (SSA), a group in which young Somalis talk about current events that affect them in Minnesota or in Somalia, and through which they stage such cultural celebrations on campus as Somali Night, a raucous night of music, song, and dance.[26] None among the three, for instance, celebrated such American holidays as Thanksgiving or the Fourth of July (aside, perhaps, from going to see fireworks). But they did warm to Somali Independence Day on July 1, when several blocks in a Somali neighborhood near the Karmel Mall fill with booths and displays showcasing Somali food and culture. "If I had been raised with it [Thanksgiving or the Fourth of July], then I would probably be more into it," said Ra'Wi Mahamud. "When it's Eid or Ramadan, that's our holiday. I generally feel excitement."

And yet, in many ways they differed little from other American college students. Mahamud, for instance, was born in Minneapolis and grew up in a family—with four brothers and a sister—that was passionate about professional sports. She played several sports in high school and pulled for the Minnesota Timberwolves, the National Basketball Association team. A young man in the trio, a Somali who was born in Nairobi and came to Minneapolis when he was three years old, said he intended to embark on a good career in the United States. "I owe something to my parents. They didn't get a degree and they worked hard," said the man, a third-year business major who asked not to be named. "I will do my best. My plan is to work in the business world, and there are a lot of things I can do with a business degree. We have Fortune 500 companies in Minneapolis."

Like Said, the young man said he would hope someday to work in Somalia, though. "I call Minneapolis home, but I feel hopeful that in twenty years, thirty years, I could leave and go to Somalia to contribute because I have an education," he said. "I would have a purpose there." Furthermore, he said that being an American for him included the ability to pray five times a day, as Islam dictates, while "trying to achieve the American dream my parents came here for. I'm not going to throw that away. . . . I love it here. I'm from Minneapolis. I was raised here." And being a black American and a Somali Muslim also meant the freedom to sit while others stood for the national anthem at sporting events—a stance he took in support of the Black Lives Matter movement and in protest of recent American policy, especially President Trump's immigration ban on Somalis and others from majority-Muslim countries.

Even as he was critical of many aspects of American politics, the young man took his American citizenship responsibilities and his advocacy for the Somali community seriously. He had volunteered as an election judge in several Minnesota elections starting when he was in high school in the Minneapolis suburb of Bloomington, helping elderly and illiterate Somalis through the voting process. And he, like many Somalis, followed current international and national affairs closely. He, like others on the university campus, felt devastated by the mid-October 2017 bombing in Mogadishu that killed 512 people, an event that led the students in the SSA to meet for discussions to share their grief and concern.

Mahamud noted that Somalis in general are politically engaged in Minnesota. They tend to vote in large numbers and pay attention, especially when Somali candidates are on the ballot. "We have to be more aware because we are such a target," Mahamud said. "The majority of Somali people are Muslims. We're black immigrants. And a lot are from low-income backgrounds, so we're disenfranchised. We don't have the luxury to be disengaged. I think people are using their civic duties to have some sort of voice."

Mahamud, who was majoring in advertising, public relations, and political science, readily listed the Somali candidates in the Minneapolis area who had won political office in the fall of 2017. She said, though, that she had reservations about how influential voting could be in affecting a system in which Somalis are such a small part. Getting involved in activist organizations that serve the community, she thought, could be a more effective means of helping her fellow Somali Americans. One of her organizations of choice was the Young Muslim Collective (YMC), a group that together with CAIR and the Muslim Justice League in October 2017 sponsored a forum session on "Resisting Surveillance" on the University of Minnesota campus, in which speakers opposed the Countering Violent Extremism program.[27] For her part, Mahamud said she was troubled by the distrust of the Muslim community that she said the CVE program bred and reflected.

Mahamud grew up in Minneapolis with a biracial neighbor and many white friends from public school, friends who accepted her with the hijab she wore regularly starting in kindergarten and then fulltime starting in about fifth grade. "I had a lot of white friends growing up, some [I'm] still really close with," she said, adding that she similarly is "around a lot of white people" at the university. Mahamud in 2017–18 served as president of the SSA, though she noted she spoke only for herself here and not for the association.

Said, for her part, felt a split in her behavior at home compared with school, even though she attended a Somali charter school from third through ninth grade and then a public high school in Burnsville, a suburb of Minneapolis. She said the feeling is common among young Somalis she knows. "Our parents are immigrants and they raised us with the same values and customs they were raised with back home in Somalia," she said. "When I went to school, I was, like, American, so to speak. That was kind of a conflict. When I was home, I spoke Somali, and I was just like I am, Somali, at home. Outside, I was more Americanized."

The students were hard-pressed to spell out the differences. But they pointed to such cultural mores as a respectful attitude toward Somali elders. Young Somalis deferentially call older Somali women "aunt," Said said, while she said many Americans want everyone to be on a first-name basis, irrespective of age. And they said they acted in a more reserved manner around older people, while feeling freer to be sarcastic and relaxed with younger Somali peers, more expressive, perhaps, than they were with white peers. "When I'm with my white classmates, we have to act the same way," Said said. She added that she never really assimilated into American culture until high school, leaving her with a split identity. Said said, "I think I coexist as both, but I more identify as Somali and then American after."

The business student said he was often the only Somali in his classes, such as in a leadership class he was then taking. Coming from a low-income family, he said it was difficult for him to relate to others in discussions of power and privilege in the class—even if the professor called on him to address such issues from his unique viewpoint. He was reluctant to do so, saying he was concerned he would be excluded by others.

For all their feelings of separateness however, the students shared many cultural elements with young non-Somalis. Mahamud, for instance, said she liked rap music, along with professional sports. Said's tastes turned to rock, hip-hop, and rhythm and blues throwbacks. Indeed, in a bit of cultural fusion, the video of Somali Night in 2017 on the SSA website was set not to Somali music but to a lively pop song by Sia Kate Isobel Furler, an Australian. That song, "The Greatest," featured the lyric: "Don't give up, I won't give up, don't give up, no, no, no . . . I'm free to be the greatest, I'm alive."

Furthermore, none of the three pointed to incidents where they had felt anti-Somali sentiments from students or others on campus. Indeed, Mahamud said whites often seemed to visit Somali restaurants near the campus. But both women said they had felt the sting of such sentiments when they were younger and before they had come to the university. Mahamud said she was riding her bike with a group of friends, at about age thirteen or fourteen, and an older white man shouted at them to go back where they came from. Fellow students said similar things to Said on a couple of occasions when she was in elementary school, once in class and once on the playground.

Anti-Somali incidents in Minnesota and across the country, however, have been rising in recent years. The Dar Al-Farooq Islamic Center, a mosque in Bloomington, Minnesota, was bombed in the predawn hours of August 5, 2017, by someone who tossed a pipe bomb into the imam's unoccupied office. No one was hurt but about a dozen people were gathered for morning prayers in a room nearby, and the office was heavily damaged, the *Star Tribune* reported. Mark Dayton, then Minnesota's governor, labeled the attack an act of terror. Minnesotans of many faiths rallied to support the mosque—with more than 1,000 people gathering there at one point—and a carpenters' union repaired the imam's office for free with donated materials. Two men from Illinois pleaded guilty in the case, saying they wanted to scare Muslims out of the country, and a third in late 2019 was awaiting trial.[28]

That same month, a man in Willmar, about ninety miles west of Minneapolis, threw a pig's foot into a Somali vendor's stand at a farmer's market, cursing the Somalis and later telling police that he didn't like Somalis or Muslims.[29] The *Star Tribune* reported that a twenty-two-year-old Somali American woman was attacked in June 2017 in the university area, suffering a concussion and being hospitalized for two days.[30] Furthermore, the newspaper said authorities reported fourteen anti-Muslim incidents statewide in 2016, nearly half of which involved bodily harm to the victims. In the most serious incident, a gunman on June 29, 2016, fired bullets into a car carrying five Somali men near the university neighborhood of Dinkytown in southeastern Minneapolis, hitting two of the men in the legs; the assailant was convicted and sentenced to thirty-nine years in prison.

The night after a Somali man, Dahir Adan, stabbed ten shoppers at the Crossroads Center Mall in St. Cloud, Minnesota, on September 17, 2016, Somalis reported seeing pickup trucks in a predominantly Somali neighborhood of the town waving Confederate flags and honking, according to an Associated Press account.[31] Reacting to the St. Cloud attack, an ice-cream shop owner in Lonsdale, a town south of Minneapolis, displayed a sign outside the shop saying "Muslims Get Out."[32] Five years earlier, the US Department of Education investigated two St. Cloud high schools after Somali students complained about derogatory comments by white students between 2008 and 2010. The department found the slurs continued into 2011 and ordered that anti-harassment efforts be put in place.[33] Adan had attended Apollo High School, one of the schools, graduating in 2014.[34]

Hostility and fear regarding Muslims in the United States dates back at least to the 9/11 attacks. Their image in the country certainly hasn't been helped by popular media, in which they've often been caricatured as treacherous and dangerous—images that may have influenced the anti-Muslim actions in Minnesota and around the country. Indeed, ever since Osama bin Laden riveted the world's attention with the attacks in New York and Washington, the media have been battlegrounds in what Oklahoma State University professor of American studies Stacy Takacs called a "very long information war."[35] The recruits in Minnesota, one could argue, merely chose one side in the dueling narratives that have played out in both news and entertainment media, as well as in material on the internet. Those launching attacks on Muslims, and some politicians, chose the other side.

In the years after Bashir and his friends were caught by the FBI, tensions between non-Somalis and Somalis (and Muslims, in general) surfaced in Minnesota electoral politics, as well. Republican gubernatorial hopeful Phillip Parrish, for instance, on his LinkedIn site said: "Minnesotans will no longer fund jihadists through the exploitation of social programs. We will no longer train ill-intended people for nefarious and terrorist activities."[36] The remark, and similar comments by the former US Naval Intelligence officer from tiny Kenyon, Minnesota, drew a rebuke from the Southern Poverty Law Center, which said his public platform "vilifies Muslims and embraces anti-Muslim conspiracies." The group reported that on the Minnesota podcast "Up and at 'Em" in November 2017 Parrish said, "In one who practices Islam, there is no separation of civilian law from a theocracy." He told the hosts that Islam in America represents "a violent, dishonest, abusive culture that is getting a pass." Further, the SPLC cited emails between Parrish and Regina Mustafa of Minnesota's Community Interfaith Dialogue on Islam in which Parrish condemned Islam as fundamentally incompatible with American law.

"I separate Islam from the word faith because faith takes belief and Islam requires only submission," the candidate stated. "I will not participate in any faith dialog because Islam is ultimately not a faith." Parrish demanded Mustafa "publicly denounce Sharia and swear to adhere to, protect, comply with, accept, and defend the United States Constitution." He suggested that as a practicing Muslim—or as he put it, "practicing Islamist"—she would be unable to do so. He also wrote, "Islam, Sharia, and the Quran are the antithesis of the U.S. Constitution."[37]

But anti-Islamic comments do not play well with some leaders in the Republican Party in the state. A February 2018 report by Minnesota Public Radio said: "There is uneasiness in segments of the Republican Party about setting a tone that the GOP is bigoted. Some party leaders have cringed amid the discussion or distanced themselves from party platform resolutions seen as outwardly hostile to immigrants or Muslims." Nonetheless, some candidates, such as former State Representative Jeff Johnson, both embraced and criticized Muslims, perhaps trying to appeal to different parts of his base. Johnson, whom the party nominated to run against Democrat Tim Walz, said he knew Muslims who were wonderful Americans, but he added that there were some who wanted to replace the Constitution with Sharia law.[38] Johnson lost the race to Walz, who was seated as Minnesota's governor in January 2019.

Reaching out to the Muslim community in Minnesota, Walz, in late March 2019, spoke at the Challenging Islamophobia Conference organized by Metropolitan State University in St. Paul by CAIR-Minnesota. "We know that our Muslim community is deeply tied into the fabric of Minnesota. You are our teachers, our doctors, our entrepreneurs, our neighbors, our brothers and sisters," the governor said. "I'm here to today to deliver a pretty simple message: hate and Islamophobia have no home in Minnesota, but you do."[39]

But Walz also said that "platitudes" would not be enough. He pledged "zero tolerance" of bullying of Islamic young people in the schools. He said he would call out "baseless attacks" on Muslims, and said his administration would "hold accountable" politicians who he said try to advance their careers by exploiting religious divisions. He said he would open human rights offices around the state to "magnify" the message of "turning against" Islamophobia. Walz referred to the mid-March 2019 shootings at the Al Noor Mosque in a suburb of Christchurch, New Zealand, in which a white supremacist killed fifty-one people, and to the bombing of the Dar Al-Farooq Islamic Center. "Christchurch could have been, and nearly was, in our backyard at Dar Al-Farooq," the governor said.

Nationally, the FBI reported 381 bias-motivated anti-Muslim offenses in 2016, up 26.6 percent from 301 the prior year.[40] Those numbers may substantially undercount the actual figures. *Vox* reported that when the US Bureau of Justice Statistics conducted surveys between 2007 and 2011 to measure hate crime overall—against many groups—it found that there were then nearly 260,000 such crimes each year, far more than the total reported by the FBI.[41] According to ProPublica, local law enforcement agencies told the FBI about 6,121 hate crimes in 2016, but estimates by the federal government's National Crime Victimization Survey put the number of potential hate crimes at almost 250,000 annually.[42] To better keep track, ProPublica in 2017 launched a national effort to gather news and information about such crimes, called the Documenting Hate Index.[43]

Anti-immigrant sentiment has been a problem in the United States for as long as the country has been open to immigrants. Over the decades, Irish, Italians, Chinese, Latinos, Jews, Catholics, African Americans, and others have felt the sting of discrimination and hostility from nativist forces at various times (as have Native Americans)—though recently such forces appear to be emboldened by President Trump, who criticized immigrants of various sorts during his campaign and who continued during his presidency to arouse hostilities to such newcomers.

But the nation's attitudes—and the feelings among immigrants—have also changed much over time. For much of the early and middle part of the twentieth century, members of various ethnic groups sought to blend into the dominant culture. Some went so far as to change their names, even change religions, as they sought to "pass" as white Anglo-Saxon Protestants or at least to stand out less, and academics spoke of America's "melting pot" culture. As ethnic pride rose and minority groups felt more comfortable in their identities, perhaps influenced by the "Black is Beautiful" efforts of the 1960s, such efforts went by the wayside—and most Americans seemed to accept the change.

The United States may now be shifting to resemble the atomized Canadian model, which academics there commonly describe as a "mosaic" of discrete identities and, often, insular neighborhoods. It again may come to look like what poet Walt Whitman in *Leaves of Grass* celebrated in the 1800s as a "teeming nation of nations."[44] Somalis, in particular, and Muslims, in general, may prove to be parts of a new American mosaic even as they make inroads into mainstream society through education, politics, and the professions.

Indeed, one hero to some Somalis in Minnesota—and a poster child for assimilation—is a Somali Canadian, Ahmed Hussen. Hussen, who the *New York Times* reported came to Canada in 1993 as a sixteen-year-old with little more than a change of clothes in a gym bag, was named Canada's minister of immigration, refugees and citizenship in January of 2017. Over the time he lived in Canada, he got himself through high school, college, and law school and was elected a member of the Canadian Parliament, the first Somali Canadian to take such an elective seat. All along the way, according to the *Times* report, he tried hard to fit in: "I wanted to be Canadian," Hussen, who was forty-one in the fall of 2017, told the newspaper. "I didn't want to be the Somali guy. I still don't."

But fitting in didn't mean turning his back on the Somali community. The newspaper reported that Hussen was active in community organizing in his government-housing neighborhood and led an advocacy group, the Canadian Somali Congress. In his law practice, he represented refugees. And he married another Somali refugee. His roots in Somalia go deep: he was the youngest of six children there. Though both his parents were illiterate, his mother prized education, and his parents insisted he migrate to Canada to join a pair of elder brothers there. Like many other Somalis, his family had fled to Kenya to escape the Somali civil war. Hussen feels he owes his adoptive country a lot. "To me, giving back to Canada is very personal," he told the newspaper.[45]

Hussen has many fans in Minnesota. When he spoke at the Humphrey School of Public Affairs at the University of Minnesota in December 2017, the auditorium was packed, according to a report in the *Star Tribune*. "He is an icon," Mohamed Amin Ahmed, a Bush Foundation fellow at the university and a Somali community leader told the newspaper. "People see him as an example of what is possible in the West."[46]

For that matter, Mohamed Amin Ahmed is an example of how Somalis could make their way in the West, even as they educated non-Somalis about their community. Ahmed runs the Average Mohamed nonprofit, which uses cartoons on YouTube and on a website—averagemohamed.com—to steer young Somalis away from extremists. He often speaks in schools, churches, and other organizations, offering a message critical of extremists and urging tolerance.[47] The Minnesota man consults with government officials on how best to battle extremism.

To foster acceptance, moreover, some Muslim organizations try to educate non-Muslim Americans about Islam. One mosque I visited during Ramadan in 2016,

Masjid Dar Al-Hijrah (meaning "Home of Migration") in the "Little Mogadishu" area of Cedar-Riverside, welcomed a Lutheran group to observe its services and then share a nighttime meal filled with Somali cuisine. Seeking to bridge the gulf between the Christians and Muslims, the mosque's imam presented a slide show in which he explained the main tenets of Islam, emphasizing its promotion of peace. Perhaps stressing their connection to the United States, the mosque's leaders in 2013 changed the name of the building housing the mosque to the Islamic Civic Society of America.[48]

The higher profiles that Somalis in Minnesota are taking have gone far toward building acceptance among many non-Somalis, even as they have alienated some. An estimated 15,000 people—many of them ethnic Somalis—gathered for each of two prayer sessions inside the sprawling U.S. Bank Stadium on August 21, 2018, in a "Super Eid" celebration marking the Muslim holiday of Eid al-Adha. While some critics on social media objected to the event, Minnesotans bearing placards saying "Love Your Neighbor" and "All Are Welcome Here" stood on the steps outside, intending to counter any protesters. (None appeared to show up, however). One Minnesota physician, Dr. Alia Sharif, told the *Star Tribune:* "I truly felt this is what America is all about. I'm an American. I can stand here at U.S. Bank Stadium and pray, and I'm welcome here."[49]

Assimilation doesn't mean that Somali Americans needed to lose their heritage. As sociologist Edward Telles wrote, in a 2006 essay in *Aztlán: A Journal of Chicano Studies,* assimilation has come to be seen among academics as "a two-way street, as immigrants and their descendants become part of the mainstream . . . at the same time the mainstream changes."[50] American culture, as reflected in areas as varied as food, entertainment, and media, changed as various ethnic groups took their places in it.

One can only wonder at how different things may have been for Bashir and his friends if they had grown up in atmospheres that stressed coexistence and bridging cultural gaps. Would they have taken different paths had they been raised with role models of successful Somalis front and center in their lives? Would the likes of Canada's Hussen have been inspirational for them, had they visited their high schools?

As athletic as they all were, would they have been inspired to make their way in Western society if they had been reared with tales of the likes of Sir Mohamed Muktar Jama "Mo" Farah, the Somali refugee who spoke almost no English when he migrated as a child to the United Kingdom and grew up to become a 2012 and 2016

Olympic gold medalist? Would online videos of the many Muslims who play soccer on the world stage have been more influential than the online recruiters for ISIS, had they been showcased for the young men in their mosque youth programming?

Plenty of Muslims and plenty of Somalis exemplify the best possibilities of assimilation, maintaining their religious and cultural identities even as they fit in with the larger societies. Their stories make for potent narratives to counter the deadly ones offered by ISIS and its likes.

CHAPTER TWENTY

Taking a Hard Look

After his near-seduction into terrorism, Bashir worked to get back on track personally and professionally. He re-enrolled at Minnesota's St. Cloud Technical & Community College during the spring of 2016, taking courses even while working with the FBI and steeling himself to testify in the trial of his friends in May and June. He was earning As and Bs in his coursework, he said, until he fell behind a bit because of the legal actions. He had to ask teachers for extensions, telling them he was working with the FBI.

He also reflected a lot on what had drawn them all into ISIS's web. The roots of radicalism, he told me after the trial, lay in a few areas. The main things that "get a young guy radical," he said, were accepting Anwar al-Awlaki's misinterpretations of Islam and listening to friends active in ISIS in Syria. Further, in Minneapolis, young Somalis intrigued with ISIS looked up to the role models of the men who earlier joined al-Shabab, hoping to liberate their ancestral homeland.

He regarded the three men who stood trial and were convicted in mid-2016—Daud, Mohamed Farah, and Omar—as leaders and recruiters. The other six who took plea deals were "soldiers," he said, adding they would go to Syria without really thinking it through. As for the appetite to fight for a radical group among young men in Minneapolis now, it has been curbed, Bashir said.

Still, he said the Somali community was wrong to turn a blind eye to potential recruitment issues. While some were quick to blame the government—and Bashir—claiming they ensnared young men who would otherwise not have attempted to go to Syria, the community instead should have tried to keep the young rebels in check, he suggested. One of the most powerful forces, he said, is a strong father figure—something he had, but several of the others lacked. "I had a dad, a father figure, who helped me," he said. His own cousins—Mohallim and the Kariye brothers—had no fathers in their lives. He said: "The time when we were radicals, it was only my dad who was trying to help me, to realize the religion, the right way."

Even the imams and sheikhs in the mosques failed the other young men, Bashir argued. As reports went public of some young men's interest in going to Syria, some could have taken them aside and taken issue with sermons by the likes of al-Awlaki. But, Bashir said, they feared touching the topic, if only because talking about it might draw unwelcome FBI interest—as they feared had happened with al-Shabab years before.

As time wore on and ISIS was routed militarily in Syria, and as reports emerged of members turning guns on their own supporters, Bashir grew more thankful that he had been spared a trip to join the group. "God saved me," he told me. The friends he turned on, too, were saved, as he said they will realize in time. Had they wound up in ISIS, they would likely be dead—perhaps even at the hands of ISIS, which proved to be anything but the ideal Islamic group he and his friends once thought it was.

Coming to that realization was difficult for Bashir, as it was for his friends who similarly repudiated violent Islamism. Changing hearts and minds, according to many experts, is a complex process, especially when dealing with impressionable adolescents and people alienated from mainstream society by poverty or cultural isolation. Moreover, each person's motivations for wanting to sign on with such groups can differ, colored by family connections to terrorist groups, the presence or absence of strong father figures or other role models, economic and professional opportunities or the lack of them, mental health, the insularity of one's community, and the powerful persuasive effect of recruiters and online propaganda.

As shown by the differences in the cases in Minneapolis, moreover, the ways to deal with would-be terrorists need to be individualized, as well. Courts, social workers, imams, and psychologists may find that some are unsalvageable, as Judge Davis appeared to conclude in sentencing one of the three men he tried to thirty-five years in prison and the other two to thirty years each—sentences that will keep them behind bars until they are well into middle age. By contrast, the sentences of the six who pleaded guilty—ranging from a couple of years served while awaiting sentencing to ten years—suggested that the men had either convinced the judge that their repudiation of radical Islam was genuine or that they could yet be turned around. While they will be under legal supervision for many years beyond their releases, they at least can look toward freedom by the time they are in their 30s.

But the court and prison systems are blunt and imperfect instruments for dealing with the malignancy of violent Islamism. For one thing, the men now serving time in prison will get no rehabilitation programming there aimed at rooting out terrorist convictions—at least not as of early 2019. Indeed, they could spread their ideas to other inmates, as has happened with Islamists in European prisons, where radicalization is an ongoing problem. An influx of radical terrorists in some such prisons "is transforming facilities designed for punishment into incubators for future terror attacks," as a *Wall Street Journal* report warned in June 2016.[1] Moreover, after their decade or more behind bars, will their anger and alienation have subsided or increased? Will they pose an ongoing danger, especially when their ability to reintegrate into society—with jobs and families—will have been weakened, perhaps permanently?

The issue goes well beyond the young Somali men now in custody, as the number of terrorists in American prisons rises above 440, as the *New York Times* reported in 2016.[2] The number of such convictions and imprisonments seems sure to grow: even as ISIS has been driven underground, some 1,000 potential terrorism investigations were still open in the United States in 2017, FBI Director Christopher A. Wray told the Senate Homeland Security and Governmental Affairs Committee in September 2017, according to *The Hill*.[3]

People imprisoned for terrorism-related offenses will get out in time, and they could do so with even more entrenched radical convictions. As a report by the Washington Institute for Near East Policy warned in March 2017:

> So far, BOP [Federal Bureau of Prisons] has been content to apply whatever programs it has in place for the general criminal population to the population of terrorism-related convicts. Moreover, within those programs participation is voluntary and nothing is tailored to the context of ideologically driven terrorism. Nor is there a program in place specifically tailored to addressing the release, restrictions, and monitoring of convicted terrorists let out from prison after serving their sentences.[4]

More recently, in his late 2018 article in the *Journal for Deradicalization,* former Minnesota federal probations chief Lowry reported that the federal prisons were holding 412 inmates with a history of involvement with foreign terrorist organizations, as well as eighty-six domestic terrorists. Some 108 of the inmates were slated for release over the following five years, he reported. Developing ways to assure that the convicts don't pose a threat to communities on their release is crucial, Lowry suggested: "If not properly managed, prisons could become breeding grounds for young jihadists and other types of extremists who, upon release to the community, may carry out terrorist acts as part of a group or as lone actors," he argued. "When incarcerated, there is a great risk that untreated, radicalized individuals will become more militant and recruit others for involvement in violent extremist activities."[5]

Managing their releases will take intense attention from teams of experts, according to Lowry. The program he devised at the behest of Chief Judge Tunheim and Judge Davis involves assessing the level of risk the terrorists pose and reviewing matters of family support, residential plans, work, and education. Once released, their ongoing supervision may include GPS monitoring, restrictions on internet use, prohibition on access to extremist materials, restrictions on media contacts, mental health counseling, lie-detector tests, drug tests, financial disclosures, and denial of a passport, as well as prohibitions on possessing weapons.

Indeed, "American Taliban" John Walker Lindh's release in May 2019 after more than seventeen years in prison—but three years early because of good behavior—raised fresh questions about the lack of programming to assure that those convicted of terrorism offenses do not pose a danger. Amid questions about whether Lindh had renounced terrorism, a federal judge in Alexandria, Virginia, imposed restrictions on him including some that Lowry had urged in such cases. Among them are the monitoring of his internet devices, mental health counseling, a ban on possessing or viewing extremist material, and denial of a passport, along with a restriction that his online communications must be conducted in English. Violations could land him back in prison. The Associated Press reported that, as recently as 2017, *Foreign Policy* magazine cited a National Counterterrorism Center report saying Lindh still advocated global jihad and wrote and translated extremist texts.[6]

Reflecting bipartisan concern about the lack of a system for dealing with releases of those such as Lindh who were convicted of terrorism offenses, Republican Senator Richard Shelby of Alabama and Democratic Senator Margaret Wood Hassan wrote a letter to the acting director of the Federal Bureau of Prisons warning that judges even lack tools to assess whether a terrorist could pose a public threat. They cited Lowry's report that suggested that neither the Bureau of Prisons nor the Federal Judiciary's probation and pretrial services have sufficient nationwide programming "to prevent incarcerated terrorist offenders from returning to violence." Further, they demanded information about what programming is available within the prisons and about processes that ensure that convicts can be reintegrated into society.[7]

Lowry described the Minnesota program as a start in developing a national approach. He suggested that it could be applied both to supporters of foreign terrorists and to violent white supremacists, whom he views as domestic terrorists who share similar senses of grievance and alienation with ISIS supporters. The program drew favorable attention in the spring of 2019 from the editorial page at the *Star Tribune*, which alluded to many of the Minnesota cases. "Early results are promising," the newspaper's editorial board wrote. "In 30 cases involving ISIS or al-Shabab-related activities, 12 of the defendants qualified for release from custody before their sentencing, and 10 successfully completed the disengagement program."[8]

Potential problems do go beyond those convicted, however. What of the friends and families of convicted terrorists, some of whom could be fellow travelers? As at least three of the men convicted in Minneapolis—Abdirahman Yasin Daud, Mohamed Abdihamid Farah, and Zacharia Abdurahman—left the courtroom separately in November 2016 on their way to terms behind bars, they flashed upward-pointed index fingers to friends in the gallery. As Prosecutor Docherty noted, according to the court transcript, this was the "tawhid" gesture referring to the oneness of God and a sign that ISIS fighters adopted as a victory and power symbol. At least one of the men got a response from friends that Docherty described as "exuberant."

The gesture could have been simply the men's way to acknowledge those who came to court to support them, as a defense attorney suggested for one of the men. And the response from those supporters may have been nothing but personal encouragement. Or, more darkly, it could have been a sign that those supporters share the men's violent Islamist convictions. Certainly, the Minnesota experience with backers of al-Shabab influencing those who later sought to join ISIS suggested that the embrace of radical ideas can be contagious and endure over time. Further, it underscored the need for authorities to keep a close eye on the friends of the convicted men for fear that they could try to follow in their footsteps with ISIS or whatever follow-on group may emerge in its wake.

Then again, the men—who were teenage naifs when they first grew infatuated with extremist Islamism—should be understood in the context of adolescence. Would their embrace of the ISIS cult have faded with time, as they approached their mid-twenties, as often happens with people who join cults as teens or early twentysomethings and who then grow up and away from the groups? As Bashir's change of heart demonstrates, personal convictions can be malleable at such times in life, but would an extended period of incarceration bolster antisocial beliefs? Did the judge, in putting some of the less culpable men behind bars for a decade, just help cement the pathological beliefs that otherwise would have died on their own? Could those beliefs have been shaken through appropriate programming outside of prison, especially since there is none inside that is likely to help the men see the world differently?

Or would the men have just faked it on the outside, secretly harboring jihadist ideology and waiting for the right time to launch a suicide attack, perhaps on a high-visibility target in the United States? They claimed to recant and, in some cases, pledged to work with moderate imams and to lecture other young Somalis to deter them from violent Islamism. But was that genuine? With his decisions to send even several of those who pleaded guilty to prison for long periods, the judge made it clear that he didn't believe in most of the men's post-conviction turnarounds. Further, with his remarks to the Somali community about the terror cell in its midst, Davis sent a message to others that such dangerous groups would not be tolerated. Society, including the Somali community, would be protected even if it meant a decade or more in prison for these individuals. And he wagered, in effect, that supervision for years after their releases will ensure that years hence they can't act on their youthful misbeliefs.

Beyond the balancing act that judges in all such cases must perform, the larger community faces tough questions, as well. What steps can society take to keep the toxic beliefs of violent Islamism away from young and impressionable people? Certainly, the schools should be vehicles for inculcating an appreciation of American values, as well as of acculturation. Are they doing that sort of work with vulnerable communities? Helping young people, dissuading them from trouble, before they wind up dealing with the court system—for terrorism or criminality—seems a far more preferable route.

But coming up with answers is difficult and is bound to alienate or infuriate some parts of the community. Is it wise to encourage—even fund with public money—self-segregated schools, such as Heritage Academy? Can programs be put in place even in such schools that foster assimilation, not isolation? Or, are young people better off by being required to attend mixed public schools, where they rub shoulders with others not like themselves (and others must learn, similarly, to accept people who may dress, eat, and believe differently)? In the cases of the Somali men convicted, more than half attended Heritage, but some attended other public schools with mixed populations or attended both at different times; in any case, their convictions gelled into support for ISIS. And even in those public schools, some of the men felt isolated and rejected by non-Somalis.

For Somalis in Minnesota, such questions are now urgent. They must police their own community members carefully to see whether younger people, perhaps friends of the thirteen plotters, have been drawn to violent Islamism. That already happened, obviously, with the shift in support for al-Shabab a decade before to the recent support for ISIS. The phenomenon could recur, since violent Islamism hasn't been stamped out and the propagandistic videos of terrorist clerics such as al-Awlaki endure.

This puts pressure on imams and teachers in Islamic after-school programs to deliver messages of tolerance and civility and to rebut the flawed theology of the Islamists. Outsiders can help, but the solution for stamping out terrorist Islamism rests within the Islamic community, as Associate Professor Abla Hasan, who teaches Arabic language and culture at the University of Nebraska-Lincoln, has argued. Syrian-born Hasan, who covers her hair and dresses traditionally but who teaches about the strong women figures and feminist elements of the Quran, has made the case in academic presentations that Muslims must defeat violent Islamism themselves.[9]

For non-Somalis in Minnesota, the challenge is to learn to accept the newcomers. The state, a creation of mostly immigrants from prior generations, has done so in the recent past in accepting large numbers of Hmong people, a group that fled Laos after the Communists took over in 1975, with many making their way to Minnesota between then and 2004. The Minneapolis–St. Paul area is home to an estimated 66,000 Hmong, who have been blending into the larger community with varying levels of success.[10] As reported by the *Pioneer Press,* many Hmong continue to struggle with poverty, poor health, and limited education, but a 2015–2016 exhibit at the Minnesota History Center, "We Are Hmong Minnesota," highlighted such successes as the 640 Hmong who now boast doctoral degrees.[11] Similarly, Somalis increasingly are climbing the professional and economic ladders, usually through education, in Minnesota.

Furthermore, non-Somali Minnesotans already open doors for Somalis through various programs, such as one that provides Somali-speaking parent liaisons in public schools, helping Somali parents to help their children to succeed in school. And young Somalis at the University of Minnesota reported that they increasingly see non-Somalis in Somali restaurants, suggesting the same sort of assimilation that has made ethnic restaurants of all sorts comfortable for people of all backgrounds. Visits by church groups to mosques also are breaking down barriers between communities.

However, only a Pollyanna would argue that the processes of acceptance and Americanization do not have a long way to go. Violence within the Somali community by Somali gangs and violence committed against Somalis by outsiders remain as painful headaches. Poverty, inadequacy in the education system, domestic difficulties within Somali homes and families, and insularity continue to dog the Somali community and affect the larger community.

The seductive power of ISIS and, earlier, of al-Shabab suggest both lingering alienation, mostly among younger people, and problems within the Somali religious world, in the mosques. Imams must teach doctrine in ways that foster tolerance of other beliefs and intolerance of violence and extremist Islamism. They can join forces with leaders in the wider community, as some have, to combat ignorance. And they must urge rejection of those in their midst who would lead young people astray.

Young people such as Bashir and his friends who have turned away from radicalism are examples of how personal attention can make all the difference. The threat of imprisonment may be a potent tool to discourage affiliation with radical groups, though it would seem a dubious deterrent for those determined to die in battle, those who seek martyrdom. For adolescent recruits, as well as those in their early twenties whose attitudes may be more malleable, personal attention by influential adults, in the end, may prove more powerful and influential than years behind bars will.

Certainly, for some of the Minnesota men, the influence of others—peers, relatives, online recruiters, older men—was profoundly damaging. Replacing such figures with healthier role models, especially early in young people's lives and educations, could make the difference between susceptibility to terrorist recruitment and a normal life. Some, no doubt, will be beyond help. But, as Bashir's experience shows, the right approach can pay off.

CHAPTER TWENTY-ONE

Moving On

While most of the Minnesota plotters who sought to join ISIS wound up in prison or under supervised release after 2016, Bashir faced his own challenges in Minneapolis long afterward. An outcast among his former peers, he was occasionally harassed by other young Somali men. Some would ridicule him on the street or in stores, taunting him while pulling out their cell phones to video their encounters.

That could have been risky for them, however, as Bashir had bulked up by joining the Army National Guard the year after the trial, a move he figured would help him take steps toward a law-enforcement career. Basic training, he recalled, was all about toughening oneself mentally and physically—constant exercise, little sleep, crawling on the ground under live fire and learning how to handle guns. Some guys, he said, didn't make it through, but he proudly did, saying he was happy to serve his country and to prepare himself to rise to the occasion whenever he might be called up.[1] After all he had been through, he said he was not cowed when he was harassed.

Marking the sharp turnaround from the ISIS terrorist he all too easily could have become, in early 2019, Bashir briefly worked as a detention officer with the Hennepin County sheriff's department. He left that post to work as a security guard.

Setting his sights on becoming a police officer someday, he also took up studies through an online college program.

As he reflected on his strange journey over the prior decade, Bashir took solace in knowing that his actions in the end had almost surely saved lives, including those of the young men he had informed on. If they had not been stopped, their lives could have ended in Syria, and they might have taken the lives of others with them, as happened with other young Somalis who left Minneapolis to join ISIS or al-Shabab. They could have done damage or killed people at home in the United States, an option suggested in some of the trial testimony. Yusuf Abdurahman, whose son Zacharia was sentenced to a decade in federal prison for his efforts to get to ISIS, acknowledged in an interview with me that Bashir's actions ironically spared his son from a worse fate.[2]

Bashir told me in a March 2019 conversation that his only regret was that he had not seen the mistakes in his beliefs earlier and so was unable to dissuade his former friends (though he did work cautiously behind his friends' backs to dissuade younger teens).[3] Indeed, Yusuf Abdurahman said he wished Bashir's father—an old acquaintance from whom he had become estranged—had tipped him off about Zacharia's activities.

Bashir, who turned twenty-four in mid-2019, was rebuilding his life, though. Early that year, his wife, Hibaq Ali, gave birth to a son, Adam, the first grandchild for Bashir's parents. Meanwhile, in the Guard, Bashir had moved up the initial ranks and planned to pursue promotion to sergeant. Harassment by other Somalis in Minnesota had largely abated by 2019, he said, partly because, with his hair trimmed close to his head, he often went about unrecognized.

Bashir still considered himself a Muslim, though he called himself a believer in "true Islam," which he said advocates peace. He occasionally went to mosque, where he said others didn't trouble him. Unlike many others who were seduced into radical Islamist beliefs and came to tragic ends, he saw a future for himself. He saw that future as possibly working in deradicalization, the importance of which he can personally bear witness to. Sadly, such expertise likely will long be needed.

Indeed, effects of the ISIS recruitment efforts continued long beyond those efforts. In October 2019, federal authorities in San Diego arraigned a Canadian cousin of Bashir's on charges related to Bashir's other Canadian cousins, the Kariye brothers. The grand jury indictment accused the man, Abdullahi Ahmed Abdullahi, thirty-four, of conspiring with longtime Bashir family friend, Douglas McAuthur McCain, and others to help the Kariye brothers and another cousin of Bashir's, along with an unnamed American from Minneapolis (possibly Bashir's cousin Hanad Mohallim), to get to Syria and to wire money to them while they were there. McCain and the others were all killed in attacks on ISIS there. Abdullahi, who had lived in San Diego and was extradited from Canada, was also accused of robbing a jewelry store in 2014 in Edmonton to raise funds for the travelers.[4]

ISIS in March 2019 lost its grip on its territory in Syria, where, over a two-year period, Western-backed military forces had shattered the group's hold on key cities and the countryside, and it was crushed in Iraq. The Syrian Democratic Forces, backed by a coalition of seventy-nine nations led by the United States, killed many of ISIS adherents in Syria and took many others prisoner. But, as news outlets including the *Wall Street Journal* reported, battle-hardened militants remained throughout Syria, Iraq, Nigeria, the Philippines, Libya, and the Sinai Peninsula; indeed, the departing US commander, General Joseph Vogel, warned that the surrender of fighters and their families in Baghouz, Syria, was a calculated moved by ISIS leaders to preserve their capabilities. Some detainees, especially women with children, were unrepentant in interviews.[5] Moreover, nearly 20,000 ISIS detainees were imprisoned in Iraq with an equal number from Syria expected to be transferred into Iraq in early 2019, in addition to unknown numbers of children born to ISIS supporters; all face uncertain futures, and many could become enemies of the West over time, experts say.[6]

ISIS continued to have footholds in the area from which it could launch attacks, as the group demonstrated lethally in early 2019 with a suicide bombing on a military convoy that killed nineteen people, including four Americans,[7] followed a few days later by a second attack on a US-Kurdish convoy[8]—both of which seemed to come in response to President Trump's claim in December 2018 that the United States had defeated ISIS and would withdraw its troops from Syria.[9] The group also remained particularly active in Afghanistan, and its presence and continued recruitment online presented a threat.[10]

Only the most naive would think the group's defeats will end Islamist terror and its radical ideology, which dates back decades before the rise of ISIS. Other radical organizations arose before ISIS, al-Qaida, al-Shabab, Boko Haram, and similar groups that now plague the West, Africa, and the Middle East. Furthermore, al-Shabab continues to put its bloody stakes into the ground in Somalia and in adjoining Kenya, even as the United States ramps up its military presence in the area. Al-Shabab in January 2019 killed at least twenty-one people, including an American, in an eighteen-hour siege in Nairobi.[11] Then, mid-July 2019, it left at least twenty-six people dead and fifty-six hurt when four of its fighters besieged a hotel in Kismayo, a southern port city in Somalia; among the dead were two journalists, one of whom was a Canadian, Hodan Nalayeh, who had returned to her native country to tell "uplifting" stories about its citizens.[12] The group killed at least seventy-nine people and wounded dozens more in a car-bombing in Mogadishu on December 28, 2019, prompting retaliatory US air strikes. A week later, on January 5, 2020, it attacked an airstrip in Kenya on the Somalia border, killing three Americans.

If past is prologue, similar groups will rise in the future, even as the remnant of ISIS continues to influence believers in its cause around the world.[13] Furthermore, hundreds, if not thousands, of ISIS fighters will in time likely make their way back to Europe and their home countries, posing a danger there.[14] Finally, the ideology that seduced Bashir and his friends, the militant form of Islam that cherry-picks bits of theology to make its apocalyptic case and is condemned by most in the Muslim world, will likely continue to be in conflict with more tolerant forms of the religion. So, understanding the appeal the militant ideology can have for young, culturally alienated young people will remain important—as will understanding the challenging process of uprooting it.

ACKNOWLEDGMENTS

This book would not have been possible, first, without the cooperation of Abdirahman Abdirashid Bashir, for whom I wish a good, long, and successful life. His journey was a tortuous one, and he shared his virtues and foibles alike with candor and thoroughness. So, too, did his father, Abdirashid Bashir Hassan.

We all owe much to the diligent work and dedication to fighting terrorism of such gifted assistant US attorneys as Charles J. Kovats Jr. While logging successes in the courtroom, he tolerated many questions from me over a couple years with equanimity and grace. Similarly, Julie E. Allyn, John F. Docherty, Greg Holloway, and Andrew R. Winter, all victors in the courts, gave generously of their time and insights. Defense attorneys who rounded out the portraits of their clients for juries and for me included Manny Atwal, Glenn P. Bruder, Marnie Fearon, Jon M. Hopeman, Bruce D. Nestor, and Kenneth Ubong Udoibok. FBI Special Agents Carson P. Green and Daniel P. Higgins epitomize professionalism, sensitivity, and astuteness. And former Minnesota federal probation chief Kevin D. Lowry tolerantly guided me through the thicket of rehabilitation procedures.

This story involved the work of many skilled hands. Federal authorities, particularly the FBI and lawyers in the US Attorney's Office in Minneapolis, did extraordinary legal and investigative work. Opposite them, defense attorneys raised crucial issues, shedding light on the complex motivations and sometimes troubled backgrounds of their clients. Journalists in Minnesota and elsewhere similarly distinguished themselves in writing about the legal action, the Somali community, and related issues. To tell this story, I relied on such people and on the insights of some exceptional Somali Americans, as well as on court records, extensive interviews, and the work of scholars who have studied terrorism, radicalization, and the Somali American community. I must also thank the brilliant educators who work with the Rift Valley Institute and who welcomed me to their annual Horn of Africa course in Uganda in July 2016, especially Davidson University Professor Kenneth Menkhaus, who schooled me in the challenges and opportunities of Somalia.

I relied on the work of many journalists, who assiduously followed the Somali cases and matters concerning the Minnesota Somali community. They demonstrated the tenacity, curiosity, and thoroughness that makes the craft a noble pursuit. Among them are Julia Edwards Ainsley, Sasha Aslanian, Brian Bakst, Julian E. Barnes, Zack Beauchamp, Peter Bergen, Tessa Berenson, Noemie Bisserbe, Lara Bockenstedt, David Brooks, Dan Browning, Ben Brumfield, Rukmini Callimachi, Greg Campbell, Mike Carter, Dominic Casciani, Margaret Coker, Isabel Coles, Helene Cooper, Rowenna Davis, Lizzie Dearden, Mike DeBonis, Jamie Dettmer, Jessica Donati, Judith Dubin, Mike Eckel, Andrea Elliott, Evan Engel, Hannah Fairfield, Zach Fannin, Farrah Fazal, James Fergusson, Amy Forliti, Rose French, David Frum, Randy Furst, Rachel Glickhouse, Chris Graham, David Greene, Shari Gross, Abdi Guled, Ted Haller, David Hanners, Andrew Harding, Julia Harte, Drew Harwell, Falih Hassan, Abigail Hauslohner, Sarah Horner, Bevan Hurley, Mukhtar Ibrahim, Faisal Irshaid. Ian Ith, Ben Jacobs, Libor Jany, Dan Joseph, Steve Karnowski, Rita Katz, Joshua Keating, Yasmin Khorram, Brendan Koerner, Mila Koumpilova, Eli Lake, Oliver Laughland, Aaron Lavinsky, Jennie Lissarrague, Helen Lock, Josh Lederman, German Lopez, Ethan Lou, Amanda Macias, Faiza Mahamud, Kirsti Mahron, Harun Maruf, Alejandra Matos, Paul McEnroe, Laura Meckler, Stacy Meichtry, Adow Mohamed, Stephen Montemayor, Kate Morrissey, Esme Murphy, Jay Newton-Small, Tony Paterson, Jesse Paul, Evan Perez, Michael M. Phillips, Catherine Porter, Kyle Potter, Shimon Prokupecz, Charlie Savage, Eric Schmitt, Nick Schifrin, Sharon Schmickle, Ken Schwenke, Somini Sengupta, Richard Sennot, Allie Shah, Ben Shapiro, Mike Shum, Abby Simons, Rachel Slavik, Kelly Smith, Felicia Sonmez, Elliott Spagat, Sheryl Gay Stolberg, Dina Temple-Raston, Brian Todd, Tad Vezner, Dustin Volz, John Wagner, Tim Wallace, James Walsh, Paul Walsh, Brandt Williams,

Katie Bo Williams, Robin Wright, Laura Yuen, Alan Yuhas, Mohamed Yusuf, and Scott Zamost. We all owe them a great debt for the impressive work they do.

I also am obliged to the scholars and authors who gave freely of their time and wisdom. These included Cawo M. Abdi, Abla Hasan, Gordon Mathews, and Ahmed Ismail Yusuf. And I thank Mary McKinley, Rooble Osman, and Jaylani Hussein for tolerating my many queries and sharing their insights. I thank Jessica "Molly" George, who aided me with research while working on her master's degree at the University of Nebraska–Lincoln. And I thank the family of the late Jerry and Karla Huse, who funded the endowed professorship I hold at UNL and whose support enabled me to undertake the research involved in this book. Finally, I am much indebted to my talented editor at Michigan State University Press, Catherine Cocks, for her patient guidance, now through two books.

While I am indebted to the many people who contributed to this effort, I bear responsibility for any errors or omissions, of course.

NOTES

Introduction

1. Abdirahman Abdirashid Bashir's name was spelled as "Bashiir" in some media reports. But he describes this as the result of a misspelling on his birth certificate, and he goes by "Bashir."

2. Islamic State of Iraq and Syria (ISIS) is also known as Islamic State of Iraq and the Levant (ISIL), referring to a broader region beyond Iraq, and by its Arabic name, Al-Dawla Al-Islamiya fi al-Iraq wa al-Sham. The last part of the latter name—"al-Sham"—refers broadly to the Levant, including Syria and the region around it. As reported by *The Independent,* the organization was founded in 1999 by Jordanian national Abu Musab al-Zarqawi as Jama'at al-Tawhid wal-Jihad and became known as "al-Qaida in Iraq" after becoming part of Osama bin Laden's network in October 2004. See Helen Lock, "Isis vs Isil vs Islamic State: What Do They Mean and Why Does It Matter?," *The Independent,* Sept. 14, 2014, http://www.independent.co.uk/. The group has also been referred to, pejoratively, as Daesh or Da'ish, based on the acronym of its original Arabic name. As reported by the BBC, "Daesh" is similar to an Arabic word meaning "to tread underfoot." See Faisal Irshaid, "Isil, Isis, IS, or Daesh? One Group, Many Names," BBC Monitoring, Dec. 2, 2015, http://www.bbc.com/news/.

3. As of the fall of 2018, federal officials in Minnesota reported handling fifty-four

defendants and offenders related to foreign terrorist organizations, plus five others related to international terrorism (but not specifically involved with foreign terrorist organizations). In addition, Somali community leaders say the number of people involved is higher because some left the United States undetected. See: Kevin D. Lowry, "Responding to the Challenges of Violent Extremism/Terrorism Cases for United States Probation and Pretrial Services," *Journal for Deradicalization* 17 (Winter 2018/19): 28–88, http://journals.sfu.ca/jd/index.php/jd/article/view/175/130.

4. Thirteen men were directly involved in the plot to join ISIS in Syria, along with several who were tangentially involved. The direct plotters included Zacharia Yusuf Abdurahman, Hamza Naj Ahmed, Adnan Abdihamid Farah, Hanad Mustafe (sometimes rendered as Mustofe) Musse, Abdullahi Yusuf, and Abdirizak Warsame, all of whom pleaded guilty when federal charges were brought against them, as well as Abdirahman Yasin Daud, Mohamed Abdihamid Farah, and Guled Ali Omar, who were found guilty of such charges. Abdirahman Bashir informed on the group for the FBI, testified against his friends, and was not charged. In addition, the plot involved three Minnesota men who made their way to Syria: Yusuf Jama and Bashir's cousin, Hanad Mohallim, both of whom were killed there, and Abdi Mohamud Nur, who is believed dead. Less directly involved were Mohamed Amiin Ali Roble, another Minnesotan who also made his way to Syria and who is also believed dead, along with Bashir's other cousins from Edmonton, Canada, Hersi Kariye, Hamsa Kariye, and Mahad Hirsi, who were killed there. A non-Somali Minnesota man, Douglas McAuthur McCain, killed in Syria, communicated with the thirteen, as did al-Shabab recruit Mohamed "Miski" Abdullahi Hassan of Minnesota, who in late 2015 defected to Somali authorities.

5. United Nations Security Council Counter-Terrorism Committee, Ninth Report of the Secretary-General on the Threat Posed by ISIL (Da'esh) to International Peace and Security and the Range of United Nations Efforts in Support of Member States in Countering the Threat, S/2019/612, (July 31, 2019), https://undocs.org/S/2019/612.

6. See in particular Jennifer Cafarella, Brandon Wallace, and Jason Zhou, "ISIS's Second Comeback: Assessing the Next ISIS Insurgency," Institute for the Study of War, July 23, 2019, http://www.understandingwar.org/report/isiss-second-comeback-assessing-next-isis-insurgency.

Chapter 1. The Seeds of Jihad

1. Abdirahman Abdirashid Bashir, interview with author, June 8, 2016, in Minneapolis. This was the first of several interviews between 2016 and 2019 from which his comments in this book were drawn.

2. Somalis typically use two or three names, though they often have many more, letting them trace their lineage back many generations. Hassan can trace his family line back for thirteen generations just by reciting his full name. Traditionally, an individual's middle name is the father's first name while the last name is the paternal grandfather's first name. See Motamedi, Jason Greenberg, Zafreen Jaffrey, Allyson Hagen, and Sun Young Yoon, *Getting It Right: Reference Guides for Registering Students with Non-English Names,* REL 2016-158 v2 (Washington, DC: US Department of Education, Institute of Education Sciences, National Center for Education Evaluation and Regional Assistance, Regional Educational Laboratory Northwest, 2016), 15–16, https://ies.ed.gov/ncee/edlabs/regions/northwest/pdf/REL_2016158.pdf.

3. Peter Bergen, *United States of Jihad: Investigating America's Homegrown Terrorists* (New York: Crown Publishers, 2016), 23.

4. Hamsa Bashir's name is also rendered as "Hamza" in some court records.

5. Transcript of Abdirahman Bashir's appearance in court on May 18, 2016, in U.S. v. Mohamed Abdihamid Farah, Abdirahman Yasin Daud and Guled Ali Omar, Case No. 15-CR-49 (MJD/FLN), 14–15.

6. "Soldier of Allah2," also called "Fighting for Jannah," source and date of origin unknown, https://www.youtube.com/watch?v=8wZx38UyKxw.

Chapter 2. A Land of Chaos

1. Catherine Besteman, *Making Refuge: Somali Bantu Refugees and Lewiston, Maine* (Durham, NC: Duke University Press, 2016), 91.

2. James Fergusson, *The World's Most Dangerous Place: Inside the Outlaw State of Somalia* (London: Black Swan, 2014), 110.

3. Cawo M. Abdi, *Elusive Jannah: The Somali Diaspora and the Borderless Muslim Identity,* (Minneapolis: University of Minnesota Press, 2015), 37.

4. Abdi, *Elusive Jannah,* 37.

5. Ahmed Ismail Yusuf, *Somalis in Minnesota* (Minneapolis: Minnesota Historical Society Press, 2012), 9.

6. Andrew Harding, *The Mayor of Mogadishu: A Story of Chaos and Redemption in the Ruins of Somalia* (New York: St. Martin's Press, 2016), 87–89.

7. Abdi, *Elusive Jannah,* 38–39.

8. Abdi, *Elusive Jannah,* 39–40.

9. Africa Watch, "Somalia: A Government at War with Its Own People" (New York: Africa Watch Committee, January 1990), https://www.hrw.org/sites/default/files/reports/somalia_1990.pdf.

10. United Nations Development Programme, "Human Development Report 2001: Somalia" (Nairobi: United Nations Development Programme, Somalia Country Office, 2001), 42.

11. Africa Watch, "Somalia," 2.

12. Fergusson, *The World's Most Dangerous Place,* 41–42.

13. The Bureau of Investigative Journalism, "Somalia: Reported US Covert Actions 2001–2016," https://www.thebureauinvestigates.com/drone-war/data/somalia-reported-us-covert-actions-2001-2017.

14. Helene Cooper, Charlie Savage, and Eric Schmitt, "Navy SEAL Killed in Somalia in First U.S. Combat Death There Since 1993," *New York Times,* May 5, 2017, https://www.nytimes.com/.

15. Michelle Tan, "Pentagon Identifies Special Operations Soldier Killed in Attack in Somalia," *Army Times,* June 9, 2018, https://www.armytimes.com/.

16. Abdi Guled, "Final Death Toll in Somalia's Worst Attack is 512 People," Associated Press, Dec. 2, 2017, https://www.apnews.com/.

17. Jessica Donati, "U.S. Says Airstrike Kills More Than 100 al-Shabaab Fighters in Somalia," *Wall Street Journal,* Nov. 21, 2017, https://www.wsj.com/.

18. Michael M. Phillips, "America's Other Endless War: Battling al-Shabaab in Somalia," *Wall Street Journal,* Jan. 17, 2019, https://www.wsj.com/.

19. Staff Sgt. Eboni Prince, "Senior U.S. Military Representative in Somali Promoted to Brigadier General," Combined Joint Task Force–Horn of Africa, June 6, 2017, http://www.hoa.africom.mil/story/21001/senior-u-s-military-representative-in-somalia-promoted-to-brigadier-general.

20. Heather Nauert, "Reestablishment of a Permanent Diplomatic Presence in Somalia," US Department of State, press release, Dec. 4, 2018, https://www.state.gov/r/pa/prs/ps/2018/12/287876.htm. See also U.S. Mission to Somalia at https://so.usmission.gov/.

21. Stephen Montemayor, "Expectations High for Somalis in Minnesota after U.S Re-establishes Permanent Diplomatic Ties," *Star Tribune,* Dec. 6, 2018, http://www.startribune.com/.

22. Ronald Reagan used the phrase, adapted from Puritan settler John Winthrop, in his election eve address in November 1980. See http://www.presidency.ucsb.edu/ws/?pid=85199.

23. Harding, *Mayor of Mogadishu,* 107.

24. Harding, *Mayor of Mogadishu,* 77–79.

25. Jie Zong and Jeanne Batalova, "Sub-Saharan African Immigrants in the United States," Migration Policy Institute, May 3, 2017, http://www.migrationpolicy.org/article/sub-saharan-african-immigrants-united-states.

26. Philip Connor and Jens Manuel Krogstad, "5 Facts about the Global Somali Diaspora," Pew Research Center, June 1, 2016, http://www.pewresearch.org/fact-tank/2016/06/01/5-facts-about-the-global-somali-diaspora/.

27. White House, Office of the Press Secretary, "Fact Sheet: Proclamation on Enhancing Vetting Capabilities and Processes for Detecting Attempted Entry into the United States by Terrorists or Other Public-Safety Threats," Sept. 24, 2017, https://www.whitehouse.gov/the-press-office/2017/09/24/fact-sheet-proclamation-enhancing-vetting-capabilities-and-processes.

28. Trump, President of the United States, et al. v. Hawaii et al., 585 U. S., ___ (2018).

29. Josh Lederman, "Trump Admin Defends New Refugee Cap of 45,000 in Coming Year," Associated Press, Sept. 27, 2017, https://www.apnews.com/.

30. Mila Koumpilova, "Minnesota Anticipates Major Drop-Off in Refugee Arrivals," Dec. 12, 2017, http://m.startribune.com/.

31. David Frum, "America's Immigration Challenge," *Atlantic,* Dec. 11, 2015, https://www.theatlantic.com/.

32. Minnesota Compass, "Groups at a Glance: Somali Foreign-Born Population," http://www.mncompass.org/immigration/groups-at-a-glance-somali.

33. Minnesota State Demographic Center, "The Economic Status of Minnesotans: A Chartbook with Data for 17 Cultural Groups," January 2016, https://mn.gov/bms-stat/assets/the-economic-status-of-minnesotans-chartbook-msdc-jan2016-post.pdf.

34. Susan Brower (Minnesota state demographer), interview with author, June 9, 2017.

Chapter 3. The First Wave

1. James Fergusson, *The World's Most Dangerous Place: Inside the Outlaw State of Somalia* (London: Black Swan, 2014), 78.

2. Fergusson, *The World's Most Dangerous Place,* 78.

3. Cedric Barnes and Harun Hassan, "The Rise and Fall of Mogadishu's Islamic Courts," *Journal of Eastern African Studies* 1, no. 2 (2007): 151–160, https://doi.org/10.1080/17531050701452382.

4. Mapping Militant Organizations, "Al Shabaab," Stanford University, http://web.stanford.edu/group/mappingmilitants/cgi-bin/groups/view/61.

5. Mapping Militant Organizations, "Al Shabaab."

6. Barnes and Hassan, "The Rise and Fall of Mogadishu's Islamic Courts."

7. Jaylani Hussein (executive director, CAIR-MN), interview with author, Aug. 4, 2016.

8. US Department of State, "Foreign Terrorist Organizations," https://www.state.gov/j/ct/rls/other/des/123085.htm.

9. According to legal records, the ten men killed were Dahir Mohamud Gure (nicknamed "Abdiwahab" or "Musab"), Shirwa Mohamud Ahmed ("Timaweyne" or "Abdirahman"), Zakaria Sharif Maruf ("Abu Muslim"), Abdirashid Ali Omar, Mohamoud Ali Hassan, Jamal Aweys Sheikh Bana, Troy Matthew Kastigar, Burhan Ibrahim Hassan ("Little Bashir"), Mohamed Osman ("Bashi"), and Farah Mohamed Beledi. Five who traveled and returned to face prosecution were Kamal Said Hassan ("Abshir"), Abdifatah Yusuf Isse ("Omar"), Salah Osman Ahmed ("Salman"), Mahamud Said Omar ("Omar Sharif" or "Abti"), and Mahdi Hussein Furreh. The al-Shabab recruits still believed alive, as of 2019, were Abdikadir Ali Abdi ("Hopkins" or "Omar"), Khalid Mohamud Abshir ("Abdullah"), Cabdullaahi Ahmed Faarax ("Adaki"), Omar Ali Farah, Mohamed Abdullahi Hassan ("Miski"), Abdiweli Isse (or Esse) ("Farhan"), Ahmed Ali Omar ("Mustafa"), and Mustafa Ali Salat. Another man, Abdisalan Hussein Ali ("Bullethead"), reportedly died in a suicide attack in 2011 on African Union troops in Mogadishu, but this has not been confirmed.

10. The eight included Ahmed Hussein Mahamud, Adarus Abdulle Ali, Saynab Abdirashid Hussein, Omer Abdi Mohamed, Abdow Munye Abdow, and three women fundraisers, Amina Farah Ali, Hawo Mohamed Hassan, and Amina Mohamud Esse.

11. US Department of Justice, "Terror Charges Unsealed in Minneapolis Against Eight Men, Justice Department Announces," press release no. 09-1267, Nov. 23, 2009, https://www.justice.gov/opa/pr/terror-charges-unsealed-minneapolis-against-eight-men-justice-department-announces.

12. US Department of Justice, "Terror Charges Unsealed in Minneapolis Against Eight Men, Justice Department Announces," press release no. 09-1267, Nov. 23, 2009, https://www.justice.gov/opa/pr/terror-charges-unsealed-minneapolis-against-eight-men-justice-department-announces.

13. David Hanners, "Somali Terror Trial: Suicide Bomber was Reluctant Terrorist, Jury Hears," *Twin Cities Pioneer Press,* Oct. 8, 2012, http://www.twincities.com/.

14. Laura Yuen, "Former al-Shabab Recruit Turned Witness to Face Deportation," Minnesota Public Radio News, Feb. 5, 2015, https://www.mprnews.org/.

15. US Department of Justice, "Four More Men Sentenced for Providing Material Support to Terrorists," press release, May 14, 2013, https://www.justice.gov/usao-mn/pr/four-more-men-sentenced-providing-material-support-terrorists.

16. Mike Carter and Ian Ith, "Somali-Born Roosevelt Grad Pleads Guilty to Terror Acts," *Seattle Times,* July 16, 2009, http://www.seattletimes.com/.

17. Sharon Schmickle, "Sudden Notoriety: Mosque in Minneapolis Draws Scrutiny from U.S. Senate, FBI and International Media," MinnPost, March 20, 2009, https://www.minnpost.com/.

18. US Department of Justice, "Federal Jury Convicts Minneapolis Man of Supporting Foreign Terrorists," press release, Oct. 18, 2012, https://archives.fbi.gov/archives/minneapolis/press-releases/2012/federal-jury-convicts-minneapolis-man-of-supporting-foreign-terrorists.

19. Brandt Williams, "Kamal Said Hassan, Mahamud Said Omar Sentenced in al-Shabab Terrorism Trial," MPR News, May 14, 2013, https://www.mprnews.org/.

20. John F. Docherty (assistant US attorney), interview with author, Nov. 9, 2017, in Minneapolis.

21. US Department of Justice, "Minneapolis Man Pleads Guilty to Terrorism Offense," press release, July 18, 2011, https://www.justice.gov/archive/usao/mn/press/jul016.pdf.

22. Dan Browning, "Alleged Minneapolis Somali Terror Recruit Is Back in Jail," *Star Tribune*, Oct. 24, 2012, http://www.startribune.com/.

23. US Department of Justice, "Four More Men Sentenced For Providing Material Support to Terrorists," press release, May 14, 2013, https://www.justice.gov/usao-mn/pr/four-more-men-sentenced-providing-material-support-terrorists.

24. Charles J. Kovats Jr. (assistant US attorney), email to author, Dec. 7, 2017.

25. Affidavit of Michael N. Cannizzaro Jr., an FBI special agent, in U.S. v. Cabdullaahi Ahmed Faarax and Abdiweli Yassin Isse, Oct. 8, 2009, https://graphics8.nytimes.com/packages/pdf/us/20091124_TERROR_DOCS/faarax.pdf.

26. FBI's "Most Wanted" list, https://www.fbi.gov/wanted/seeking-info/providing-material-support-1/cabdulaahi-ahmed-faarax/view.

27. Jay Newton-Small, "An Alleged Terrorist's Family Waits in Hope and Fear," *Time*, Sept. 27, 2013, http://time.com/.

28. *Congressional Hearing to Testify at a Hearing Entitled: Violent Islamist Extremists: "Al Shabaab Recruitment in America," before the S. Comm. on Homeland Security and Government Affairs* (2009) (statement of Osman Ahmed, on behalf of the victim families), https://www.hsgac.senate.gov/imo/media/doc/031109Ahmed.pdf?attempt=2.

29. Alexander Lee, "Who Becomes a Terrorist?: Poverty, Education, and the Origins of Political Violence," *World Politics*, 63, no. 2 (April 2011): 203–45

30. Brian Todd, "Family Learned over Internet That Son Was Killed," CNN, July 24, 2009, http://www.cnn.com/.

31. Allie Shah and Dan Browning, "Emotional Mom of Slain Somali Man Says Son Just Vanished," *Star Tribune*, Oct. 4, 2012, http://www.startribune.com/.

32. Mohamoud Ali Hassan, "Essay by Mohamoud Hassan" (posted on Facebook in May 2007 under the name of Bashir Caydid Maxamed), *New York Times*, July 10, 2009, http://www.nytimes.com/.

33. Andrea Elliott, "A Call to Jihad, Answered in America," *New York Times,* July 11, 2009, https://www.nytimes.com/.

34. Al-Katai'b Media, "The Path to Paradise: From the Twin Cities to the Land of the Two Migrations," part 1, http://jihadology.net/2013/08/07/al-kataib-media-presents-a-new-video-message-from-%e1%b8%a5arakat-al-shabab-al-mujahidin-the-path-to-paradise-from-the-twin-cities-to-the-land-of-the-two-migrations/.

35. *Congressional Hearing to Testify* (Ahmed).

36. Laura Yuen and Sasha Aslanian, "Minnesota Pipeline to al-Shabab," Minnesota Public Radio News, November 2011, updated Sept. 25, 2013, http://minnesota.publicradio.org/projects/ongoing/somali_timeline/.

Chapter 4. Blind Devotion

1. Jaylani Hussein (executive director of CAIR-MN), interview with author, Aug. 4, 2016.

2. Hon. Yusuf Hassan Abdi (member of the Parliament of Kenya), interview with author, July 18, 2016, in Nairobi.

Chapter 5. A Cautionary Tale

1. Abdirashid Bashir Hassan, interview with author, Aug. 2016, in Minneapolis.

2. Kirsti Marohn, "Fact Check: How Somali Names are Chosen," *SC Times,* Feb. 22, 2016, https://www.sctimes.com/.

3. Ahmed Ismail Yusuf, *Somalis in Minnesota* (St. Paul: Minnesota Historical Society Press, 2012), 20–27.

4. Minnesota State Demographic Center, "The Economic Status of Minnesotans: A Chartbook with Data for 17 Cultural Groups," January 2016, p. 17, https://mn.gov/bms-stat/assets/the-economic-status-of-minnesotans-chartbook-msdc-jan2016-post.pdf.

5. Minnesota Compass, "Groups at a Glance: Somali Foreign-Born Population," http://www.mncompass.org/immigration/groups-at-a-glance-somali.

6. Stefanie Chambers, *Somalis in the Twin Cities and Columbus: Immigrant Incorporation in New Destinations* (Philadelphia: Temple University Press, 2017), 140–141

7. Cawo M. Abdi, *Elusive Jannah: The Somali Diaspora and the Borderless Muslim Identity,* (Minneapolis: University of Minnesota Press, 2015), 188–189

8. Chambers, *Somalis in the Twin Cities and Columbus,* 141.

9. Minnesota State Demographic Center, "Economic Status of Minnesotans," 19.

10. Abdi, *Elusive Jannah,* 184–185

11. US Department of Justice, "Investigation into Sex Trafficking of Juveniles Results in Federal Indictment Charging 29 Persons," press release, Nov. 8, 2010, https://archives.fbi.

gov/archives/memphis/press-releases/2010/me110810.htm.

12. Travis Loller, "Tenn. Judge Acquits Three of Sex Trafficking," *San Diego Union-Tribune,* Dec. 19, 2012, http://www.sandiegouniontribune.com/.

13. Amy Forliti, "Somali Community Wants Its Youth to Look beyond Gangs," *Twin Cities Pioneer Press,* Feb. 6, 2011, updated Nov. 12, 2015, http://www.twincities.com/.

14. Evan Andrews, "7 Infamous Gangs of New York," June 4, 2013, The History Channel, http://www.history.com/news/history-lists/7-infamous-gangs-of-new-york.

15. Federal Bureau of Investigation, "History of La Cosa Nostra," https://www.fbi.gov/ investigate/organized-crime/history-of-la-cosa-nostra.

16. FBI National Gang Intelligence Center, "2015 National Gang Report," https://www.fbi.gov/ file-repository/national-gang-report-2015.pdf/view.

17. Al Valdez, "Tracing the Roots of Black Gang Rivalry," *Police,* Aug. 1, 1996, http://www. policemag.com/.

18. Gordon Mathews, interview with author, Aug. 2017, in Hong Kong.

Chapter 7. Why ISIS?

1. *Encyclopaedia Britannica Online,* s.v. "caliphate" by Asma Afsaruddin, https://www. britannica.com/.

2. Analysts have looked to earlier research on cults to enhance their understanding of recruitment. See Daniel Koehler, "Methods, Sources, State of the Art," in *Understanding Deradicalization: Methods, Tools and Programs for Countering Violent Extremism* (Oxon and New York: Routledge, 2017), 10–64.

3. Saul Levine, *Radical Departures: Desperate Detours to Growing Up* (New York: Harcourt, Brace, Jovanovich, 1984), 10–11.

4. Julie E. Allyn (assistant US attorney), interview with author, Nov. 9, 2017, in Minneapolis.

5. Randy Furst, "Minneapolis Family Worries That Son, 20, Is Headed to Syria," *Star Tribune,* June 4, 2014, http://www.startribune.com/.

6. Mike Eckel and Harun Maruf, "'Why He Chose to Leave This Good Land?': Islamic State Beckons and Somali Americans Again Struggle with Radicalization," Voice of America, Nov. 20, 2014, https://www.voanews.com/.

7. Scott Shane, "From Minneapolis to ISIS: An American's Path to Jihad," *New York Times,* March 21, 2015, https://www.nytimes.com/.

8. Eckel and Maruf, "'Why He Chose to Leave This Good Land?'"

9. Stephen Montemayor, "Sister of ISIL Co-conspirator Testifies He Planned to Die for the Cause," *Star Tribune,* May 17, 2016, http://www.startribune.com/.

10. Exhibit 53 in U.S. v. Mohamed Abdihamid Farah, Abdirahman Yasin Daud, and Guled Ali

Omar.

11. Saul Levine (psychiatrist), phone interview with author, July 4, 2016.

12. Levine, *Radical Departures,* 38.

13. James. R. Lewis, *Cults: A Reference and Guide,* 3rd ed. (Sheffield, UK: Equinox, 2012), 44.

14. Rodney Stark and William Sims Bainbridge, *The Future of Religion: Secularization, Revival, and Cult Formation* (Berkeley: University of California Press, 1985), 395.

15. Jonah Goldberg, *Suicide of the West: How the Rebirth of Tribalism, Populism, Nationalism, and Identity Politics Is Destroying American Democracy* (New York: Crown Forum, 2018), 356.

16. Lena Slachmuijlder, *Transforming Violent Extremism: A Peacebuilder's Guide,* 1st ed., (Washington, DC: Search for Common Ground, 2017), 10, https://www.sfcg.org/transforming-violent-extremism-peacebuilders-guide/.

17. Kevin D. Lowry (former chief US probation officer, Minnesota federal court), phone conversations with author, March 26, 2018, and July 27, 2018.

18. Paul Joosse, Sandra M. Bucerius, and Sara K. Thompson, "Narratives and Counternarratives: Somali-Canadians on Recruitment as Foreign Fighters to Al-Shabaab," *British Journal of Criminology* 55, no. 4 (2015): 811–832, doi:10.1093/bjc/azu103.

19. Zakaria Amara, "Deradicalisation—The Boy Who Built His Dreams on Sand," *insidetime,* March 1, 2019, https://insidetime.org/deradicalisation-the-boy-who-built-his-dreams-on-sand/.

20. Center for Law, Brain and Behavior at Massachusetts General Hospital, "Brain Science is Reforming Juvenile Justice, Policy and Practice," http://clbb.mgh.harvard.edu/juvenilejustice/.

21. Leah Somerville (associate professor of psychology at Harvard University; Center for Law, Brain and Behavior, Massachusetts General Hospital), phone interview with author, March 14, 2018.

22. The dead among the second wave of people, those who joined or sought to join ISIS, included Douglas McAuthur McCain, Abdifatah Ahmed also known as Abdirahmaan Muhumed, Yusuf Jama, along with Bashir's Minnesota cousin, Hanad Mohallim, and Canadian cousins Hamsa Kariye, Hersi Kariye, and Mahad Hirsi. Also killed in Syria was Mohamud Mohamed Mohamud, whose father lived in Minnesota. Abdi Mohamud Nur, another Minnesota traveler, is believed dead. Other travelers include Mohamed Amiin Ali Roble, who is believed dead, and Yusra Ismail, whose fate in 2019 was unknown. Another Minnesota traveler, Abdelhamid al-Madioum, turned up, injured, in a prison in northeastern Syria in September 2019.

Chapter 8. A Special Case

1. Transcript of direct examination by Glenn P. Bruder, U.S. v. Mohamed Abdihamid Farah, Abdirahman Yasin Daud, and Guled Ali Omar, trial vol. 13, Case No. 15-CR-49 (MJD/FLN), May 26, 2016, 35.

2. Transcript of direct examination by Bruder, *Farah, Daud, and Omar,* 26.

3. See Abby Simons, "New Gun Charge against Man Convicted of Threatening FBI Agents," *Star Tribune,* June 30, 2015, http://www.startribune.com/.

4. Transcript of sentencing hearing, U.S. v. Guled Ali Omar, Case No. 15-CR-49 (7) (MJD/FLN), Nov. 16, 2016, 26.

5. Transcript of sentencing hearing, *Guled Ali Omar,* 31 . Here is more of Winter's statement:

> Make no mistake, the government views this defendant as extraordinarily dangerous. He not only talked about how the kuffar [non-Muslims] are going to get it, America's time is coming, he had a plan for it and he was going to get over to Syria and then he was going to provide the routing information so his ISIL brothers could come back and, as he says, do crazy damage here. It is a great opportunity. So he's dangerous at that macrolevel. He also is the one that was talking about bringing a pistol with him to the border of Mexico, in case somebody tried to stop him, he could shoot them. . . . At the end of the day, we have a man, he is not a boy, he is not a kid, who presents a very, very unique case. He's been convicted of conspiring to commit murder outside the United States. He's been convicted of conspiring to provide material support. He's been convicted of two separate and distinct attempts to do so, has denied these up and down with insane lines, and, of course, using financial aid, attempting to use financial aid, to fund. He lies. He denies. He counter-accuses. He claims racial and social prejudice. He attempts to ride the coattails of the hardships of others, like his parents, in order to excuse his own criminal behavior and only when backed into a corner does he attempt to offer false contrition as he has done today. You can't fix manipulative. You can't fix deceitful. And you can't fix Guled Omar. Not in a manner that's consistent with public safety. Ultimately, this defendant has blood on his hands, Your Honor. He's got blood on his hands from people he's helped get overseas who are dead.

6. Transcript of sentencing hearing, *Guled Ali Omar,* 26–27.

7. Transcript of direct examination by Bruder, *Farah, Daud, and Omar,* 6 (quoted throughout this chapter).

8. Laura Yuen, "Guled Omar: The Path to ISIS and the Story You Haven't Heard," Minnesota

Public Radio News, Dec. 22, 2016, https://www.mprnews.org/.

9. Wendell Berry, *What Are People For? Essays* (Berkeley, CA: Counterpoint, 2010).

10. Transcript of sentencing hearing, *Guled Ali Omar,* 8–10. Here is more of Bruder's statement:

> Guled never really felt like he fit in, either in Islamic society, at his mosque, or
> in western society. You heard his testimony at trial, and you heard that although
> he had friends at school, not one of them ever visited his home, nor was he
> ever invited to theirs. The PSR [pre-sentence report] indicates that Guled felt
> inadequate and powerless. That's not atypical of first generation Somali youth.
> The PSR recounts the abuse and the violence that Guled experienced growing
> up, violence that was actually shocking even to a veteran probation officer.
> I think that comes through clearly in the report. Guled found his identity
> and sense of purpose with his co-defendants, all of whom were swayed by
> professionally produced ISIS propaganda videos. . . . And then on top of that,
> something that's specifically mentioned in Mr. Omar's PSR, you've got the
> veneer of intellectual respectability and theological correctness prepared by
> the al-Awlaki videos that are equally available on the internet. Mr. Omar says
> that he watched those and was heavily influenced by those. I think it becomes a
> little bit more understandable why someone—how someone like Guled Omar,
> who delights in playing with his young nephews and caring for them and his
> family views him as a source of strength, somebody who is very caring and
> compassionate, who empathizes with refugees, could be influenced by those
> videos, whether it's al-Awlaki or the ISIS videos, to want to try to have some—
> find some sense of meaning in his life, meaning beyond smoking marijuana and
> using the potpourri of drugs that he admits to using during this period of time.

Chapter 9. Peer to Peer

1. Dina Temple-Raston, "For Somalis in Minnesota, Jihadi Recruiting is a Recurring
   Nightmare," National Public Radio, Feb. 18, 2015, http://www.npr.org/.

2. Amy Forliti, "6 Men from Minnesota Charged with Trying to Join Islamic State Group,"
   U.S. News & World Report, April 21, 2015, https://www.usnews.com/.

3. Al-Katai'b Media, "The Path to Paradise: From the Twin Cities to the Land of the Two
   Migrations," part 1, http://jihadology.net/2013/08/07/al-kataib-media-presents-a-new-
   video-message-from-%e1%b8%a5arakat-al-shabab-al-mujahidin-the-path-to-paradise-
   from-the-twin-cities-to-the-land-of-the-two-migrations/.

4. Amy Forliti, "Struggling Minneapolis Man, Facing Child Support, Goes to Syria to Fight

for Islamic State," *U.S. News & World Report,* May 20, 2015, http://www.usnews.com/.

5. Stephen Montemayor, "Feds Have At Least Six Open Cases Looking at ISIS Support in Minnesota," *Star Tribune,* Sept. 9, 2017, http://www.startribune.com/.

6. Ben Hubbard, "'What Is Going to Happen to Us?' Inside ISIS Prison, Children Ask Their Fate," *New York Times,* Oct. 23, 2019, http:www.nytimes.com/. Also, Holly Williams, "American inside Syrian Prison Says He Was Recruited to ISIS Online," CBS News, Sept. 17, 2019, http:www.cbsnews.com/.

Chapter 10. A Woman's Place?

1. US Department of Justice, "Minnesota Woman Charged with Stealing Passport to Travel to Syria," press release, Dec. 2, 2014, https://www.justice.gov/usao-mn/pr/minnesota-woman-charged-stealing-passport-travel-syria.

2. Paul McEnroe, "St. Paul Woman Charged with Stealing Passport to Travel to Syria," *Star Tribune,* Dec. 3, 2014, http://www.startribune.com/.

3. Jamie Dettmer, "Jihadists Turn to Mainstream Matchmaking Site for Partners," Voice of America, May 1, 2017, https://www.voanews.com/.

4. Bevan Hurley, "The Jihadi and Me: Conversations with 'Bumbling' Kiwi Jihadi Mark John Taylor," *Sunday Star Times,* Dec. 18, 2016, http://www.stuff.co.nz/world/middle-east/87592895/the-jihadi-and-me-conversations-with-bumbling-kiwi-jihadi-mark-john-taylor.

5. Office of the Spokesperson, US State Department, "State Department Terrorist Designations of El Shafee Elsheikh, Anjem Choudary, Sami Bouras, Shane Dominic Crawford, and Mark John Taylor," media note, March 31, 2017, https://www.state.gov/r/pa/prs/ps/2017/03/269306.htm.

6. Mike Ives, "New Zealand Won't Revoke ISIS Member's Citizenship, but He May Face Charges," *New York Times,* March 4, 2019, https://www.nytimes.com/.

7. Dettmer, "Jihadists Turn to Mainstream Matchmaking Site for Partners."

8. Dettmer, "Jihadists Turn to Mainstream Matchmaking Site for Partners."

9. Erin Marie Saltman and Melanie Smith, "'Till Martyrdom Do Us Part': Gender and the ISIS Phenomenon," Institute for Strategic Dialogue (2015), https://www.isdglobal.org/wp-content/uploads/2016/02/Till_Martyrdom_Do_Us_Part_Gender_and_the_ISIS_Phenomenon.pdf.

10. Saltman and Smith, "Till Martyrdom Do Us Part," 9.

11. Saltman and Smith, "Till Martyrdom Do Us Part," 13.

12. Saltman and Smith, "Till Martyrdom Do Us Part," 20–27.

13. Laura Burnip, "Hotbed of Terror: How Manchester Bomber Lived Streets away from

Notorious 'Terror Twins,' a Top ISIS Recruiter and More Than a Dozen Known Jihadis,"
Sun, May 24, 2017, https://www.thesun.co.uk/. Also see Mark Townsend, Daniel Boffey,
Kate Connolly, and Ben Quinn, "The Race to Find the Manchester Terror Network,"
Guardian, May 28, 2017, https://www.theguardian.com/; Sean O'Neill, Fiona Hamilton,
Fariha Karim, and Gabriella Swerling, "Huge Scale of Terror Threat Revealed: UK Home to
23,000 Jihadists," *Times,* May 27, 2017, https://www.thetimes.co.uk/.

14. Saltman and Smith, "Till Martyrdom Do Us Part," 20–27.

15. Asne Seierstad, "My Daughters Ran Away to Join Isis: The True Story of a Dad Who Faced
Torture and Terror to Find His Children," *Sunday Times,* March 4, 2018, https://www.
thetimes.co.uk/.

16. Lizzie Dearden, "Isis Austrian Poster Girl Samra Kesinovic 'Used as Sex Slave' before
Being Murdered for Trying to Escape," *Independent,* Dec. 31, 2015, http://www.
independent.co.uk/.

17. Tony Paterson, "Austrian 'Jihad Poster Girls' Tell Friends: We Want to Come Home,"
Independent, Oct. 13, 2014, http://www.independent.co.uk/.

18. Rita Katz, "From Teenage Colorado Girls to Islamic State Recruits: A Case Study in
Radicalization via Social Media," *Insite Blog on Terrorism and Extremism,* Nov. 14, 2014,
http://news.siteintelgroup.com/blog/index.php/entry/309-from-teenage-colorado-girls-
to-islamic-state-recruits-a-case-study-in-radicalization-via-social-media.

19. Middle East Media Research Institute, "Top Female ISIS Recruiter Revealed to Be
American from Seattle," May 1, 2015, https://www.memri.org/jttm/top-female-isis-
recruiter-revealed-be-american-seattle.

20. Amanda Macias, "Major ISIS Online Recruiter Identified as a Journalism Student in
Seattle," *Business Insider,* April 30, 2015, http://www.businessinsider.com/.

21. Greg Holloway (assistant US attorney), interview with author, July 20, 2015, in Denver.
Holloway was involved in prosecuting several terrorists and would-be terrorists,
including Shannon Maureen Conley, a convert to Islam from the Denver area who, in a
January 2015 plea deal, was sentenced to four years in prison after she attempted to leave
the United States to join ISIS in April 2014, when she was nineteen. Conley subsequently
condemned ISIS's brutality.

22. Ben Brumfield, "3 Denver Girls Played Hooky from School and Tried to Join ISIS,"
CNN, updated Oct. 22, 2014, http://www.cnn.com/. The article contains a link to
the Arapahoe County Sheriff's Department runaway child reports at https://www.
scribd.com/fullscreen/243901601?access_key=key-luderqtQz5qlo470uXCU&allow_
share=true&escape=false&viewmode=scroll&irgwc=1&content=10079&campaign=
Skimbit%2C%2Ltd.&ad_group=87732X1540624X77383b9e78aea6ea0fd873c968dc5d6e

&keyword=ft750noi&source=impactradius&medium=affiliate.

23. LeakSource, Aug. 19, 2014, and Sept. 2, 2014, https://leaksource.wordpress. com/2014/08/19/graphic-video-islamic-state-beheads-american-journalist-james-foley/.

24. Jesse Paul, "Analyst Group: Colorado Teens Spoke with Top Islamic State Terrorists," *Denver Post,* Oct. 29, 2014, updated April 26, 2016, http://www.denverpost.com/.

25. Alexander Meleagrou-Hitchens, Seamus Hughes, and Bennett Clifford, *The Travelers: American Jihadists in Syria and Iraq* (Washington, DC: Program on Extremism at the George Washington University, 2018), 17, https://extremism.gwu.edu/sites/g/files/ zaxdzs2191/f/TravelersAmericanJihadistsinSyriaandIraq.pdf.

26. Eric Schmitt and Somini Sengupta, "Thousands Enter Syria to Join ISIS despite Global Efforts," *New York Times,* Sept. 26, 2015, https://www.nytimes.com/.

27. Richard Barrett, "Beyond the Caliphate: Foreign Fighters and the Threat of Returnees," The Soufan Center, Oct. 2017, p. 7, http://thesoufancenter.org/research/beyond-caliphate/.

28. Barrett, "Beyond the Caliphate," 26.

29. Isabel Coles, "Hard-Core Islamic State Members Carry Ideology from Crushed Caliphate," *Wall Street Journal,* March 18, 2019, https://www.wsj.com/.

Chapter 11. Brotherhood

1. See Bill Chappell, "Judge Vacates Terrorism Convictions of Man Who Had Trained with Paintball Group," NPR, July 20, 2018, https://www.npr.org/.

2. See William McCants, "ISIS Fantasies of an Apocalyptic Showdown in Northern Syria," Brookings Institution blog *Markaz,* Oct. 3, 2014, https://www.brookings.edu/blog/ markaz/2014/10/03/isis-fantasies-of-an-apocalyptic-showdown-in-northern-syria/.

3. Laura Yuen, Mukhtar Ibrahim, and Sasha Aslanian, "Called to Fight: Minnesota's ISIS Recruits," MPR News, March 25, 2015, https://www.mprnews.org/. The eight men who attended Heritage, in some cases transferring in from diverse public high schools, were Abdirahman Bashir, Zacharia Abdurahman, Abdirahman Yasin Daud, Adnan Farah, Mohamed Abdihamid Farah, Hanad Abdullahi Mohallim, Abdullahi Yusuf, and Abdirizak Warsame.

4. Phone interview with a Minnesota school group official, May 4, 2017.

5. Affidavit of Nicholas L. Marshall, FBI special agent, in U.S. v. Mohamed Abdihamid Farah, Adnan Abdihamid Farah, Abdurahman Yasin Daud, Zacharia Yusuf Abdurahman, Hanad Mustafe Musse, and Guled Ali Omar, April 18, 2015, https://extremism.gwu.edu/sites/ extremism.gwu.edu/files/Daud%20Criminal%20Complaint.pdf.

6. Kenneth Ubong Udoibok (attorney), interview with author, May 17, 2017, with additions

and corrections by email, September 25, 2017.

7. Jon M. Hopeman (attorney), interview with author, Feb. 6, 2017.

8. Yusuf Abdurahman, interview with author, March 21, 2019.

9. Angella LaTour (director of community affairs, US Attorney's Office), interview with author, Nov. 29, 2017.

10. Alejandra Matos, "Minneapolis School District Takes Over Heritage Academy," *Star Tribune,* Oct. 28, 2015, http://www.startribune.com/.

11. Mukhtar Ibrahim, "Heritage Academy Students Walk out in Protest over Firing, Demand Leadership Change," MPR News, Jan. 8, 2016, https://www.mprnews.org/.

12. Ted Haller, "Minneapolis Public Schools to Take Over Troubled Contract School," Fox 9 News, Oct. 26, 2015, http://www.fox9.com/.

13. Somali American Parents Association, 2015 Form 990, available from the 990 Finder at The Foundation Center, http://990s.foundationcenter.org/990_pdf_ archive/263/263120451/263120451_201512_990.pdf.

14. Mila Koumpilova, "Somali-American Father Shares with Parents the Painful Lessons He Learned in Minnesota," *Star Tribune,* Dec. 28, 2016, http://www.startribune.com/.

15. Kelly Smith and Paul Walsh, "Food Fight Erupts into Melee at Minneapolis South High School," *Star Tribune,* Feb. 15, 2013, http://www.startribune.com/.

16. Mary McKinley (executive director, Heartland Democracy Center), phone interview with author, May 4, 2017.

17. Dina Temple-Raston, "He Was Caught Trying to Join ISIS, Now He's in Jihadi Rehab," National Public Radio, May 16, 2016, http://www.npr.org/.

18. McKinley, email to author, Sept. 28, 2017.

19. Data from Minneapolis Public Schools, "Graduation Rate," 2013–2018, https://insights. mpls.k12.mn.us/SchoolBoardPortal/graduation.html.

20. Minneapolis Public Schools Graduations 2018, streamed on Vimeo, https://livestream. com/iDreamTV/MPSGRAD2018/videos/176386535.

21. Dina Temple-Raston, "He Wanted Jihad. He Got Foucault: Why Would an American Teenager Leave the Comforts of Suburbia to Fly to Syria and Join ISIS?," *New York,* Nov. 27, 2017, https://www.nytimes.com/.

22. Ahmed Amin (assistant principal), phone interview with author, April 8, 2019.

Chapter 12. The Caravan Beckons Again

1. Superseding indictment, U.S. v. Hamza Naj Ahmed, Mohamed Abdihamid Farah, Adnan Abdihamid Farah, Abdurahman Yasin Daud, Zacharia Yusuf Abdurahman, Hanad Mustofe Musse, and Guled Ali Omar. Available at https://extremism.gwu.edu/sites/

extremism.gwu.edu/files/Daud%20Superseding%20Indictment.pdf.

2. McCain's brother, Marchello Dsaun McCain, in 2016 pleaded guilty to lying to the FBI about his knowledge of his brother's plans to travel to Syria. He admitted to helping his brother go by letting him use a debit card belonging to his wife to pay for the trip, and to various gun-possession charges. See R. Stickney and Associated Press reports, "San Diego Man Admits to Lying to FBI about Brother's Ties to ISIS," 7 San Diego, https://www.nbcsandiego.com/. Marchello McCain was sentenced to ten years in federal prison. See US Department of Justice, "Brother of San Diego Man Killed Fighting for ISIS Sentenced to 10 Years for Terrorism Related Charges and Illegal Firearms Possession," press release, Jan. 12, 2018, https://www.justice.gov/opa/pr/brother-san-diego-man-killed-fighting-isis-sentenced-10-years-terrorism-related-charges-and.

3. Federal authorities in October 2019 extradited a thirty-four-year-old Canadian, Abdullahi Ahmed Abdullahi, to San Diego to stand trial for conspiring with Douglas McCain to aid Bashir's cousins and at least two Americans to join ISIS. See US Justice Department "Canadian National Extradited to San Diego to Face Terrorism Charges," press release, Oct. 25, 2019, https://www.justice.gov/usao-sdca/pr/canadian-national-extradited-san-diego-face-terrorism-charges.

4. Steve Karnowski, "Minnesota Man Changes Plea to Guilty in Islamic State Case," Associated Press, April 14, 2016, https://apnews.com/.

5. Transcript of direct examination by Glenn P. Bruder, U.S. v. Mohamed Abdihamid Farah, Abdirahman Yasin Daud, and Guled Ali Omar, trial vol. 13, No. 15-CR-49 (MJD/FLN), May 26, 2016, 78.

Chapter 13. The Glory of the Shahid

1. Muslim Public Affairs Council, "Religious Views on Suicide: Perspectives from World Religions," https://www.mpac.org/programs/anti-terrorism-campaign/islamic-views-regarding-terrorism-and-suicidem/religious-views-on-suicide.php.

2. See Rowenna Davis, "Bin Laden: The War in His Words," *Guardian,* May 2, 2011, https://www.theguardian.com/.

3. David Brooks, "The Culture of Martyrdom: How Suicide Bombing Became Not Just a Means but an End," *Atlantic,* June 2002, https://www.theatlantic.com/.

4. Haim Malka, "Must Innocents Die? The Islamic Debate over Suicide Attacks," Brookings Institution, March 1, 2003, https://www.brookings.edu/articles/must-innocents-die-the-islamic-debate-over-suicide-attacks/.

5. Palestinian Media Watch, "Hamas Leaders: We Love Death like Israelis Love Life," July 30, 2014, http://palwatch.org/main.aspx?fi=1046&fld_id=1046&doc_id=12234.

6. Homer, *The Iliad of Homer,* trans. Alexander Pope (London, 1899; Project Gutenberg, 2006), bk. 15, p. 280, http://www.gutenberg.org/files/6130/6130-h/6130-h.html.

7. Louis Rawlings, *The Ancient Greeks at War* (New York: Manchester University Press, 2007), 196.

8. John H. Miller, *American Political and Cultural Perspectives on Japan: From Perry to Obama* (Lanham, MD: Lexington Books, 2014), 41.

9. History.com Editors, "First Kamikaze Attack of the War Begins," *History,* A&E Television Networks, Nov. 16, 2009, http://www.history.com/this-day-in-history/first-kamikaze-attack-of-the-war-begins.

10. See Nancy Bartlit and Richard Yalman, "Japanese Mass Suicides," Atomic Heritage Foundation, July 28, 2016, http://www.atomicheritage.org/history/japanese-mass-suicides.

11. Qais bin Zayed, "Islam Does Not Tolerate the Killing of Innocents," IslamWeb.net (English), Dec. 12, 2012, http://www.islamweb.net/en/article/113432/islam-does-not-tolerate-the-killing-of-innocents.

12. "Qu'ran, Hadith and Scholars: Jihadists," WikiIslam, Aug. 13, 2013, https://wikiislam.net/wiki/Qur%27an,_Hadith_and_Scholars:Jihadists. Denise Chow, "What Does Islamic Faith Promise Martyrs?," Live Science, March 29, 2010, https://www.livescience.com/6237-islamic-faith-promise-martyrs.html.

13. Brian Fishman, "Suicide as a Weapon in Iraq," in *Suicide as a Weapon,* ed. NATO Centre of Excellence–Defence Against Terrorism (Amsterdam: IOS, 2007), 67.

14. Eli Lake, "The Palestinian Incentive Program for Killing Jews," Bloomberg View, *National Post,* July 1, 2016, http://nationalpost.com/.

15. Margaret Coker and Falih Hassan, "Iraq Prime Minister Declares Victory over ISIS," *New York Times,* Dec. 9, 2017, https://www.nytimes.com/.

16. See Robin Wright, "The Ignominious End of the ISIS Caliphate," *New Yorker,* Oct. 17, 2017, https://www.newyorker.com/.

17. Chicago Project on Security and Terrorism (CPOST), Suicide Attack Database, Oct. 12, 2016, https://cpost.uchicago.edu/.

18. BBC Monitoring, "Dabiq: Why Is Syrian Town So Important for IS?," Oct. 4, 2016, http://www.bbc.com/.

19. Aaron Y. Zelin, Jihadology, http://jihadology.net/category/dabiq-magazine/.

20. Joshua Keating, "ISIS's End-of-the-World Problem," *Slate,* Sept. 13, 2017, http://www.slate.com/.

21. Brooks, "The Culture of Martyrdom."

22. Adam Lankford, "What You Don't Understand about Suicide Attacks," *Scientific American,*

July 27, 2015, https://www.scientificamerican.com/.

23. Scott Zamost, Yasmin Khorram, Shimon Prokupecz, and Evan Perez, "Chattanooga Shooting: New Details Emerge about the Gunman," CNN, July 20, 2015, http://www.cnn.com/.

24. Ariel Merari, Ilan Diamant, Arie Bibi, Yoav Broshi, and Gloria Zakin, "Personality Characteristics of 'Self Martyrs'/'Suicide Bombers' and Organizers of Suicide Attacks," *Terrorism and Political Violence* 22, no. 1 (Dec. 19, 2009): 87–101, https://doi.org/10.1080/09546550903409312.

25. David Lester, "Female Suicide Bombers: Clues from Journalists," Suicidology Online, Nov. 14, 2011, http://www.suicidology-online.com/pdf/SOL-2011-2-62-66.pdf.

26. William McCants, *The ISIS Apocalypse: The History, Strategy, and Doomsday Vision of the Islamic State* (New York: St. Martin's Press, 2015), 161–164.

Chapter 14. Breaking Down

1. Carson P. Green (FBI special agent), interview with author, Nov. 8, 2017.

2. Amy Forliti, "AP Exclusive: Bridge Collapse Survivor Linked to IS in Syria," May 27, 2016, https://www.ap.org/en-us/.

3. Oliver Laughland, "Somali Americans Divided as FBI Informant Testifies against Friends," *Guardian,* May 27, 2016, https://www.theguardian.com/.

4. "Wallahi" is an idiom that has been translated as "I swear to Allah."

5. See Paul McEnroe, Abby Simons, and Libor Jany, "From the Heartland to Jihad: How a Group of Young Men from Minnesota Were Drawn into ISIL's Campaign of Terror," *Star Tribune,* Sept. 20, 2015, http://www.startribune.com/.

Chapter 15. A Very Real Threat

1. Rukmini Callimachi, "Clues on Twitter Show Ties Between Texas Gunman and ISIS Network," *New York Times,* May 11, 2015, https://www.nytimes.com/.

2. Dan Joseph and Harun Maruf, "American Al-Shabab, Nabbed in Somalia, Denies IS Links," VOA, Dec. 8, 2015, https://www.voanews.com/.

3. Charles J. Kovats Jr. (assistant US attorney), email to author, Dec. 7, 2017.

4. Abigail Hauslohner and Drew Harwell, "As Unassuming Life before a Suspect's Rampage in a Minnesota Mall," *Washington Post,* Sept. 19, 2016, https://www.washingtonpost.com/.

5. The term "as-sahabah," apparently misspelled in his post, refers to companions of the Prophet Muhammad

6. Ben Shapiro, "The Ohio State Terrorist Saw Himself as a Victim of Islamophobia," *National Review,* Nov. 30, 2016, http://www.nationalreview.com/.

7. Kate Morrissey, "Edmonton Attack Suspect Had History in San Diego Immigration Detention," *San Diego Union-Tribune,* Oct. 17, 2017, http://www.sandiegouniontribune.com/.

8. Ethan Lou, "Somali Refugee Faces Terror Charges in Canada Stabbing, Car Attacks," Reuters, Oct. 1, 2017, https://ca.reuters.com/.

9. CBC News, "Man Charged in Edmonton Attacks Was Ordered Deported from U.S. in 2011," CBC Radio Canada, Oct. 3, 2017, http://www.cbc.ca/.

10. "Abdifatah Aden," Counter Extremism Project, https://www.counterextremism.com/extremists/abdifatah-aden.

11. Alexander Meleagrou-Hitchens, Seamus Hughes, and Bennett Clifford, *The Travelers: American Jihadists in Syria and Iraq* (Washington, DC: Program on Extremism at the George Washington University, 2018), 73–74, https://extremism.gwu.edu/sites/g/files/zaxdzs2191/f/TravelersAmericanJihadistsinSyriaandIraq.pdf.

12. Amy Forliti, "Minnesota Terror Case Shows Challenge of Predicting Attacks," Associated Press, Feb. 17, 2018, https://www.apnews.com/.

13. Tad Vezner and Sarah Horner, "'You Guys Are Lucky I Don't Know How to Build a Bomb,' St. Kate's Arson Suspect Allegedly Said," *Pioneer Press,* Jan. 19, 2018, https://www.twincities.com/.

14. St. Catherine University, "Arson Incident Update," press release, Feb. 7, 2018, https://www.stkate.edu/news-and-events/news/arson-incident-update.

15. Indictment, U.S. v Tnuza Jamal Hassan, 2018, http://kstp.com/kstpImages/repository/cs/files/HASSAN%20Indictment(1).pdf.

16. Vezner and Horner, "'You Guys Are Lucky I Don't Know How to Build a Bomb.'"

Chapter 16. Straight Out of Hollywood

1. Carson P. Green (FBI special agent), interview with author, Nov. 8, 2017.

2. Warfa in 2016 returned to Somalia to be elected to the Somali Parliament.

3. Judith Dubin, Greg Campbell, Mike Shum, and Evan Engel, "ISIS in America: The Terror Trial That Shook Minnesota," Vocativ, Nov. 17, 2016, https://www.youtube.com/watch?v=wQW0N69fKXE.

4. See photo gallery by Aaron Lavinsky, published alongside Stephen Montemayor, "ISIL Defendants Either Were Part of a 'Wholehearted' Conspiracy or Were Entrapped by Government Agents," *Star Tribune,* May 31, 2016, 2017, http://www.startribune.com/.

5. Stephen Montemayor, "Minneapolis Terror Trial Opens with Tension over Lawyer, Jury," *Star Tribune,* May 10, 2016, http://www.startribune.com/.

6. The phrase, sometimes rendered as "Wallaahi, Billaahi, and Tallaahi," means "all

perfect praise to Allah" and can mean one swears by Allah or makes an oath to Allah, according to Islamweb. See "Meaning of Wallaahi, Billaahi and Tallaahi," Islamweb.net (English), Aug. 25, 2012, http://www.islamweb.net/emainpage/index. php?page=showfatwa&Option=FatwaId&Id=185289.

Chapter 17. The Backlash

1. Stephen Montemayor, "Minneapolis Mother Who Sent Payments to Al-Shabab Receives Rare Federal Probation Sentence," *Star Tribune,* April 26, 2017, http://www.startribune. com/.

2. U.S. Department of Justice, "Two Women Sentenced for Providing Material Support for Terrorists," press release no. 17-344, March 31, 2017, https://www.justice.gov/opa/pr/two-women-sentenced-providing-material-support-terrorists.

3. Stephen Montemayor, "Minnesota Woman's Al-Shabab Guilty Plea Unveiled, Linked to Virginia Terrorism Case," *Star Tribune,* July 1, 2016, http://www.startribune.com/.

4. For the Group of Fifteen's discussions, see Joint motion to close defendant's guilty plea and seal the transcript of the hearing, U.S. v. Amina Mohamed Esse, Case No. 14-CR-00369 MJD, June 30, 2016, Document 19, http://kstp.com/kstpImages/repository/cs/files/AminaEsse.pdf. For Sheikh Hassan Hussein's support for ISIS, see Avraham Ben Adam, "Al Shabaab 'Spiritual Leader,' Sheikh Hussein, Pledges an Oath of Allegiance to ISIL," Strategic Intelligence News, March 23, 2015, http://intelligencebriefs.com/al-shabaab-spiritual-leader-sheikh-hassan-hussein-pledges-an-oath-of-allegiance-to-isil/. Also, see Yasmin Juma, "Al Shabaab Cleric Gives Daesh Stamp of Approval," Hiiraan Online, March 19, 2015, https://www.hiiraan.com/news4/2015/Mar/98655/al_shabaab_cleric_gives_daesh_stamp_of_approval.aspx.

5. Charles J. Kovats Jr. (assistant US attorney), interview with author, May 17, 2017.

6. Amy Forliti, "Minnesota Woman Gets Probation for Supporting Al-Shabab," *U.S. News & World Report,* April 26, 2017, https://www.usnews.com/.

7. Elliott Spagat, "Somali Woman Gets Prison for Terror Support," *San Diego Union-Tribune,* Dec. 11, 2012, http://www.sandiegouniontribune.com/.

8. Indictment, U.S. v. Amina Farah Ali and Hawo Mohamed Hassan, Case No. CR 10-187 PJS/FLN, 2010, https://www.investigativeproject.org/documents/case_docs/1355.pdf.

9. Sentencing appeal, U.S. v. Amina Farah Ali, No. 11-3512 (U.S. Court of Appeals for the Eighth Circuit, June 4, 2012), https://ecf.ca8.uscourts.gov/opndir/12/06/113512P.pdf.

10. Allie Shah and Rose French, "Defendant in Somali Terror Case Changes Stance on Standing," *Star Tribune,* Oct. 5, 2011, http://www.startribune.com/.

11. Dan Browning, "Judge Reinstates Contempt Charges against Somali Woman," *Star*

Tribune, Sept. 18, 2012, http://www.startribune.com/.

12. Richard Sennot, video with "Two Rochester Women Get 10, 20 years for Aiding Somalia Terrorists," written by Randy Furst, *Star Tribune,* May 17, 2013, http://www.startribune.com/.

13. Stephen Montemayor, "Guilty Verdicts Returned against All Three Defendants in ISIL Trial," *Star Tribune,* June 4, 2016, http://www.startribune.com/.

14. Julie E. Allyn (assistant US attorney), interview with author, Nov. 9, 2017, in Minneapolis.

15. Council on American-Islamic Relations, "CAIR Countering Violent Extremism (CVE) Brief Questions Effectiveness of Program," Feb. 12, 2015, https://www.cair.com/press-center/press-releases/12850-cair-countering-violent-extremism-cve-brief-questions-effectiveness-of-program.html.

16. *Memorandum of Understanding between the United States Attorney's Office for the District of Minnesota and the Somali American Taskforce,* May 11, 2015, https://www.justice.gov/usao-mn/file/764306/download.

17. Stephen Montemayor, "Two Minneapolis Nonprofits Get Federal Grants to Counter Extremism," *Star Tribune,* Jan. 13, 2017, http://www.startribune.com/.

18. Ben Jacobs and Alan Yuhas, "Somali Migrants Are 'Disaster' for Minnesota, Says Donald Trump," *Guardian,* Nov. 7, 2016, https://www.theguardian.com/.

19. Ka Joog Organization, "Fear and Uncertainty," Facebook, Feb. 1, 2017, https://www.facebook.com/kajoog.org/posts/1561873447164107.

20. Esme Murphy, "Somali Youth Group Ka Joog Turns Down $500K Grant, Cites Trump," WCCO CBS Minnesota, Feb. 2, 2017, http://minnesota.cbslocal.com/.

21. See US Attorney's Office, District of Minnesota, "Community Outreach," updated Aug. 24, 2017, https://www.justice.gov/usao-mn/community-outreach, and "Somali American Parent Association & Ka Joog," January 2017, https://www.justice.gov/file/992806/download.

22. U.S. Attorney's Office, District of Minnesota, "Building Community Resilience," press release, updated April 27, 2017, https://www.justice.gov/usao-mn/building-community-resilience.

23. Statement by Youthprise, May 10, 2017, https://youthprise.org/wp-content/uploads/2015/12/CVEStatement.pdf. The organization describes itself as "a leading youth-centered philanthropic organization in Minnesota. Youthprise invests in the future of Minnesota by investing in youth. Our focus is reducing disparities with and for youth. Our core strategies include funding, capacity building, policy advocacy and research."

24. Julia Edwards Ainsley, "White House Budget Slashes 'Countering Violent Extremism' Grants," Reuters, May 23, 2017, https://www.reuters.com/.

25. Julia Harte and Dustin Volz, "U.S. Government Narrows Focus of Counter-extremism Programs," Reuters, June 23, 2017, https://www.reuters.com/.

26. See Department of Homeland Security, "DHS Countering Violent Extremism Grants," June 23, 2017, https://www.dhs.gov/cvegrants.

27. Mary McKinley (executive director, Heartland Democracy Center), phone interview with author, Feb. 28, 2018.

28. McKinley, phone interview with author, Oct. 10, 2017.

29. Leader of Minnesota nonprofit, email to author, Oct. 11, 2017.

30. Ainsley, "White House Budget Slashes 'Countering Violent Extremism' Grants."

31. Jonathan Challgren, Ted Kenyon, Lauren Kervick, Sally Scudder, Micah Walters, Kate Whitehead, Jeffrey Connor, and Carol Rollie Flynn, "Countering Violent Extremism: Applying the Public Health Model," *Georgetown Securities Studies Review,* Oct. 2016, 11, http://georgetownsecuritystudiesreview.org/wp-content/uploads/2016/10/NSCITF-Report-on-Countering-Violent-Extremism.pdf.

32. Dominic Casciani, "Analysis: The Prevent Strategy and Its Problems," BBC News, Aug. 26, 2014, http://www.bbc.com/.

33. Chris Graham, "What Is the Anti-terror Prevent Programme and Why Is It Controversial?," *Telegraph,* May 26, 2017, http://www.telegraph.co.uk/.

34. Open Society Justice Initiative, *Eroding Trust: The UK's Prevent Counter-extremism Strategy in Health and Education* (New York: Open Society Foundations), 6, https://www.justiceinitiative.org/uploads/f87bd3ad-50fb-42d0-95a8-54ba85dce818/eroding-trust-20161017_0.pdf.

Chapter 18. The Judge

1. James Walsh, "Calm and Commanding, on the Bench and Off," *Star Tribune,* July 21, 2008, http://www.startribune.com/.

2. See "Foreign Intelligence Surveillance Court, Foreign Intelligence Surveillance Court of Review, Current and Past Members, May 2017," http://www.fisc.uscourts.gov/sites/default/files/FISC%20FISCR%20Judges%20May%202017.pdf.

3. Sentencing hearing, U.S. v. Mohamed Abdihamid Farah, Case No. 15-CR-49(2) (MJD/FLN), Nov. 16, 2016, 54.

4. Sentencing hearing, U.S. v. Abidrahman Yasin Daud, Case No. 15-CR-49 (MJD/FLN), Nov. 16, 2016, 29–30.

5. Judge Michael J. Davis, phone conversation with author, March 26, 2019.

6. See US Department of Justice, "Nine Twin Cities Men Sentenced For Providing Material Support to ISIL," press release, November 16, 2016, https://www.justice.gov/usao-mn/pr/

nine-twin-cities-men-sentenced-providing-material-support-isil.

7. University of Minnesota Law School, "Judge Michael J. Davis ('72) Wins Sarah T. Hughes Civil Rights Award," October 25, 2016, https://www.law.umn.edu/news/2016-10-25-judge-michael-j-davis-72-wins-sarah-t-hughes-civil-rights-award.

8. Federal Judicial Center biography of Judge Davis, https://www.fjc.gov/history/judges/davis-michael-james.

9. Stephen Montemayor, "Federal Judge Michael Davis Receives National Civil Rights Award," *Star Tribune,* October 18, 2016, http://www.startribune.com/.

10. Maajid Nawaz, *Radical* (London: W. H. Allen, 2012), 275–276.

11. Mukhtar Ibrahim and Laura Yuen, "Attorney Defending Mpls. Man Departs ISIS Terrorism Case," MPR News, April 1, 2016, https://www.mprnews.org/.

12. Mukhtar Ibrahim, "Feds: Defender of Minnesota ISIS Suspect 'Preaching Jihad,'" MPR News, March 28, 2016, https://www.mprnews.org/.

13. Farrah Fazal and Jennie Lissarrague, "Teen to Terrorist: Adnan Farah's Transformation," KSTP-TV Channel 5 News, October 2016, http://kstp.com/.

14. Judith Dubin, Greg Campbell, Mike Shum, and Evan Engel, "ISIS in America: The Terror Trial That Shook Minnesota," Vocativ, November 17, 2016, https://www.youtube.com/watch?v=wQW0N69fKXE.

15. Hanad Musse's middle name is spelled "Mustafe" in some legal documents and "Mustofe" in others. Here, we adopted the spelling used in the transcript of his sentencing.

16. Stephen Montemayor, "First of Minnesota's ISIS Defendants Wins Release from Federal Halfway House," November 9, 2017, *Star Tribune,* http://www.startribune.com/.

17. Sentencing hearing, U.S. v Abdullahi Mohamed Yusuf, File No. 15-CR-46 (MJD), November 14, 2016, 6.

18. Dina Temple-Raston and David Greene, "Jihadi Rehab May Be an Alternative to Prison for Young ISIS Recruits," NPR, November 28, 2017, https://www.npr.org/.

19. Dina Temple-Raston, "He Wanted Jihad. He Got Foucault," *New York,* Nov. 27, 2017.

20. Manny Atwal (federal public defender), conversation with author, May 16, 2017, in St. Paul, Minnesota.

21. Atwal, conversation with author, November 9, 2017, in Minneapolis.

22. Kevin D. Lowry (former chief US probation officer, Minnesota federal court), phone conversations with author, March 26, 2018, and July 27, 2018.

23. Brendan I. Koerner, "Can You Turn a Terrorist Back into a Citizen?," *Wired,* January 24, 2017, https://www.wired.com/.

24. Lowry, phone conversation with author, May 29, 2019.

25. Final report to the Court concerning sentencing nationwide following convictions

for providing material support to terrorist organizations, U.S. v. Hamza Naj Ahmed, Mohamed Abdihamid Farah, Adnan Abdihamid Farah, Abdirahman Yasin Daud, Zacharia Yusuf Abdurahman, Hanad Mustofe Musse, and Guled Ali Omar, Case No. 15-CR-49 (MJD/FLN), November 1, 2016, Document 698. Congress raised the maximum sentence for material support from 15 years to 20 years while the Minnesota cases were pending.

26. Kelly A. Berkell, "Risk Reduction in Terrorism Cases: Sentencing and the Post-conviction Environment," *Journal for Deradicalization* 13 (Winter 2017/18): 276–341, http://journals. sfu.ca/jd/index.php/jd/article/view/131. The journal is edited by Daniel Koehler.

27. Lowry, phone conversation with author, May 30, 2019.

28. Berkell, "Risk Reduction in Terrorism Cases," 318.

Chapter 19. A Closed World?

1. For a video about the mall, see Rachel Slavik's report for WCCO/CBS Minnesota, "Finding MN: Karmel Plaza," Jan. 17, 2016, https://minnesota.cbslocal.com/2016/01/17/finding-minnesota-karmel-plaza/.

2. For a video tour of the mosque and mall, see Hamza The Linguist (screen name), "The Somali Mall/A Visit to Karmel Mall," YouTube, June 24, 2016, https://www.youtube.com/watch?v=4-AqRtNHHpY.

3. Cawo M. Abdi (sociologist, University of Minnesota), interview with author, August 3, 2016, in Minneapolis.

4. See the Somali American Police Association website at http://mexsolution.com/sapa/.

5. Steve Karnowski, "Cop Who Shot 911 Caller Gets 12½ years; Apologizes in Court," Associated Press, June 7, 2019, https://www.apnews.com/.

6. Emily Witt, "How Ilhan Omar Won Over Hearts in Minnesota's Fifth," *New Yorker,* Aug. 15, 2018, https://www.newyorker.com/.

7. Tara Law, "Congressional Rules Changes Allows Head Scarves, Religious Headwear on House Floor," *Time,* Jan. 6, 2019, http://time.com/.

8. Zack Beauchamp, "The Ilhan Omar Anti-Semitism Controversy, Explained," *Vox,* March 6, 2019, https://www.vox.com/.

9. Mike DeBonis, Felicia Sonmez, and John Wagner, "House Overwhelmingly Passes Broad Measure Condemning Hate in Response to Rep. Ilhan Omar's Alleged Anti-Semitic Comments," *Washington Post,* March 7, 2019, https://www.washingtonpost.com/.

10. Sheryl Gay Stolberg, "House Votes to Condemn All Hate as Anti-Semitism Debate Overshadows Congress," *New York Times,* March 7, 2019, https://www.nytimes.com/.

11. Ilhan Omar, "Ilhan Omar: We Must Apply Our Universal Values to All Nations. Only Then

Will We Achieve Peace.," *Washington Post,* March 17, 2019, https://www.washingtonpost.com/.

12. See Maggie Haberman and Sheryl Gay Stolberg, "In Attacking Ilhan Omar, Trump Revives His Familiar Refrain Against Muslims," *New York Times,* April 15, 2019, https://www.nytimes.com/.

13. Ilhan Omar, "Ilhan Omar: It Is Not Enough to Condemn Trump's Racism," *New York Times,* July 25, 2019, https://www.nytimes.com/.

14. See Bari Weiss, "King Bibi Bows before a Tweet," *New York Times,* Aug. 16, 2019, https://www.nytimes.com/. Also see Ari Hoffman, "Israel Was Right to Bar Tlaib and Omar," *Forward,* Aug. 15, 2019, https://forward.com/.

15. Sentencing materials filed by attorney Bruce Nestor, U.S. v. Abdirahman Yasin Daud, November 9, 2016, https://www.snopes.com/uploads/2019/01/Yasin-Daud-Ilhan-Omar-letter.pdf.

16. Isaak Osman Rooble, interview with author, March 19, 2019, in Minneapolis.

17. See Abdi Warsame's biography on a Minneapolis government website, http://www.ci.minneapolis.mn.us/ward6/about-warsame.

18. See Associated Press, "Hussein Samatar, 45; Pioneering Somali Public Official Dies," *Pioneer Press,* Aug. 25, 2013, http://www.twincities.com/.

19. Sentencing Materials filed Nestor, *Abdirahman Yasin Daud.*

20. Lara Bockenstedt, "Fartun Ahmed Is First Somali American Woman Elected to a School Board in the Country," *Lakeshore Weekly News,* November 16, 2017, http://www.swnewsmedia.com/.

21. CCX News, "Candidate Profiles: Hopkins School Board, Fartun Ahmed," YouTube, Oct. 18, 2017, https://www.youtube.com/.

22. Tessa Berenson, "Donald Trump: Minnesota Has 'Suffered Enough' Accepting Refugees," *Time,* Nov. 6, 2016, http://time.com/.

23. Betsy Hodges, "Donald Trump, You Need to Know a Few Things about Minnesota," Facebook, Nov. 6, 2016, https://www.facebook.com/betsy.hodges.7/posts/10209449694173952?pnref=story.

24. Amy Forliti, "Somali Diaspora: Blast Won't Stop Effort to Rebuild Homeland," Associated Press, October 23, 2017, https://apnews.com/.

25. Libin Said, interview with author, Nov. 9, 2017, in Minneapolis.

26. For a video of Somali Night at the University of Minnesota in the spring of 2017, see SSA, "Somali Student Association-UMN is at Northrop," Facebook video, https://www.facebook.com/ssaumn/videos/1200777623377737/.

27. For a video about the group's session, see YMC, "Resisting Surveillance Forum Part 1," Oct.

13, 2017, https://livestream.com/accounts/12767816/events/7798789/videos/164221424/ player?width=640&height=360&enableInfo=true&defaultDrawer=&autoPlay= true&mute=false. Also, see https://resistingsurveillance.org/2017/11/02/minneapolis-forum-connects-surveillance-across-midwest-massachusetts-and-the-uk/.

28. Amy Forliti, "2 Militia Members Admit Role in Attack on Minnesota Mosque," Associated Press, Jan. 24, 2019, https://apnews.com/.

29. Forum News Service, "Minnesota Man Faces More Charges for Throwing Pig's Foot into Somali Food Stand," *Pioneer Press,* October 19, 2017, http://www.twincities.com/.

30. Stephen Montemayor and Faiza Mahamud, "Rattled by Hate Incidents Here and Abroad, Minnesota Muslims Take New Precautions," *Star Tribune,* June 24, 2017, http://www.startribune.com/.

31. Kyle Potter, "Minnesota Somalis Recount Racial Tensions after Mall Attack," Associated Press, September 20, 2016, https://apnews.com/.

32. Paul Walsh and Shari Gross, "'Muslims Get Out' Sign Will Stay, Says Business Owner, despite Vandalism," *Star Tribune,* September 20, 2016, http://www.startribune.com/.

33. See a letter from Dave Blom of US Department of Education's Office of Civil Rights, Midwestern Division, Chicago, to Bruce Watkins, superintendent of the St. Cloud Area School District, November 16, 2011, https://www2.ed.gov/about/offices/list/ocr/docs/investigations/05101146-a.pdf.

34. Abigail Hauslohner and Drew Harwell, "As Unassuming Life before a Suspect's Rampage in a Minnesota Mall," *Washington Post,* September 19, 2016, https://www.washingtonpost.com/.

35. Stacy Takacs, *Terrorism TV: Popular Entertainment in Post-9/11 America* (Lawrence, Kansas: University Press of Kansas, 2012), 1.

36. Phillip Parrish, "Minnesotans Will No Longer Fund Jihadists," LinkedIn, https://www.linkedin.com/in/phillip-parrish-598a498a/.

37. Rachel Janik, "Minnesota Gubernatorial Candidate Denounces Islam as 'Incompatible' with the U.S. Constitution," Southern Poverty Law Center, January 16, 2018, https://www.splcenter.org/hatewatch/2018/01/16/minnesota-gubernatorial-candidate-denounces-islam-incompatible-us-constitution.

38. Brian Bakst, "Anti-immigration Gubernatorial Candidate Finds Support at Republican Caucuses," MPR News, Feb. 7, 2018, https://www.mprnews.org/.

39. Tim Walz, speech at the third annual Challenging Islamophobia Conference, March 28, 2019, C-Span, https://www.c-span.org/.

40. FBI Uniform Crime Reporting Program, *2016 Hate Crime Statistics,* table 4, https://ucr.fbi.gov/hate-crime/2016/tables/table-4.

41. German Lopez, "A New FBI Report Says Hate Crimes—Especially against Muslims—Went Up in 2016," *Vox,* Nov. 13, 2017, https://www.vox.com/.

42. Ken Schwenke, "Why America Fails at Gathering Hate Crime Statistics," ProPublica, December 4, 2017, https://www.propublica.org/article/why-america-fails-at-gathering-hate-crime-statistics.

43. Rachel Glickhouse, "Track News Stories About Hate with the Documenting Hate News Index," ProPublica, August 18, 2017, https://www.propublica.org/article/track-news-stories-about-hate-with-the-documenting-hate-news-index.

44. Walt Whitman, preface to *Leaves of Grass* (New York, 1855).

45. Catherine Porter, "In Canada, an Immigration Minister Who Himself Is a Refugee," *New York Times,* September 6, 2017, https://www.nytimes.com/.

46. Mila Koumpilova, "Canada's Immigration Minister Warns against Illegal Crossings at Minnesota's Northern Border," *Star Tribune,* December 8, 2017, http://www.startribune.com/.

47. See Average Mohamed website at https://www.averagemohamed.com/.

48. Anduin Wilhide, "Dar Al-Hijra Mosque, Minneapolis," MNOPEDIA, Minnesota Historical Society, June 28, 2017, modified October 17, 2017, http://www.mnopedia.org/place/dar-al-hijrah-mosque-minneapolis.

49. Chris Bowling, "Thousands Join in 'Super-Eid' Celebration at U.S. Bank Stadium in Minneapolis," *Star Tribune,* August 21, 2018, http://www.startribune.com/.

50. Edward Telles, "Mexican Americans and the American Nation: A Response to Professor Huntington," *Aztlán: A Journal of Chicano Studies* 31, no. 2, (Fall 2006): 10.

Chapter 20. Taking a Hard Look

1. Noemie Bisserbe, "European Prisons Fueling Spread of Islamic Radicalism," *Wall Street Journal,* July 31, 2016, https://www.wsj.com/.

2. Hannah Fairfield and Tim Wallace, "The Terrorists in U.S. Prisons," *New York Times,* April 7, 2016, https://www.nytimes.com/.

3. Katie Bo Williams, "FBI Has 1,000 Open Domestic Terrorism Investigations: Director," *The Hill,* September 17, 2017, http://thehill.com/.

4. Washington Institute Study Group, "Defeating Ideologically Inspired Violent Extremism," *Transition 2017: Policy Notes for the Trump Administration,* edited by Matthew Levitt (The Washington Institute for Near East Policy, 2017), 16, http://www.washingtoninstitute.org/uploads/Documents/pubs/Transition2017-CVE-6.pdf.

5. Kevin D. Lowry, "Responding to the Challenges of Violent Extremism/Terrorism Cases for United States Probation and Pretrial Services," *Journal for Deradicalization* 17 (Winter

2018/19): 76, http://journals.sfu.ca/jd/index.php/jd/article/view/175/130.

6. Matthew Barakat, "'American Taliban' John Wallker Lindh Is Released from Prison," *Associated Press*, May 23, 2019, https://www.apnews.com/.

7. Senators Richard Shelby and Margaret Wood Hassan, letter to Hugh Hurwitz (acting director, Federal Bureau of Prisons), May 17, 2019, https://www.hassan.senate.gov/imo/media/doc/OversightLetter-BOP-final-190517.pdf.

8. *Star Tribune* editorial page, "Attacking Terrorism at Its Domestic Roots," *Star Tribune,* March 8, 2019, http://www.startribune.com/.

9. Hasan made this argument in a presentation at the University of Nebraska-Lincoln on January 24, 2018, titled "The Muslim Ban: Patriotism or Xenophobia." Hasan's doctorate is in the philosophy of language, and she did her undergraduate training in philosophy at Damascus University before Syria slipped into civil war.

10. See "We Are Hmong Minnesota," which details an exhibit at the Minnesota History Center in St. Paul, http://www.mnhs.org/media/kits/hmong.

11. "40 Years after Arrival, Minnesota Hmong Tell Their Story," *Pioneer Press,* March 5, 2015, https://www.twincities.com/.

Chapter 21. Moving On

1. Abdirahman Abdirashid Bashir, interview with author, May 16, 2017, in Minneapolis.

2. Yusuf Abdurahman, interview with author, March 21, 2019.

3. Bashir, interview with author, March 19, 2019, in Minneapolis.

4. Indictment, U.S. v. Abdullahi Ahmed Abdullahi, S.D. Cal., Case No. 17CR0622-W, March 10, 2017, Document 1, https://extremism.gwu.edu/sites/g/files/zaxdzs2191/f/Abdullahi%20Indictment.pdf. See also US Department of Justice, "Canadian National Extradited to San Diego to Face Terrorism Charges," press release, Oct. 25, 2019, https://www.justice.gov/usao-sdca/pr/canadian-national-extradited-san-diego-face-terrorism-charges.

5. Isabel Coles, "Hard-Core Islamic State Members Carry Ideology from Crushed Caliphate," *Wall Street Journal,* March 18, 2019, https://www.wsj.com/.

6. See Charles Lister, "Trump Says ISIS is Defeated. Reality Says Otherwise," *Politico Magazine,* March 18, 2019, https://www.politico.com/.

7. Eric Schmitt, Ben Hubbard, and Rukmini Callimachi, "ISIS Attack in Syria Kills Four Americans, Raising New Worries About Troop Withdrawal," *New York Times,* January 16, 2019, https://www.nytimes.com/.

8. Vivian Lee and Rukmini Callimachi, "Bombing in Syria Targets U.S.-Led Military Patrol," *New York Times,* January 21, 2019, https://www.nytimes.com/.

9. See Rukmini Callimachi, "Described as Defeated, Islamic State Punches Back with Guerrilla Tactics," *New York Times,* January 21, 2017, https://www.nytimes.com/.

10. See Michael M. Phillips, "In One Corner of Afghanistan, America Is Beating Islamic State," *Wall Street Journal,* December 10, 2017, https://www.wsj.com/; and Sune Engel Rasmussen, "Online Propaganda Builds Islamic State Brand in the Face of Military Losses," *Wall Street Journal,* August 26, 2018, https://www.wsj.com/.

11. Michael M. Phillips, "America's Other Endless War: Battling al-Shabaab in Somalia," *Wall Street Journal,* January 17, 2019, https://www.wsj.com/.

12. Hussein Mohamed and Anemona Hartocollis, "At Least 26 Dead in Somalia Hotel Attack Claimed by Shabab," *New York Times,* July 13, 2019, https://www.nytimes.com/.

13. For a list of organizations the United States has designated as terrorist groups, see "Foreign Terrorist Organizations," US Department of State, https://www.state.gov/j/ct/rls/other/des/123085.htm.

14. See Noemie Bisserbe, "France Cracks Down on Islamic Extremism in Prisons and Schools," *Wall Street Journal,* February 24, 2018, https://www.wsj.com/; and Stacy Meichtry and Julian E. Barnes, "Europe Balks at Taking Back ISIS Fighters," *Wall Street Journal,* February 13, 2018, https://www.wsj.com/.

SELECTED BIBLIOGRAPHY

Abdi, Cawo M. *Elusive Jannah: The Somali Diaspora and the Borderless Muslim Identity.* Minneapolis: University of Minnesota Press, 2015.

al-Berry, Khaled. *Life is More Beautiful Than Paradise: A Jihadist's Own Story.* Cairo: The American University in Cairo Press, 2016.

Bergen, Peter. *United States of Jihad: Investigating America's Homegrown Terrorists.* New York: Crown Publishers, 2016.

Besteman, Catherine. *Making Refuge: Somali Bantu Refugees and Lewiston, Maine.* Durham: Duke University Press, 2016.

Byman, Daniel. *Al Qaeda, the Islamic State, and the Global Jihadist Movement: What Everyone Needs to Know.* New York: Oxford University Press, 2015.

Chambers, Stefanie. *Somalis in the Twin Cities and Columbus: Immigrant Incorporation in New Destinations.* Philadelphia: Temple University Press, 2017.

Crenshaw, Martha, and Gary LaFree. *Countering Terrorism.* Washington, DC: Brookings Institution Press, 2017.

Fergusson, James. *The World's Most Dangerous Place: Inside the Outlaw State of Somali.* London: Black Swan, 2014.

Goldberg, Jonah. *Suicide of the West: How the Rebirth of Tribalism, Populism, Nationalism, and Identity Politics is Destroying American Democracy.* New York: Crown Forum, 2018.

Hansen, Stig Jarle. *Al-Shabaab in Somalia: The History and Ideology of a Militant Islamist Group,* New York: Oxford University Press, 2016.

Harding, Andrew. *The Mayor of Mogadishu: A Story of Chaos and Redemption in the Ruins of Somalia.* New York: St. Martin's Press, 2016.

Husain, Ed. *The Islamist: Why I Became an Islamic Fundamentalist, What I Saw Inside, and Why I Left.* New York: Penguin Books, 2009.

Koehler, Daniel. *Understanding Deradicalization: Methods, Tools and Programs for Countering Violent Extremism.* New York: Routledge, 2017.

Levine, Saul. *Radical Departures: Desperate Detours to Growing Up.* New York: Harcourt, Brace Jovanovich, 1984.

Lewis, James. R. *Cults: A Reference and Guide.* 3rd ed. Sheffield, UK: Equinox, 2012.

Lister, Charles R. *The Syrian Jihad: Al-Quaeda, The Islamic State and the Evolution of an Insurgency.* London: Hurst, 2015.

McCants, William. *The ISIS Apocalypse: The History, Strategy, and Doomsday Vision of the Islamic State,* New York: St. Martin's Press, 2015.

Nawaz, Maajid. *Radical.* London: W. H. Allen, 2012.

Seierstad, Asne. *Two Sisters: Into the Syrian Jihad.* Translated by Sean Kinsella. New York: Farrar, Straus and Giroux, 2018.

Stark, Rodney, and William Sims Bainbridge. *The Future of Religion: Secularization, Revival, and Cult Formation.* Berkeley: University of California Press, 1985.

Takacs, Stacy. *Terrorism TV: Popular Entertainment in Post-9/11 America.* Lawrence, KS: University Press of Kansas, 2012.

Yusuf, Ahmed Ismail. *Somalis in Minnesota.* Minneapolis: Minnesota Historical Society Press, 2012.

People Interviewed

Cawo M. Abdi

Yusuf Abdurahman

Julie E. Allyn

Ahmed Amin

Manny Atwal

Abdirahman Abdirashid Bashir

Susan Brower

Glenn P. Bruder

Michael J. Davis

John F. Docherty

Marnie Fearon

Carson P. Green

Abla Hasan

Abdirashid Bashir Hassan

Yusuf Hassan Abdi

Daniel P. Higgins

Greg Holloway

Jon M. Hopeman

Jaylani Hussein

Charles J. Kovats Jr.

Angella LaTour
Saul Levine
Kevin D. Lowry
Ra'Wi Mahamud
Gordon Mathews
Mary McKinley
Bruce D. Nestor

Rooble Osman
Libin Said
Leah Somerville
Kenneth Ubong Udoidok
Andrew R. Winter
Ahmed Ismail Yusuf

INDEX